WILD VOICES

Mike Cawthorne began hill-walking on Ben Nevis aged seven, and has been climbing mountains ever since. He has worked as a teacher, professional photographer and freelance journalist. His first book, *Hell of a Journey: On Foot through the Scottish Highlands in Winter* (2000, new edition 2007) was short-listed for the Boardman Tasker Prize for mountain literature. His second book, *Wilderness Dreams*, was published in 2007. He lives in Inverness.

WILD VOICES

*Journeys through Time
in the Scottish Highlands*

Mike Cawthorne

BIRLINN

First published in 2014 by Birlinn Ltd
West Newington House
10 Newington Road
Edinburgh
EH9 1QS

www.birlinn.co.uk

ISBN: 978-1-78027-192-7

British Library Cataloguing in Publication Data
A catalogue record for this book is available from the
British Library

Contents

Illustrations

Maps

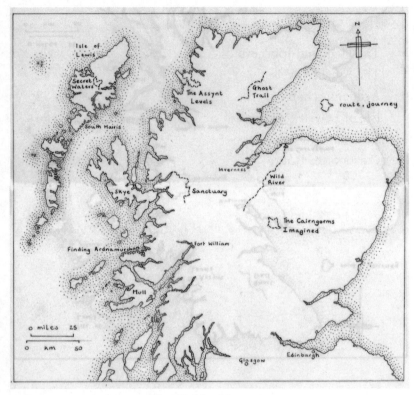

The Highland Journeys

Preface

In the anonymity of a hillslope above Loch Monar in Wester Ross is a water-filled cleft. I stumbled across it one blazing hot day in April. It was cool and shady in there. I sat for a while, then I began to follow it upstream, picking over polished stones and feeling along water-smoothed sides. It went deep into the hill and at the same time opened out. A small waterfall spilled onto a great angular rock that had once belonged to the side of the mountain. The whole world was there. The story of a stream and a hill in its making. Though I have searched I never found it again, but it runs clear in my mind and I know that out there somewhere the stream still goes around rocks and over pebbles and collects in pools and sings in voices and holds in its watery palm the sun and sky.

Which is how I remember it at any rate. Probably the great conundrum of outdoor writing, maybe any writing, is to bridge the gulf between what we see and feel and what we are able to capture on the page and present to the world. In that spirit are undertaken the journeys in this book, tales of adventure on foot and by canoe through some of the last wild places in Scotland. Each journey is haunted by another writer, someone whose passion for a region was for me a large part of its appeal. I wondered how my experience would differ from those of, say, Iain Thomson, or Rowena Farre. In the case of novelist Neil Gunn the experience I am sharing is that of the fictional Kenn. Gunn's lyricism chimes with his subject matter – a boy seeking the source of a river, and himself. I hoped that by entering into the spirit of a similar journey – on this occasion by following the River Findhorn – I might have an insight not only into the character of Kenn but discover a truth about the river, and maybe even about life.

The exploration of the lochans of Assynt deepened my belief that, regardless of ownership, here is a place so beautiful and unspoilt it cries out for legislative protection. We cannot any longer rely on benevolent landowners to keep out developers with their wind-farm and hydro proposals. Canoeing the extraordinary loch system there was an adventure partly inspired by the poet Norman MacCaig, who wrote prolifically about this area and often passed his long holidays here. A part of Assynt was one of the first in the Highlands to come under community ownership when it was purchased by local crofters in 1988. But MacCaig in his long poem *A Man in Assynt*, which predates the community buyout, asks whether something so ancient in provenance and beautiful and open to all can in fact be 'owned'. This raises the question, does ownership matter? It certainly does to cash-strapped crofters.

In Ardnamurchan there is probably no greater dichotomy than that between how locals view a place and the experience of visitors. Or at least there was. It is about as far west as you can reach in mainland Britain, a peninsula of achingly beautiful beaches and a stark rocky coastline. But don't worry it for a living. Alasdair Maclean's parents were the last crofters here to try and it nearly broke them. The author needs metaphors when weighing his own and his parents' experience, and perhaps to make it palatable for the reader he somehow manages to elevate their story to the level of a fable, though underlying his elegant narrative are sweat and tears and crushed hopes. It informed deeply my own trek around the wild Ardnamurchan coast.

Rowena Farre's tale of growing up with her aunt Miriam on a remote croft in the shadow of Ben Armine in Sutherland before the war, along with a menagerie that included a seal, a pair of otters and a pet squirrel, is altogether happier. She and her aunt embraced their isolation and revelled in the solitude, drawing what they needed from the land, and Miriam's allowance. The idyll painted by Farre was lapped up by reviewers and thousands of readers, but a few questioned the book's authenticity. A copy had lain for years on my parents' bookshelf, and later in life I realised I knew the empty moorland of the story's backdrop. Setting out to uncover its truth or otherwise would also give me an opportunity to revisit, perhaps for the last time, a truly wild area before its industrialisation by huge wind turbines.

Like many who love wild places I am torn on the issue of wind farms. To do our bit to moderate the effects of global warming probably requires the expansion of this form of energy, yet I am saddened when our diminishing portions of wildland are used for this purpose.

It is a dilemma that author and environmental campaigner Alastair McIntosh is only too aware of. Focusing largely on his native Hebrides, he catalogues our appalling history of disconnection with the natural world, but he offers hope as well, with tales of opposing the corporate interests behind the Harris superquarry and supporting the Isle of Eigg community buy-out. McIntosh's vision is for humanity to readjust its relationship with nature. I'd long wanted to explore the lochs of Lewis, close to where McIntosh had lived as a child. What, I wondered, did his message hold for these quiet, rarely-visited backwaters?

Maybe a deep attachment to any one place can only be nurtured through a prolonged stay in that place. Iain Thomson spent five years in the mountain fastness at the west end of Loch Monar, living with his family in a small croft that was then one of the remotest dwellings on mainland Scotland. Thomson's memoir has an overriding elegiac quality, for reasons that become apparent.

Living remotely and usually self-sufficiently in the Highlands had been the norm for millennia, though it was unusual by the time Thomson took up his posting in the mid-1950s, and virtually unheard of when his book appeared some twenty years later. Readers, including this one, were fascinated. I wondered if books like Thomson's tap into an age-old yearning for the wild and lonely places, whether our present day stravaigings there are just that. And I discovered something else. The land the author so lovingly portrays and was forced to leave is now more developed, more moribund and emptier than at any time since prehistory.

Thomson is a great watcher of the seasons, but what if that ability is denied you? Does it lessen the hill experience? The mountaineer and poet Syd Scroggie believed not, and we have his words as proof, vivid accounts of his extraordinary blind walks and climbs. On these journeys Syd found something beyond the visual or physical. He loves wildness, but would have been unaware of the huge turbines that now press against the boundaries of his beloved Cairngorms, unless he happened to bump into one. Syd's focus is on an inner, almost mystical experience, triggered by sounds and textures and the elemental, that he attempts to distill in his poetry. When attempting to follow in his footsteps, I was led astray. Much to Syd's delight I am sure.

So on each journey, alone or with a friend, I travelled with a ghost, a literary companion if you like, who offered a fresh perspective and a different story. All these writers enriched my experience, adding layers to my understanding. They made me laugh and gasp and nearly cry and sometimes be annoyed. If at times they struggle to convey the depth and meaning of their attachment to a place then they share that failing with the rest of us. We all struggle. Our offerings are painfully incomplete.

Note on Authors

All authors are referred to by their surnames, with two exceptions: when referring to Alasdair Maclean I use 'Alasdair' to distinguish him from his father, and I use 'Syd' for Syd Scroggie because I knew him personally.

Acknowledgements

I am very grateful to Francis Byrn for his excellent hand-drawn maps, and to Alastair McIntosh, author of *Soil and Soul*, who allowed me to quote generously from his work.

Dedication

This book is dedicated to the memory of Clive Dennier

Wild River

It's difficult to know where the river ends and the sea begins. Probably there isn't such a place.

Two of us and the ghost of a third were standing on a kind of peninsula at the edge of Findhorn Bay, the river opening out from behind and to our left, the bay ahead. The ground was sun-dried that day, but water would soon be there from the front and back – more from the back – greater amounts of tree debris and brash had been dumped by the river than styrofoam and plastic left by the sea. A place at the margins, unsure of its future, like the lands beneath the man-made Culbin Forest a mile across the bay.

Late in 1694 a huge storm swept the coastal sand dunes and sent them across the surrounding farmland, which was then an alluvial and high-yielding area known locally as the 'granary of Moray'. The storm was just the tipping point, and in a few weeks the entire estate comprising sixteen farms and a mansion house became a wasteland of drifting sand. Fresh dunes blocked the River Findhorn, damming its waters into a huge lake. With no way out, the waters rose and after some years broke through and carried away the small port of Findhorn, a centre for shipping and mercantile trade. Today not the slightest trace of it remains.

Neither of us could visualise such ruin as we gazed over the bay on a warm sunny morning, the air lively with gulls and oystercatchers, families of ducks bobbing on the water, white-sailed dinghies moving slowly at the opposite side. On the coast beyond the narrow entrance to the bay and the present-day village of Findhorn is a substantial sand bar, and I suppose at the start of this journey we should have been there, not here, facing out to sea, looking across the Moray Firth to Sutherland and beyond to Caithness, 'land of exquisite light', which is how the writer Neil Gunn described his home country. Gunn was born there in 1891 and lived his early years in the village of Dunbeath; the river rising on the moors and flowing through its small harbour became the central focus for one of his most evocative works, *Highland River*.

Highland River haunted me from its first reading. At its core is the story of a boy, Kenn, and his relationship with a river. A pivotal event early in the tale is when nine-year-old Kenn lands a huge salmon with only cunning and bare hands, and from then on, as Gunn writes, 'the river became the river of life for Kenn'. It grew in his consciousness and was like a thread that joined somehow the delight and wonder of his world, the goodness of his life, the unspoken love of his parents and the close-knit community of the fisher village. Even during the depths of horror of the First World War, amid the mud and blood and bombs of the trenches, the river rose before him 'with the clearness of a chart'. Two decades later, with his parents now dead and their old home lived in by strangers, he returns to the river of his youth, this time in a bid to reach its source in the distant moors, a place he'd dreamed of but never seen. A final journey of aching sadness and discovery takes him not only to the source of the river but into the mystery of his own heart.

Like the best literature, *Highland River* reaches beyond its own time and sings in the memory. In ways I couldn't altogether fathom, it swayed my view of the world. Kenn came out of the pages and into my life, a ghostly companion on many trips, a figure who grew in my mind until he shadowed my footfalls across the Highlands and beyond; yet he was also someone about whom I had misgivings. I thought he might join me on another exploration, this one on his own familiar ground. To what extent, I wondered, would my experience of a river grant me a glimpse into Kenn's world, and bring something imaginatively drawn from the page into the bright, sharp-edged world of the senses?

My desire to follow the Findhorn from its outspill here to its beginnings deep in the Monadhliath Mountains would also provide a chance to solve a small riddle. Writers about the Findhorn have long disagreed on the exact location of the river's source. I thought that by simply following the riverbank, always taking the larger branch wherever the channel divided, would eventually get me there. A few lines hidden away in *The Old Statistical Account of Scotland* claim that the fountainhead lies close to the summit of Carn Ban, 3,045 feet, where a stream issues from Cloiche Sgoilte, a 'cloven stone', a large rock with fissures in it.

It was an image to hold onto, at least, and I carried it as we turned away from the bay, leaving the briny marsh and rot, and followed a river that ran gently, making little sound beyond a murmur of tiny bubbles. After a mile or so we eased around a bend and it was suddenly fast; not quite rapids but with an urgent swirl on its reddish surface, the water hurrying past stony banks with an unending clucking and something lower – a stone-roll coming from deep. So close to the sea and crossing land that was virtually flat I'd expected a broad and lazy spill, but it was narrow and jumpy and bristling. Small drifts of foam spoke of a tumult higher up, and when I stopped to place my hand in its current I felt the icy cold of recent snowmelt.

The Findhorn chugged through a corridor of alders and birch, all green with new leaf, as were the giant hogweed that were uncoiling along the bank. White-flowering anemones brightened the shady places and the sward by our feet was lush and thick with wild flowers. At some distance from a main road and with only the sound of water in our ears it was peaceful walking, and we felt buoyant in ourselves at the start of this journey, if a little cumbered with our loads. The path was wide and well-beaten, from the endless footings of fishermen we assumed, but fresh tyre marks in the mud told another story. Sure enough, after a few minutes there came the rising pitch of a revving engine, a sound that in seconds drowned all others. A trail bike sped towards us. We pressed against a bush as it flew by, upriver, the noise receding, then rising again as the rider gunned down and back along the opposite bank, bumping and whining past an angler who looked resignedly at the water. When something choked the noise there was a second of absolute silence before the river and bird-sound and soft whorl of breeze came back to us.

Crossing the footbridge at Broom of Moy, we skirted regular fields of oilseed rape and more stands of hogweed, reaching a railway bridge where we spoke to a man and woman who lived a short walk from this spot. 'Ah, the bikes.' The lady's face hardened and she told us a modern tale of young teenagers who built fires by the river, drank themselves stupid and shouted obscenities into the night. We'd seen the charred driftwood and ash piles.

A mile further on we waited out a shower beneath the flood arch of Forres Bridge and listened indifferently to the drumbeat of lorries and cars overhead. This bridge, built in 1923, replaced a rather grander structure, a chain bridge with gothic towers at each end.

As we set off again I paused for something. Nick, my companion, turned and looked back. Earlier that year a snowstorm had swept Inverness, leaving the usual chaos in its wake, but I had been thinking of spring when I phoned Nick about the Findhorn.

'You said something about this river a while back,' he'd remarked.

'I probably did, but where?'

'In Qatar.'

'Qatar?' I thought for a moment. 'Yeah, I remember.'

A peat-tinged Highland river and a city in the desert, there could be no greater contrast. I recalled the day for other reasons. I was on a teaching contract and the father of one my students invited me for a day in the desert with his friends and some falcons. It was a pretty macabre spectacle, not like the gentle falconry practised here. A fat pigeon was released, given a few seconds of freedom, then a peregrine spurted off like a missile and the end was a distant puff of feathers. Not my thing, but I remember the space and silence of the desert as we sipped tea at sundown, long shadows cast by the dunes and a coolness I had never found in the city. It reawakened something – a river running serpentine from the moors and through the woods to the sea. The Findhorn. I'd told Nick about its wild spates and hidden gorges and its birth among the strange high country of the Monadhliath, the 'grey hills'.

While it's easy to paint word pictures of the unknown, the allure was different for each of us. And while I had the company of a ghost, Nick knew nothing about it.

I pulled a cord on my rucksack and went on, following Nick though not his movements. He was struggling. His sack was full and taut and I thought the weight was cramping his gait. I noticed how he crow-footed around a big stone that I took in one step, and every incline elicited a soft grunt. Then he went through some yellow-flowering broom and disappeared.

A track came to our path from Dalvey. At the end of it were parked cars belonging to fishermen, and looking upriver we could see maybe a dozen figures, most on the banks but a few standing midstream in two or three feet of water, clad in waders and jungle fatigues and casting and floating their flies in a single action. They were all after salmon.

Then in one short step the riverbank changed from flattened grass and openness to a steep slope so densely wooded we could hardly get onto it. After the easier strolling of the first stretch we now fought for every yard, over or around fallen and half-fallen timber which all seemed to have died downslope and crossways to where we wanted to go. Though we tried hard it was impossible to twist our bodies through oaks and birch that grew thick to the river's edge, their barriers making us detour half a dozen times in a minute. Nick struggled to keep up the pace. A noose of bramble took his leg and he kicked madly to get free, spitting out curses that I'd never heard before. A sort of temperate jungle had evolved here with sub-storeys of vegetation that appeared to be living on and through each other. Coils of ivy hung from overhead branches and tied themselves around trees with a kind of suffocating menace. At its densest, little light came through the branches and the air smelt old and damp. Fungus and parasitic growths were everywhere, as if the place was rotting from the ground up. In fact these woods make up the outliers of the great Darnaway Forest, a hunting ground for variously rich and noble families down the ages. It may have been easier going on the crest of the slope, but we hardly gave it a thought, keeping to the river, which though still broad, was now more hemmed in and ran through a well-defined valley.

Just as we began to weary, from the slope grew a lovely outcrop of pale rock, Old Red Sandstone that rose up in a barrel-like curve and was wonderfully smooth to touch. Soon after, the woods thinned, the steep bank rode inland and we stepped onto a gorgeous pebble beach, almost white in the sunshine, and rested. The river kinked at this point, and facing us at the crook on the other bank was a modest sandstone cliff, with growing from it a number of old and twisted oaks, having a tenure which appeared extraordinarily fragile. They overlooked a dark pool, almost still but for slow eddies that gave the water a viscous quality.

After this the river ran as straight as a river could run; in more than a mile the banks hardly varied and our view was compressed as if we were gazing through a telescope. To our right the land opened to the Meads of St John, an area of near-level farmland which I read had been cleared of trees in medieval times. Beyond a field of wheat was a low ridge dotted with stumps of more recently felled trees, and behind this the pressing forest. For a minute we had the company of some ancient-looking oaks, each one an island of sadness with hollowed-out trunks and missing limbs. A farmers' track finished at a turning circle and through some trees came the acoustic of rapids, made deeper and louder by sun-bright cliffs on the far side. We got to the bank for a better look. From the pool beneath the cliffs the river fell in a noticeable step, the peaty waters narrowing and running white and cider-coloured until finding a new level. On a nearby beach half-buried in river sand was a huge tree stump. There was something disturbing about its appearance, stripped of bark and truncheoned by a thousand rocks in their passing. It made me wonder.

Kenn's life changes when he is sent to fetch water from the well. The well is at the bottom of a bank by the river, and reaching it he sees a large salmon plough across the current. It settles in a pool on the far side. In the silence that follows 'all his ancestors came to him', and driven by some compulsion he puts aside somehow his fears, primal fears of creature-strength, of gamekeepers and lawcourts, and goes for the salmon. With stones picked from the riverbed he hounds the fish, wading and crawling and scooping more stones and attacking with such frenzy the salmon cannot stop or rest even for a moment – 'inwardly a madness was rising in him, an urgency to rush, to hit, to kill'. As the saga unfurls, Kenn has the wounded and bleeding fish trapped in shallow water, and there is a moment when he grabs it by the gills, a salmon almost as long as he, and wrestles it ashore.

I feel Kenn's battle with the salmon doesn't quite work for the modern reader. It's too brutal, too unsporting, not to mention that salmon are now an increasingly rare and protected feature of our rivers. Gunn was writing about the attitude of a boy in a Highland community of the early 1900s. Salmon were plentiful and poaching a way of life, certainly one means of putting food on the table. Kenn's epic struggle, though, was much more – a rite-of-passage towards mature boyhood; it was somehow a duel that cemented his linkage with the 'Old Folk' of his ancestors, the Picts and broch-builders and their hunting instinct. This one event transformed the way he thought about the river, now *his* river, running through him like a thread of hope and lending a strength that he would one day draw upon.

Sluie Gorge couldn't be far now, and I hoped we would get there before nightfall. More bare rock, more sandstone, the Findhorn curling on a meander and seeming to sink in on itself as wooded land on both banks climbed higher and more steeply. A noisier, faster river, more authoritative; it broke easily as it brushed past islets of pale stone and over shallows. If earlier the Findhorn presented an equal show of turbulence and quiet, now it was all movement.

Woodland came down to brush the water's edge again and the merging lent a growing sense of remoteness to the valley. Time slipped by largely unregistered. We'd seen nobody since the anglers at Dalvey, hours ago. Our desire was always to keep to the bank, but when forced to seek easier ground, as sometimes we were, the river was reduced to fragments and glimpses; water-sound was still there, but it came to us dimly, filtered by all the undergrowth. When we found it again we saw a man midstream casting a rod. There was such a simple rhythm to his action, like a type of callisthenics that was in complete harmony with the flow, and we watched not wanting it to be broken by a fish or some distraction. I don't think he was aware of us as we slipped by, on a good path at last and approaching a sheer and overhanging cliff. The walls seemed mechanically carved. There were layers of different sandstones, and in between these, gravels and conglomerate like a hardened soup. We probed its base until it banked against the dark of the river, not what we had hoped for, especially now in the gloom of evening. Retracing our steps until the valley side eased to about forty or forty-five degrees we monkeyed up, holding to roots and clawing and finding better angles. Then to my surprise we stumbled upon a disused switchback trail buried under years of leaf-mould. It wound and climbed through a stairwell of old trees and took us, breathing heavily, to a path high above the great cliffs. Nick was exhausted.

We had reached a wide terrace, some large beech trees, and soft and sheltered among them were level spaces, any of which would work for a small tent and bivouac. In a few minutes a spot we had chosen largely at random was colonised, made home.

After the bustle of cooking and eating and some chat, I lay back and opened my head to the river which came to me broken and hollow, and to other sounds. I looked up through the canopy to shards of sky.

In the deep shade of the woods night came upon us prematurely. Nick's shadow moved in the green glow of his tent, then he settled and all was still. Tiredness had brought us to this glade and now in some magical way everything about it seemed right. 'Going from the mouth to the source,' Gunn writes, 'may well seem to be reversing the natural order . . . Yet that is the way Kenn learned his river and, when he came to think of it, that is the way he learned life.'

The greater part of *Highland River* presents a middle-aged Kenn looking back on a childhood spent in and around a tight-knit fishing community. The sea has a strong if ambivalent presence in the text, as a material provider and sustainer but also one prone to spasmodic violence, and though Kenn feels its pull it is the river that captures his imagination. After his great battle with the salmon he works deeper into the valley, on forays with a friend, Beel, and his brother, Angus, to rabbit-bait, poach and to explore the birchwoods, the Pictish broch, and all the ways of the river. He wanted the 'river knowledge' that Angus had, and in time he went beyond it.

Here is not just an evocation of youth but something more profound, a memoir of the things which, though dimly observed at the time, have stayed most in his mind. Sledging with friends in winter he remembers, not the beauty of a snowy night or the sparkle of frost, but simply 'a stillness and Arctic whiteness'. Kenn is moved by what he barely understands, the information received by his senses having an effect on him akin to music. Gunn's narrative is unusual in that at times it rolls out like an internal monologue; Kenn's mind-journeys transcend time, so his childhood, wartime and later experiences are pulled into a continual present.

The next day, from our campsite we tracked upstream, when suddenly the river narrowed to almost nothing; it hooked and cramped along a dense shading of contours – the Sluie Gorge, caused by the river working down into hard igneous rock. It is so deep it is almost subterranean, so that even the noise coming to us high on the rim was cave-like and echoing. White, disturbed water ran past more or less continuously, not just driven by the gradient but because it was jammed in and urged along in a single direction. The wonder we found was a graded path on the cliff-edge that led through scattered woodland, heather and blaeberry and mirrored every turn of the gorge. When occasionally it came to a clearing we stole out and marvelled at the wider scene, steep forests dropping to rock walls a hundred feet high or more, sheer or tiered with trees clinging to them in every attitude. A window to an undisturbed past; a rare thing even in Scotland. Nick whistled in appreciation.

'You can imagine,' I said, 'the first humans coming here and seeing more or less the same view, standing just where we are.'

'Who were they, the Picts?'

'No, much earlier. Hunters for sure. This river would have been bursting with salmon and these woods thick with game. Like us they probably worked upstream from the coast, maybe having come over by sea from Doggerland.'

'Dogger . . . what?'

'After the last Ice Age a large part of the North Sea was land, a prehistoric hunting ground covered in oak-woods. Fishing boats have been picking up artefacts and wood from the seabed for years.'

Rubbing one of his eyes, Nick thought about this for a moment.

'Yeah, that's interesting. I didn't know that . . . but I do worry sometimes about the stuff that lives in your head.'

In a few places estate owners had fashioned steps and attached iron railings for paying fishermen to reach the bank. There was nobody about so we went down. The river could not have been more than twelve feet wide and in the middle the stream-bed came through as a sharp ridge, splitting the flow and making both channels run in a complete frenzy.

For a short time the cliff path left the river as it went vaguely into a side-gorge, the way hard to see beneath leaf-fall. This was miles from the nearest road, and I wondered who ever came this way. From what I could see it was like a coastal chine remembered from childhood, dank and airless, with all manner of ferns and mosses. We climbed out to a thickly wooded hill, Dun Earn, once operating as a Pictish fort, then went back to riding the high path that snaked and stretched on a natural course and carried us lightly and in rhythm with the river, now seen only in flashes through the trees; heard more than seen, a low thunder that climbed the canyon walls and hung in the woods like a fog. It rose in pitch as we passed the outspill of the River Divie, and again as we sloped through even-aged conifers to where two large teeth tore at the current. The main flow was trapped in a kind of *cul de sac*, with nowhere to go but roll back on itself in confusion and escape in a wild step down. We stood for a moment as if mesmerised, then moved on to a spot not far upstream, where the river came out of a rapid and was faced with a bottleneck of about seven or eight feet. Here the entire Findhorn is squeezed through. The spot is known as Randolph's Leap.

A grim little tale clings to this place and I asked Nick if he would like to hear it. Why not, he said, we need a break anyway. So I told of the dispute between two powerful families, the Cummings and the Earl of Moray, who lived on opposite sides of the Findhorn. Sometime in the thirteenth century, an attack by a thousand-strong force led by Alastair Cumming was thwarted and chased back by Thomas Randolph, who was fighting for the Earl. Most were hacked to pieces by Randolph's men at or near this spot as they forded the river. Cumming and a few companions escaped and hid in a cave, but were all later smoked out and beheaded.

Nick listened while chewing a sandwich, but history, certainly this brand of it, held little appeal for him. He finished eating and looked about, unmoved. Maybe the account sat ill with the beauty of this place; the clash of steel, the chaos and savagery of men fighting and killing waist-deep in bloodied water. Somehow none of it belonged here. More likely it reinforced a suspicion that most written history is the hyperbole of the victors, overblown accounts of rulers and rogues and bloodletting.

The Findhorn is probably no different. The other parallel histories of family stories handed down orally about the folk who lived and loved and moved here, are largely, I suspect, unrecorded and forgotten. The untapped subconscious of memory is another storehouse, though it has no dates, no events or personages, just a quiet intuition of atmosphere, wordlessly lingering in the spirit of these places.

Above the Leap the river quietened. Conifers packed the bank with the thickness of a palisade, so we climbed and puffed and found a rough track that had seen nothing mechanical on it for years. Muddy seeps were taking it away piece by piece and our route was interrupted time and again by fallen trees. I felt most had came down in storms, and there was violence about their lying, snapped or forced over, with roots skywards holding stones and earth, still living.

If the planted pinewoods were largely sterile places, the birch groves crawled with life – ferns and lichens along outstretched branches, wild honeysuckle bushing around crowns of trees, fungi and moss taking the windfall at our feet. Oak, yew, and willow also grew there, and the water-loving alder.

Wherever we neared the bank there was brash. Since the tidal reach of Findhorn Bay we'd seen it, a latticework of dead grasses, twigs, small branches, animal remains; all arranged in long contours by the bank and on the soft upstream of boulders and tree crowns, a tangible evidence of the last spate. In narrow places we noticed clumps of it wrapped tight around branches that were shoulder-height and more, dried-out effigies of once green things that had been stranded there for years. They were a sign and had an ominous quality that we both could grasp.

When a choice was presented between following the old track or fighting the bank, we disagreed as to which was preferable. Nick rested on an abutment at a curve in the river, overlooking a bar of the palest stones. Ahead we could see the high grey arch of Daltulich Bridge growing from two sides of forest. After a brief discussion we took the south bank, the wilder side according to the map. A path of sorts fingered along the water's edge to the last reach of fishermen, then gradually petered out in a wilderness of conifers. The next mile took an hour, our upstream as slow as the river's downstream. The Findhorn faced sullen to the overcast sky, dark in its reflection and showing just an odd boulder; the stream was quietest since the great pool of Sluie.

Escaping the firs we came to a clear-felled area and went about negotiating armies of sawn crowns and discarded timber. Both of us were tiring, Nick more so. He grumbled again we'd taken the wrong bank. A lovely open stretch of fields appeared soon enough, though, where we could walk straight to Logie Bridge and see a couple of cars whose noise lingered as we crossed and rejoined the woods, on the left bank again.

After leaving Sluie every step presented new ground to me. I had read two lovely old books about the Findhorn, one by George Bain published in 1911, and another by Thomas Henderson from 1932, but for an accurate impression of this untrodden land I relied on maps, thinking beyond the colours and key symbols. Rivers run with contours, so I studied their loops and curves, the pattern of their spacing, but the landscape I conjured up out of them fell short of what I had expected. I felt the maps had missed something or maybe I was reading them wrong, that the loops and symbols were like some runic script I could not decipher. But then I suppose even the best map can never offer more than the bare bones. The living tissue and detail and beauty of a place only come into being with our presence there.

My map-gazing had showed an intriguing mile of bunching and twisting contours on the final section before Dulsie Bridge, a gorge of sorts. I wondered what this meant for our plan of reaching this landmark by dark. Nick wanted a path, a good one, or he else he would camp soon, and he wasn't arguing. His rucksack, he reminded me, was only a tad lighter than yesterday's.

The path was good, and it varied, one minute leading through a shag-carpet of woodrush and tree boughs, the next to a bouldery shore with dark puddles. After the brief openness of Logie the river found its valley again. Conifered slopes crowded inwards, light dimmed, colours grew muted, mustard-colour of gorse against grey rock walls. The river corridor narrowed and the path now crept along a small ledge only a few feet above the waters. Ardclach Church was around this spur, but we came upon it suddenly and almost unexpectedly, a green place in the nook of a bend. There was the church and adjoining meadow and a small road winding steeply down the valleyside. No cars and no one on the meadow. The church itself was all boarded up. Three yew trees lived in the small cemetery and on the minister's grave yellow narcissi bloomed.

In the next few miles the Findhorn reached a peak of such loveliness we forgot our tiredness and moved as if in a kind of trance. Nowhere does the river snake and twist more or change its flow from stepped white to calm so quickly. Pine and broadleaf trees grew on the canyon walls at impossible angles and the darkening afternoon lent the place something northern and arboreal. A softness as well, I think because the river had made its own way and life had followed it down.

For an age our path picked along the water's edge, losing itself among miniature beaches and greasy stones, then climbing steep and narrow to ride over a spur and down again to Daltra and a broadening valley. The ground spread to pasture and a ridge in the distance. Then we seriously gained height. The cliffs on our side rose more sheer and I couldn't see for sure where the path went. It reached so high that when we stared down the river filled the entire frame. At this point it narrowed to little more than a ledge scratched on the cliff face and we had to cling to rocks so that, when facing the cliff, our faces were level with little plants that grew there – primroses, wild strawberry and saxifrage. Where a burn came from the side, lying among moss and brookweed was a dying bird, a kestrel.

I felt some regret as we pulled out of the gorge, even as we climbed into evening sunshine that bathed everything in a diffuse orange glow. Half an hour later we leaned on the bridge at Dulsie and looked sixty feet down to the river sloughing past, the surface heavy like oil. A thundering came from upstream rapids. It was good to reach the old crossing point; we could stop here, but I felt the day had more to run. Even so, when I suggested to Nick a place a mile and a half further I was surprised that he agreed.

We crossed and turned and went towards the noise, and from a high vantage point peered over a torrent that in the half-light had a ghostly quality. The Findhorn bottled here into the tightest corner of its course, looping back on itself in a trail of white and calming before rolling towards the bridge. Day visitors leave their cars in a small lay-by to view the spectacle, and over the years have made a path. A smaller path carried on somewhat further and plunged to the bank. We tried to work along it but in no time we were bending around the ironwork of trunks and boughs and mangrove-like roots, all trace of the path gone.

With night came the old urgency and I forged ahead in a callous and self-absorbed way, arming aside branches. I was only aware that Nick was right behind when a branch whipped back into his face and he swore loudly. The trees left the bank to bluffs and terraces, which reduced us virtually to rock-climbing until we abandoned the river and climbed steeply, holding onto nothing more substantial than moss-backed wood and rotting vegetation.

Away from the river night closed around us, and as the angle relented, trees clothed the slope. A few of them seemed troubled, their bark cankered and rucked into small blocks, all thrown into sharp relief by our passing torch beams. Their branches were hung with feathery lichen that glowed like magnesium in the battery light. We footed through the softness, so tired now, not entirely sure where we were, down what might have been a field; but there were birch huddled in groves and grass so high it was more like savannah. A water-sound from our left was different in tone to the Findhorn. The Tor Burn, I was sure of it.

I crossed it slowly using stone islands; Nick waded and splashed, not really caring. Let's camp, he said. I ran my torch over the ground. From the amount of debris it was certainly a spot that flooded regularly. Okay, this looks fine. We'd found a kind of hollow, on a corner of turf where the tributary met the Findhorn. Around us was a thicket of young birch with larger trees on some raised ground, and these screened us so effectively that even had it been day we could not have seen beyond them. This lent a feeling of cosy seclusion, but also a sense of being overlooked. At first I don't think Nick was aware of this. I felt it strongly.

As water boiled we got our shelters up, then gathered brash and dry wood for a small fire which Nick raised on some nearby rocks. The day's long unravelling began as we sat back to enjoy the tea. In ten minutes we were able to spoon a large meal from plastic plates as the fire grew and radiated its warmth. The desiccated stuff left by the river flared up, sending light into the shadows and bringing out all the hollow features on Nick's face. His hair was tousled and matted and his grin had a life-affirming quality, not just approving this spot where the rivers joined, but our walk in general and this day and the last hours especially, the quiet magic of the Findhorn.

'One of my best days,' he said, 'and I've got it all here.' He pressed a finger to his temple.

'Let it run through you,' I said.

'Do you mean the river? . . . no, don't explain. No more of that. I don't want to wake up with your chewed-up ideas in my head. I'm dreaming about women tonight.'

'Okay, just listen to it, then.'

We did, at least I did, to the water running over thousands of pebbles, an unending whirring, but when

I listened more deeply there were always single notes beyond, something swallowing, like a stone dropped into a pool, a sound on the fringe yet so pervasive it reached over the rapids and under them and, if you allowed it, grew in your mind.

Then a sound that was completely different. You hear new sounds because of their anomaly and this one we both registered immediately – a loud *crack*, and it came from behind. Nick swung round.

'What the hell was that?'

We stood and waved our torches at the surrounding dark, the beams catching the white of birch-bark. Beyond that they couldn't penetrate, there was a wall of blackness.

'Probably some animal. A deer maybe.' I was pretty convinced.

Nick continued searching, his light more powerful than mine, though I noticed he didn't stray from his position by the fire.

Then we heard it again and both jumped. It was different in key, probably because it was closer, and louder. Moving away from the fire we scouted in small orbits, not entirely sure what was going on. We scanned the dark behind the birch and cast light where before had been shadows. I withdrew to our patch to sort a few things, and for some minutes heard Nick's soft footfalls in the brash and saw his torch flashes. He needed to be sure. I built the fire up with more branches that I broke to length, in a quiet way if that's possible. Nick on his return was pensive.

'This fire,' he said, 'it lights us up like a beacon. You could see us from miles.'

'Who could?'

'Someone out there.'

'Who's someone?'

'Someone, anyone.'

'Yeah, they might, but I seriously doubt it. And if someone was out there, why would they be sneaking up on a couple of guys camping by a river?'

My logic must have worked because he said no more, not out loud at any rate. I turned in with him still hunched over the fire. I left my bivvy open – I can't remember why, though maybe it wasn't something I did consciously, and I remember Nick sitting by the fire, a dark meditative figure whose head appeared to be smoking. For a moment he seemed to bow his head like a supplicant, though he was probably just digging at the embers. I could guess his thoughts. Beyond a sensation of being overlooked, which I'd reassured myself was due to our having chosen to camp in a slight hollow, I shared none of his concerns that we were the focus of some malevolence. And yet I could not fully account for my own disquiet. It was a recurrence of something old and it came from deep, as if some faint lingering of an evolutionary trait that equipped outrforebears had been reawakened. I have felt it before but it was strong here. When my mind did eventually slow enough for sleep it was broken and thin, and as soon as dawn brightened the eastern sky we gathered up our things and left.

In a short and revealing chapter Kenn, in one of his monologues, weighs the influence on him of his Pictish ancestors. He reaches beyond the plain facts of local history and genealogy to something in his imagination felt at particular moments when exploring the river valley. Alone before a broch or on a path through a birchwood, he remembers a premonition, a moment of 'exquisite panic' or 'sheer delight'. It was an interior world now

dimmed by the preoccupations of adulthood. By returning to his own land and walking to the source, Kenn
hoped he might rediscover this delight, 'he would recapture not merely the old primordial goodness of life but its
moments of absolute ecstasy'.

I only realised afterwards that we'd passed the night
close to the vitrified hill fort at Dunearn. There is little
to see for your efforts, just a shorn hilltop with a hint of
something that might have been old walls. Nothing at all
remains of an ancient chapel on the northern aspect. The
quarried stone, I'd read, was recycled as boundary walls
for nearby farms. Dunearn takes from the old name of
the Findhorn, the Earn, probably the name of a pagan
goddess, long forgotten. Findhorn is simply 'white river'.

I don't know if any of this mattered to us at the time,
but as we journeyed upriver we saw more clearly the reach
of history into the present. Particularly now as we left the
woods and entered a more open stretch known as the
Streens, from 'scian' in Gaelic meaning 'bridle'. Though
the Findhorn is a flood-river, its fertile niches and shelter
gave the first settlers a chance, and dotted along the valley, if we were to look, are rings of stone, tumuli, cairns,
hut circles. At one place, Carnoch, 'Field of Cairns', local
people practiced deasil, which is going around the hill
three times with the sun for luck. Past habitations overlap
here, the stone monuments of the Neolithic, the Pictish
forts, the later ruined farms and homesteads which you
see everywhere in the Highlands. All bear dumb testimony
that brought a poignancy and aliveness to the place.

After leaving the Tor Burn there was a half mile of
narrows and rapids, then it all changed at a quaint old
footbridge, the river growing to a width we'd not seen
since the first morning, maybe thirty or forty yards across.

It stretched out and ran quieter when compared to the gorges. There were still steep valley sides, but also space for meadow and rough pasture.

For no other reason than that it was roadless, we'd decided to keep to our bank – I didn't want to walk one step on tarmac if I could help it – and as far as I could see it was also deserted. There were dwellings with placenames, but they stood isolated and I guessed were just ruins, cut off by the river. The era when this valley was cultivated, beginning with the Neolithic and stretching to the last century, is over. In places you can see the old fields which once held oats and edible tubers, but now they are only grass. It was lush about our feet and for the most part made for good walking, though when the river bit into our hillside we pushed upslope and struggled over some rough. The Findhorn woods which had been almost seamless since the beginning of our hike now thinned, replaced by leggy gorse and broom and leagues of rust-coloured heather that drew away to distant moors.

Dalbuie was a ruin, so was Knockandhu. Dynachan Lodge, further up and across from us, seemed the hub of the fishing and shooting fraternity. A man not far from the lodge stood on the bank like a heron and watched us pass. He didn't move for some minutes. I was tempted to wave, which I do almost always and without thinking, but there was something vaguely accusatory about his bearing. I suppose only a trickle of people not in some way connected with the estates come this way. Two folk heading upstream, you might wonder about their business.

We could see the changes in river features were geology related. After the granite and gneiss of the middle section the river now ran over gravels; the only granite was the stones across the bed trailing small white scarfs of water. They drifted by as we marched on like a pair of regular troopers, sometimes together on the flats, or in file, maybe rolling on a little too fast for the scenery. We followed our chosen bank, each corner opening out another stretch of river that some distance ahead came from a fold in the hills. We passed one boarded-up house and saw nobody all afternoon.

From the high moors a cold wind soughed, mixing with river noise so the two came and went with the breeze. Oystercatchers swung low, dragging their misshapen shadows over the waves. Families of ducks swam off at our approach. Caught by current and wind, in an instant they were sluiced away and scattered, then in a matter of seconds, and as if their feathers concealed little magnets, they reassembled. I marvelled at this and their genius of riding waves two or three times their height.

Crossing our portion of sky sometimes was a lone buzzard. I pointed it out to Nick and he queried whether it might not in fact be an eagle. But it was a buzzard, no doubt, and as the miles went by it graced the leagues above us and drew lines as if conveying some message. For all its dumb animal instinct it was still the object of my envy. I wanted to shuck off my tiredness to ride its wheel of freedom and see the Findhorn below as a thread of silver in a green corridor, flowing northeast from its cradle in the hills to almost disappear in the woods and gorges of Dulsie and Sluie, spilling finally across Petty to the sea. Then to course higher into the blue, the river now just a faint groove in a great swelling of tan moor from Dava to the Monadhliath, the eye drawn further across Strathspey to the rising wall of the Cairngorms with its white flanks of Braeriach and Coire an Lochain. Rolling with the mountains for a minute, then down to the valley again, watching for any life. Two tiny figures by the river approaching the narrows at Shenachie.

To soar is the oldest dream of man, and in a vision the middle-aged Kenn returns to his old haunts on the wings of a buzzard. Homing in on a sun-bright strath, he sees movement on the riverbank, a young boy wholly absorbed in his adventure: 'he peers into pools, he pokes under stones, he examines rabbit burrows, he listens, he looks about him, he wanders on'. The boy cannot hear the singing of the buzzard's wings as he is so utterly taken, not just with his carefree adventure but by the wonder of his discoveries, the quality of which seemed to drip with mystery. As the older Kenn looks on, he realises with heartbreak that his years away from the river had made him forget what it was like to be young. If only he could reach down and touch the boy on the shoulder and whisper, 'Don't you know me, Kenn?' But the little boy had gone.

At Shenachie the valley sides drew together and reached down a thousand feet and pressed the river so tight it struggled to get through, its voice rising in pitch and running faster than we'd seen it do for some time. A strong wind funnelled through the gap and I was surprised at how cold it felt; Nick's face was blood-pinched. Since we had started at sea level spring had painted its fresh green along the valley, but now it was stalling. There was something of winter in the long lines of flood-mulch where the slope reached up, and in the river rubbish left on the plain. Then the moorland withdrew, the valley opened and we saw the river coming towards us, wide and shallow and singing over a great bed of shingle. This was the beginning of Strathdearn, threshold of the upper Findhorn.

That was for tomorrow; for now, after hours of marching against a building wind, we needed to stop. I looked at the map. A shelterbed showed on the small hill ahead. The trees would be good, I thought, but I was also drawn to it by the words *cairn* and *field system*, which denoted an echo of earlier footfalls. We took ourselves up. The field markings were easy to miss and there was nothing save a pile of stones, but I had a notion why thousands of years ago people might have thought this an important spot. At every quarter the land drew away; we could see up and down the valley and through a window to the northwest where the Funtack Burn joined the Findhorn, then further out to a ring of moorland. At a time when the straths were thickly wooded, here was an old vantage-point and maybe the axis of a small kingdom; any stranger approaching, like us, would know it. It was remembered and I was glad of it.

It said much about Nick that in the morning he came through the vestibule of his small tent, yawned, looked around, put a toothbrush to his mouth and waved a finger at a watercourse I'd barely noticed the evening before. It wriggled from some hills to the east and cut past and below us maybe a quarter of a mile away.

'That river,' he said, chewing his words. 'Remind me. Is that the Findhorn?'

I was not really surprised. I'd realised a while ago that although we walked the same ground we came to it from different paths. For much of the time Nick expressed only the vaguest interest in where he was. Places whose names I might have mouthed were soon forgotten. Where was Dulsie? Where were the Streens? I think he harboured a suspicion that a name repeated too often could somehow narrow a place, mask its essence. For him it was about the quality of living. He came with few preconceptions and left with memories all the richer. Maybe I needed to see it more his way, to shed the names and lose the language as the river sloughed off its human influence; today the last houses, tomorrow only small grey ruins from the shieling times, then nothing but the solitude of the moor. Kenn feels this strongly when he climbs beyond the uppermost tumble of stones to the river's source. 'Time is gone. Human relationship was gone. He had entered into the non-human, not only in the moor but in himself.'

Nick only needed to rotate himself a little to see the sweep of the river as it curled a long meander round our hill and looped back under the A9 trunk road and railway viaduct at Tomatin. Wide and expansive, we could see its passage around individual rocks, the small stitches of current, though its sound was weaker and brought to us unevenly by the breeze.

Our morning ritual of map-gazing showed Strathdearn as a broad green corridor that extended and climbed southwest for maybe twelve miles, until the valley sides met and the wildness of the moor began. Over this the Findhorn wavered and stalled, more interested in sidewards than seawards movement, imprisoned and wriggling like a snake in a pipe. Only when we unfolded the map sheet corner to corner did we see the staggering area which fed into the valley, a great blanch of moorland everywhere drained by rivers. A Findhorn spate washes through the imagination; no British river has risen faster or carried more. Given a cloudburst or rapid snowmelt the first pulse can reach the lower gorges as a six foot wall of water. In 1829 the river rose fifty feet at Dulsie. We'd seen its flood shadow everywhere. It explained why the regular brash lines were so high, why few houses were sited on its banks.

A small public road runs up Strathdearn. It keeps above the plain on the left bank and strings together the scattered dwellings all the way to Coignafearn Lodge. Avoiding this we footed along the opposite bank, the river tea-coloured, shallow over shoals, deep by peaty bends. Its colours came out more in the shallows, but at certain angles it also carried the flinty-white of sky and dark moor. As yesterday a constant breath of cold came onto us. It broke further the already broken water and urged on the swift current.

At Clune we found brief shelter amongst some trees. When I eyed the route ahead and saw only twists and half-loops that went contrary to the valley I suggested to Nick that for a while at least we take the rough track, if only to make some easy distance. He didn't need persuading. In any case the water was never more than ear-cupping distance away.

At a whitewashed lodge, voices came from an open garage. A child's bicycle lay abandoned on the front lawn. A little further on an ageing farm worker was repairing an old dyke. All day toiling in the wind had brought out the colour in his face. He was the first person we had spoken to since the couple near Forres. 'Ain't nothing where you're going,' he said, 'just a river and a whole lot of emptiness.' He warned there would be rain tomorrow.

Then we left the track and found the bank again. We walked against the wind, towards rising moors that were mostly hidden from our sightline; and this went on for a couple of hours, the water and land changing slowly or hardly at all unless you particularly noticed something.

The work rate had a dulling effect and I stayed mainly in my head. I think it was the same for Nick, though my thoughts were more about Kenn. He doesn't have to deal with this purging wind and he doesn't miss a thing: 'As the seasons went on,' Gunn writes, 'Kenn adventured not merely further up the river but also into a more intimate knowledge of the reaches he knew.'

It was an intimacy that would help him survive the horrors of the trenches. But not his brother. Angus had emigrated to Canada, and at the outbreak of the war signed up with the Canadian military. Kenn was a British Gunner and somehow, during a lull in the fighting, he managed to find his brother, who was employed as a sniper. 'They painted me up all green and then I lay behind a boulder . . . potting away at the Germans . . . you would hear a squeal, just like a rabbit.' Kenn hadn't seen his brother in years, and they talked and laughed about family and home, but when Kenn delved into their adventures on the river, the salmon poaching and dodging keepers, Angus drifted a little. He saw no profit in reminiscing, he lived only in the 'now'. Recognising this, Kenn showed nothing in his face, but underneath, 'there was a nerve thread of pain . . . it was the old river in a shadowy land. A land it would never flow out of'. This was a premonition, and Angus would soon be dead.

The river as metaphor is a recurrent idea in the story, though not always employed in a traditional way. At different times Kenn has the river running eternally, 'old as the hills . . . is the river that flows through the straths of time'. He compares it with a chart or a human nervous system; or it is a symbol showing the inexorable flow of human progress, and its stagnation is a sign that 'our river took the wrong turning somewhere', he says. As an adult

Kenn is drawn to the idea of a lost age, a past era when man lived in greater harmony with nature, in stark contrast to the complexity and alienation of modern life. The clear-running river carries intimations of this time, and its Pictish echoes particularly resonate with Kenn, who is himself an inheritor of that race, a pilgrim in search of its forgotten memories. By returning to the river and exploring it up to its crystal beginnings he hopes to recapture a little of the lost goodness of mankind.

In a last preamble before he leaves for the river, Kenn, now a professional scientist, talks with Radzyn, a Pole and a much older scientist. When Radzyn inquires gently about Kenn's desire to reach the source of his boyhood river he naturally asks what he expects to find there. 'Nothing,' Kenn replies, adding, 'I think I look for too much'. The discussion moves on to an art versus science debate, Kenn arguing in favour of his profession, saying, 'I believe the scientist is the one who with certainty is going to make war impossible'.

At this point the reader understands that this is not necessarily Kenn speaking, but his creator, Neil Gunn. It is hard to disagree with some critics that many of Gunn's lifelong beliefs are expressed through the fictional Kenn, and this highlights a few contradictions as well. In common with many writers of the thirties who lived through an era of industrial breakdown and looming war, Gunn was greatly attracted to the idea of a 'Golden Age'. He was a convinced socialist, a Scottish nationalist, indulged a liking for Stalin's Soviet Union, and was interested in the anarchist writings of Peter Kropotkin. A distrust of authority and belief in the right of individuals to make their own choices is a theme that runs through *Highland River*. 'We were a fairly communal folk . . .' Kenn says during the conversation with Radzyn, until we were thoroughly debauched by predatory chiefs and the like. A feeling lingers that the poor have always been wronged – it's time they were freed.'

But there are also the tensions between individual and society. While Kenn holds his village and upbringing in great affection, acknowledging the strength they have given him, he is ultimately drawn away on a solitary quest for self-knowledge and renewal at the lonely fountain-head.

Highland River was published in 1937 to critical acclaim, at least in the newspapers and periodicals of the time. Later commentators have taken a more guarded approach, and as new material is added the modern researcher has plenty to consult. As I discovered. In the end I grew weary of reading literary critiques, not because I couldn't face what I so admired being 'explained' away, but rather that such criticism often missed the point. It is a paradox that some truths are found only in our emotional response to them. I can accept that Kenn's outlook has much in common with Gunn's, but I can't warm to the idea that Kenn, for instance, is not fully an individual but more 'an archetypal Scottish boy from an archetypal Scottish village' (a boy strong enough at the age of nine to pull a 30lb salmon from a river, and who later finished first in the Northern Counties bursary exam). Nor does it matter to me that the book, apparently, lacks a strong storyline or, as one critic wrote, is simply about 'male possession', that it digresses wildly and drifts into awkward phraseology.

These are all empty words and they fall away with the others, taken by passing winds or carried downstream like old brash. When all is said we are left with the lonely integrity of Kenn as he sets out in the dew of morning on his last journey.

For some miles the river didn't appear to be falling much, it just washed across a wide basin, while the slopes on both sides rose higher and were fractured into outcrops. Beyond one of these two birds traced patterns against a white sky. A pair of eagles. I knew this was a favoured haunt. We craned our necks as we walked, and when I peered to the land ahead something else caught my eye: a small dark object which after a minute had matured into a figure. It was standing stock still and apparently waiting for us.

'Who's that?' I said.

There was unease as we approached. I strained to get sense of what I was seeing.

'Bloody hell,' Nick said, 'it's a scarecrow or something, made of wire, I think.'

A load of galvanised fence wire had been twisted in such a way as to represent a lifesize figure, a man. Some effort had gone into this, I thought, but why? He stood vigil by a pond. What fooled us was the dark Crombie overcoat and hat. His head was in fact completely hollow save for a couple of spent shotgun shells for eyes. To one of his arms a fence post had been attached, and tied to its end was a small white rag that shook and snapped in the wind.

'Can't be much to do around here,' Nick laughed, but I found the figure faintly menacing and its image stayed in my head as we traversed the great river-flats and pasturage, then at last crossed to the left bank and Coignafearn Old Lodge, where the tarmac road ended. No one was about and it was very quiet apart from the river and a

sigh of wind. I thought it strange that what had so har-
ried us and been such a drag on progress should make
so little noise. It came straight from the grey sky and
never let up; indeed as the lodge receded it seemed to
grow in vigour. Yet I had a sense of being reeled to the
centre of this barren land, pulled to its heart. It may have
been something to do with the perspective of valley that
drew the eye naturally, but I think it was more an age-old
human curiosity for what lay around the next bend or
spur, a never before seen stretch of running river, almost
the same but contrasting in small degrees – in the assem-
bly of rocks that forced a different flow, a fresh pattern,
a newer pitch. Small changes that chimed with an old
longing and a kind of wonder that settled over me. We
went on like this until a haze of tiredness began to make
our gait crooked and our strides slower as if we neared
the end of the day.

Dalbeg was the place I had in mind, a little-used bothy
sixteen-hundred feet above sea level and four miles from
the last occupied house. A friend who'd visited recently
said it was in 'pretty poor nick', which sounded fine, and
in anticipation we gathered windfall from around the
gnarly birch on our hillside. What couldn't be lashed to
our sacks we balanced like yokes on our shoulders, struggling comically the last few hundred yards as the rain
came on.

Everything about Dalbeg spoke of abandonment,
but as we pushed through the rickety door I knew we'd
caught it right – a stale rush of wood-smell, candle-wax
and something charred. The smells were not strong, probably because the wind came straight through glassless
windows and sent little dust spirals across the wooden
floor. In the other gloomier room, part of the floor had

rotted away and we shuffled about uneasily. Wall plaster
crumbled at a touch and came away to show green growth
on the old masonry. What lent the place life, or at least
a memory of life, were names scribbled and emblazoned
on walls and panelling, some dating back nearly 80 years.
The earliest of these were small and neatly handwritten:
a name, date, maybe a role – a ghillie or ponyman, local
folk with names like Macleod, Mackenzie, Geddes. Later
inscriptions were more scrawled and reflected the self-
consciousness of the age – 'will we ever find what we
are looking for' one said. Or they were unappreciative –
'Rainy weather. Shit Scotland. Two Germans. July 1986'.
I'd been in the Monadhliath then, and remembered a
bright day of sun and cloud shadow, but it was a poor
month.

I swept the floor with half a broom, Nick fixed the
open windows by stretching plastic from old bags and
securing it with his walking poles, nails driven in with
the back of a stone. Small gestures, but it lent the place
a sense of home. Night drew down from the moors, the
rain stopped. I emptied every food packet we had into
our largest skillet and brought it to a simmer, then gazed
across at Nick as he dug around in the fireplace with
the eye of his head torch. With flood mulch he prepared
a kind of bird's nest, delicately roofing this with twigs
and larger pieces as if model-making or stacking cards.
I don't know anyone who puts more time and care into
fire-building. The payoff came when the edifice breathed
out yellow flames, brightening our home to its four corners and distorting everything with moving shadows. The
warming room creaked out its stiffness as if waking from
a long sleep. We talked in strange empty-room voices or
sat in quiet torpor and watched the fire bloom, touched

by a magic that made everything seem possible. Sometimes the fire popped and sparked, so we inched away,
closer to the window sheeting that sucked to the draw
of the breeze and to something that was always there, a
melody of running water. It grew with listening, reaching over the fire-crackle and wind and flooding the mind
until it was the only sound I could or wanted to hear.

It was so bright first thing I thought we must have
overslept. The Findhorn ran by through a shadowed
alleyway or glided past sunlit rocks and carried a blue
reflection of sky on its surface. Above the bothy gulls,
oystercatchers, and lapwings signed their presence and
danced in the peculiarities of the breeze. The quality of
atmosphere was born of the mountains. We mooched
with mugs of tea and sponged up the warmth and slowly
limbered up towards an idea of moving. I felt rejuvenated
by our arrival here, expectant at what lay ahead. Nick
stretched his large frame, then sat on the bank staring for
some minutes at nothing in particular, before wandering
back over to me, by which time I had the map unfolded
on the grass. We needed a discussion about the source
and our map presented options. At first Nick was only
mildly interested. Maps were my department. Then something caught his eye.

'Look at this branch.' His finger ran along a blue
line that spilt a mile up the valley, growing fainter as it
climbed the contours and wormed west until it finally lev-
eled. 'Here.' His finger rested where the line stopped, or
began, somewhere I could tell was unimaginably bleak,
a nameless watering-ground of mosses and seepways. 'I
reckon this is our source.'

At least one writer on the Findhorn agrees with the
notion that the source must be the tributary that has its

beginning at a point furthest west. For others there is no one source, but countless springs and streamlets that have their births on the watershed.

'It's not the highest,' I said, 'and anyhow, surely *this* is the main flow.' My river reversed south until it broke into many feeder tributaries, all ending in a no-man's land that I could also clearly picture. I was looking for something else, though. A small lochan tucked in close to the summit of Carn Ban, a collecting pool for the last land of the Findhorn basin.

'Lochan Uisge?' Nick queried.

'That's it.'

'What does it mean?'

' "Loch of Water", I think.'

'What about the cloven stone?'

'I don't know.'

'Can we find it?'

'We can try.'

At the meeting of waters a short distance away, even a traveller without a map would instinctly take the left channel; the valley trended that way, it reached further and cut a narrow wedge all the way to the southern crest and the highest ground. But it was a different river now, its volume quite halved, banks closer together, the river-sound lighter and more fractured, with stray notes coming like a whisper of voices. Every so often it was met by feeder burns from one side or other that zipped down the steep flanks of the valley. Where it broke over bedrock it showed a pure whiteness we'd not seen even in the fury of the gorges, and at quiet pools we saw through to pebbles on the bed and a purity only faintly coloured by the earth. It was of the mountains now, and so far removed from what tumbled through the lower reaches or ran

through the Streens or across Strathdearn. And I finally
realised the futility of trying to give it a human space; its
reality too changing ever to be snared by abstract description, or measured. It ran detached from all and for itself,
unknowing even of the creatures and plants that lived in
its sphere.

Some of those plants had struggled of late. Gaunt
birch and ash growing from behind boulders were only
just coming to leaf, with a few still bare. Among the grass
and heather by the bank, wildflowers were trying to open
– purple saxifrage, marsh violet, the pale lilac of spotted
orchid. Higher slopes still oozed the flattened pale yellow
of a winter recently gone, or were dotted with old pockets
of snow that fed the burns left and right. Crossing one, we
came to something the map didn't show, a roofless shieling with thick walls built on a small elevation of moraine
or river terrace. A summer dwelling-place only, I would
think, a crumbling reminder of the era of transhumance
when, for unrecorded centuries, cattle were driven to the
high pastures each spring and folk lived half their lives
in these remote places. Summer habitation here at the
margins and elsewhere gave even the loneliest valleys a
human story, and when the old ways died the stories died
as well. At this place on this day, if there was any vestigial
memory of those times I could never know it.

When Kenn considers the 'prehistoric walls' of the last
ruin before the open moor, something is resolved as to
his own identity and that of the Picts. 'I am the Pict,' he
says in a moment of revelation. But I think this is a way-
ward note and fits ill with the text, as if Gunn himself had
crowbarred something in for the sake of polemic. Kenn's
whole life-tale, from catching the salmon to reaching the
source, unfurls as a journey towards understanding and

self-knowledge; he carries the memory of the beauty of his river to the science laboratory in a quest for a greater truth. The nurturing of a brilliant mind and the moments of absolute delight by the river were both inspiration and a counterpoint to his scientific work. Kenn doesn't need the myth of a Golden Age or the affiliation of a tribe and a era we know virtually nothing about. He only needs the river, his river or any river, a rocky torrent in the Himalayas or just a little Madagascan creek coming from a spring in the forest. Kenn is Everyman, and his example is for us. We have the same question and carry the same hope, that walking to the source will bring all our life-threads together, a rediscovery of life's goodness and a glimpse of the secrets of our own heart.

Yesterday's forewarning came in the shape of darkening cloud and greater wind presence. A pouring sound was a waterfall that fed a nameless burn on our left, then we came to an extraordinary kink in the main channel where it twisted back on itself and traced an almost perfect 'U', the geological reason for which I couldn't fathom.

The gain in height was more or less constant now. Everywhere save our valley route was loaded with steepness; it came right to the river so that to follow each bend we walked at angles and crabbed and slipped and held to nuggety rocks and crossed on stones in two or three dry steps. The crossing and re-crossing was a joy, and we did it whether needing to or not. After days of watching from the banks, now we could watch from the middle, stand in the current and feel its press. From here it was a different river.

When it split I knew, though I'm not sure how, but here was our burn, and if our intuition needed any support the map gave it. Enough water was carried down to suggest the melting of a great snowfield or our promised lochan, and we made our first steps to follow it. In its slow making our chosen burn had eaten into the mountainside, and confined us to peering down at it from the rim, mostly white in almost continual falling. The tone of it, though, was deeper somehow. The pattern of a sheer plunge and collecting pool repeated itself, and we climbed until the greater Monadhliath came into the frame, snow-spotted moors stretching for uncounted miles north to a desolate land under ragged clouds. The wind gusted and switched. Spots of rain. Not far now.

Kenn was here before us, and there came a time when his river went into the ground, or rather came from it. He lowered his head and listened: 'Faintly he heard the surge of stream . . . but listening more acutely, he realised what he heard was the surge of the rivers of his own blood'.

Feeder burns joined, but it was easy to follow our stream and we needed no other guide, the infant river coming over the curve of the land and so narrow it was just a nook-line in the peat. I looked over at Nick, folded the map and put it away. I should have done that a while ago, but had somehow missed the signs.

What lifts *Highland River* from a tale fixed in time and place to a fable for our age, or any age, is the moment Kenn leaves the last ruin and enters the non-human world of the river's final reaches. As if emerging from a chrysalis he at last breaks free of the author's philosophical grasp, escaping his creator, shedding the race polemic, the Jungian influences, the old myths and opens himself to the river's magic. Kenn's voice is the river's voice, and the last miles are filled with haunting and allusions and a trail of few clues and then, at the end-place, a final twist so we cannot really know what happens. It is unrevealed, though in some ways it appears to be only the beginning. 'The inexorable search for truth . . . an unending spiritual drive into the unknown. Man's greatest of all poaching forays leading him to what inconceivable water-heads?'

Kenn fades but the Findhorn was still here, flowing so gently and slowly and so narrow we could step over it at will. At some point it emerged like a spring from a large snowdrift. We traced its murmur and here were its last curves and mini-meanders and the last sound of softly running water. Lochan Uisge came upon us quite suddenly. Footing a small lip to some stones, we pulled up and looked across the tear-shaped lochan, its surface creased by thousands of ripples. It was small and unremarkable, and hardly matched the longed-for place I carried in my mind. Just another pool tucked away on a Scottish hillside. A few tiny burns soaked into it, and I thought about looking for the 'cloven stone', but knew in my heart this was it, the birth-waters, the wellhead.

If it all came together in a second it was in an image of Nick. A near-silhouette on the edge of the lochan stooping and cupping his hands and drinking. Like a sacramental receiving and a bow to the unknowable.

The Assynt Levels

I had the map spread out on the table. It was a map of land but it showed an enormous amount of blue and gave the impression of an area half underwater, like the remnants of a great flood where all the hollows and troughs had refused to drain. I thought there might be as many as two hundred lochs and lochans crowded here, but what attracted the eye was how they presented and configured, how they clustered or went along valleys or were isolated, shaped by what the land could offer. In fact when I looked closely, most were joined by narrow necks or burns that ran down the levels, and this suggested that something subterranean was happening, involving soakways and seeplines and hidden peat channels, all connected in some way to create a labyrinth that my map could only hint at. It probably explained why I couldn't see any settlements or roads or even a path that divided the place or went anywhere in particular. It was a space only for fishermen or local shepherds or solitaries. At no point west of Quinag was the land particularly high, though neither did it blanch entirely or lose its contours. But it was the lochs that drew me. Their shapes and especially their islands, sometimes shaded green which denoted a tree cover stretching back to the last Ice Age.

Is here to be found the last relics of a Scotland before humans came? I realised I must see these places before they changed or were gone. And not just from the shoreline. I wanted to find their water's edge and reach the islands and pass nights among the old stands. By doing

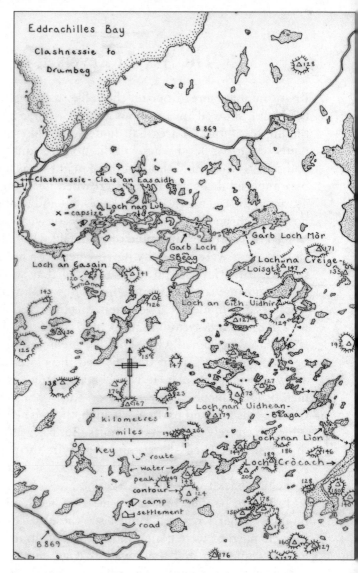

Eddrachilles Bay
Clashnessie to
Drumbeg

B 869

Clashnessie - Clais an Easaidh

× = capsize   Loch nan Lub

Garb Loch Mòr

Garb Loch
Beag

Loch na Creige-
Loisgte

Loch an Easain

Loch an Eich Uidhir

N

Loch nan Uidhean-
-Beaga

kilometres

Loch nan Lion

miles

Key

Loch Cròcach

route

water→

peak

contour→

camp

settlement

road

B 869

The Assynt Levels.

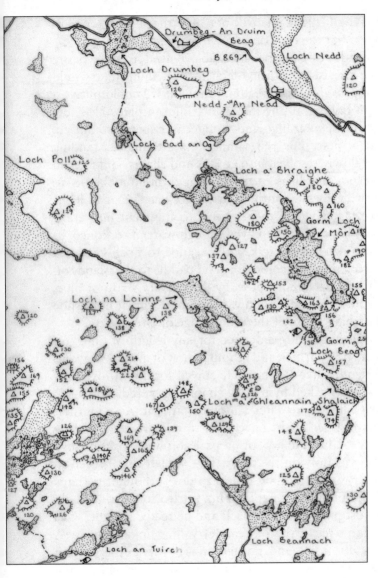

so maybe I might uncover not only the reason for their survival but the root of my own fascination.

The idea of a journey by canoe evolved from the desire to see one island on one loch to something that would encompass the entire region. I thought If I could puzzle a way of linking all the major lochs into a plausible route it would be a strange and wonderful experience indeed. What at first appeared a random scattering of standing water slowly resolved into groups and chains, and I began to see possible lines of travel, though none looked easy. From Clashnessie on the coast, a necklace of small lochs arced inland where they seemed to fragment into crazy jigsaw shapes, but there was enough water, I reckoned, to see two determined folk with a canoe to Loch Crocach, and from there we could drag and paddle to the islands on Loch Beannach. Somehow, by using every scrap of blue, we would bear north and west again in a great horseshoe and perhaps finish at the little village of Drumbeg.

To portage an open canoe for any length of time you need a good partner, and I thought first of my old stravaiging friend, Clive Dennier. He stayed locally in Inverness and when I asked by text he simply answered, 'why not'. I gave Clive some dates and left it at that. As a journalist his instinct might have been to enquire just what he was in for, but the joys of preparation were lost on Clive and it was only on the day before we left that I received another text, 'Anything I need to do?' I thought perhaps I should phone and explain, but settled for texting back, 'No. Just pack your rucksack and be ready at eight.'

I don't recall the old car ferry that linked Inverness to the Black Isle, but my father says it was there when we first went north in a Jowett Javelin in the mid-sixties. It had certainly gone when I took off on my own some fifteen years later, the new Kessock Bridge spanning this ancient water route and taking me over then, as it did us this morning, rattling north in my work van. With a canoe strapped to the roof I felt the vehicle lurch and drag a little, and the engine complained just a tad more than usual. Clive kept up a constant stream of news and trivial chat. I'd not seen him for a calendar month and we still hadn't properly discussed the trip.

'Are you going to let me into your little secret and tell me what I'm in for?' he said.

'No secret. You only have to ask.'

'Well, for starters, how many lochs are on that itinerary of yours?'

'Not sure exactly. Maybe three dozen. It depends on our route.'

Clive was quiet for a minute as we accelerated away from the Tore roundabout, the road climbing steadily to a crest from where on most days the peaks of Strathfarrar, Fannichs, and Ben Wyvis fill the windscreen like the poster on a wall in a dentist's waiting room, though today we only saw great banks of cloud and wisps of showers ahead.

'That's hell of a lot of dragging.' He looked thoughtfully at the landscape. 'I suppose it's being that age, the wrong side of forty and all that. I go to the gym and kick a football, but as you know I spend most of my time at a keyboard. And I probably eat the wrong food and like to drink a little too much. You reckon on five days' hauling? I know I said I wanted something, but I'm not sure if my system's ready for *that*.'

I'd heard this before.

'Relax. We'll go as slow as we need to. I want to take time to really explore this place, you know, look under a few stones, have a poke about. I would bet some of those lochs have never seen a canoe, at least not the smaller, remoter ones.'

'There's a reason for that.'

'Which is?'

'Why would anybody take one there?'

I ignored the jibe and smiled.

'Pioneering in the wilds of Assynt. Come on, how does that sound?' I repeated it for effect.

'I know how it's going to feel. I pretty much dislocated my shoulder last time I did something like this with you. Can't we rig up that dog of yours?' Clive turned and cast about in the dark of the van. 'Whaddya say, Holly?' Holly was a Hungarian Vizsla, at the cusp of middle age herself. In the rear-view mirror she uncoiled herself, raised her muzzle and tilted her head in vague expectation.

Clive laughed. 'She's too posh to pull.'

Rain smeared the windscreen and we saw little of the Fannichs, even in the interludes between showers. Only when we dropped to Ullapool did the curtain lift, and there were green fields with cattle and smart newbuilds with B&B signage; then the road ran north and climbed to the great barrenlands of Assynt. The radio station we'd been listening to faded. The rain came again. A big German car with twin exhausts gunned past, leaving only the drone of diesel and the soft beat of wipers. Clive looked in the direction of Stac Pollaidh, but there was little to see save shifting clouds. We passed a few wind-harassed lochans, and on one was a small island choked with dwarf trees. It seemed incongruent with the landscape, as if borrowed from an older time and set here in the present.

'These islands,' Clive said, 'why the fascination?'

I composed myself. 'I want to see what's left.'

'Of what?' Clive seemed genuinely bemused.

'Of whatever there was. Look at this empty land. Look what we've done to it.'

'We did that?'

'We, our forebears, everyone. We now have this tree-less waste, which in a way I love, of course, and would hate to see it covered in turbines and dams, but it used to be so much richer. Imagine this landscape even two thousand years ago? All manner of wild animals lived here, and natural woodland stretching as far as your eye could see and I bet there were plenty of humans around as well.'

'You think we'll find the last wolf or maybe Balu the Bear living on an island somewhere in Assynt?'

I laughed. 'No, of course I don't, but as far as I can tell these islands have largely escaped the boot of man, probably because of their location which meant nobody could be bothered to clear-fell or graze them. If you like, they've fallen through the net and we have them as they are meant to be. That's a rare thing in this country, don't you think?'

At Ledmore junction we swung north, the rain now coming on more heavily. Clive had been quiet for a few minutes, which was not like him.

'You said about people living here,' he said. 'That's true. There was a cattle economy and plenty of farming tradition which goes way back. People lived in places that today might seem remote, and I've read that islands were often used as burial sites, a place safe from the threat of scavenging wolves. There's a whole human history here we know nothing about.'

'That's probably true, but in the remoter areas the map suggests otherwise.'

'Alright, let's say we do find these islands in a wild or semi-wild state. What if a local farmer is grazing his sheep on them? It's his land. Most of that area is North Lochinver Estate and owned by crofters, and has been since the buy-out in 1992.'

'The Assynt Crofters Trust, I know.'

'It's their land. They bought it, admittedly largely with donations from the general public, but they own it and can do with it as they please and don't go thinking anyone can tell them otherwise. They're none too keen on advice from outsiders or the John Muir Trust or even the Government. Let's not forget their ancestors were dumped off the land by the lairds and factors to make way for sheep.'

Clive was right, of course. In fact Assynt as a whole suffered two phases of clearances, first in 1812 when fifty families were cleared and resettled in coastal areas, and again in 1819-20, when agents for the Duke of Sutherland evicted eighty-six families.

'You know my sympathies are with the crofters,' I said, 'they always will be, but I have a problem when you talk of title and ownership. I can't get my head around anyone owning a mountain, not a millionaire or company or charity or, and, I'll be shot for saying this, even a crofter. It's been sitting there doing its thing for millions of years, and for an individual or group to claim absolute ownership, I mean, beyond anything written on a legal document, smacks of arrogance. It's nonsensical. In the life of a landscape we are just passing shadows.'

'You need to join the real world.'

'You mean the fantasy one we left behind?'

Clive refused to be drawn, and went on, 'Look, from what I can gather nobody gets rich from crofting. They're hanging on to their government support like any farmer, and if some wind farm or hydro developer offers them a slice of that subsidy they pick up for renewables then I bet they'll be tempted. Every local who sold an incomer a property that's now a holiday home was tempted. They may love their land and feel some bond to it but like any farmer they'll want to squeeze it, and if that means burning or spraying chemicals or covering it with tracks and turbines then so be it. Principles are fine but they can't pay the bills.'

'You're a cynical old hack'.

'No, a realist. John Muir Trust have the neighbouring Quinag estate, and they want to restore the land to the way it was before humans, like one of those islands, which is fine with me, but I do know there's been some bad blood over the amount of deer being culled. Too many, according to the crofters. Detrimental to their earnings from stalking and venison they say. Which might sound rich coming from a group traditionally against field sports. You can get all philosophical about ownership and rail against what humans are doing to the planet, but in the end it boils down to scratching a living like anyone else. Those lines from that poem, how do they go . . .'

'You mean – "Who owns this landscape?/The millionaire who bought it or/the poacher staggering downhill in early morning/with a deer on his back . . ." It's by Norman MacCaig.'

'That's the one, but how often have I heard or read that? I bet the fellow didn't have to make a living from the land. These intellectual types . . .'

'Careful now. MacCaig is fondly remembered in these parts. He was a strong supporter of the crofters.'

'Fine, but promise me one thing?'

'If I can.'

'Promise you won't go quoting poetry at me. I'm on holiday, remember.'

The few cars we saw came up and overtook us. We were in no hurry. Every trip has its own pace; this one would be slow. October fitted with this, always the best month in the Highlands. The great midge swarms have collapsed, yet the days still retain plenty of light and the colours come to a blaze of ripeness. Autumn was around us now on the coast road from Lochinver, in the bronze of dying bracken and flame-red of rowan berries. As the road climbed we caught windows to a wider landscape of low brown hills, which in places surfaced into outcrops and pavement with monolithic boulders. Only in the shelter of burns or beneath a small cliff were there pockets of woodland, showing as fingers of softness in the grain of the land. We passed a couple of narrow lochs that could only be described as water-filled fissures, and another whose shores meandered wildly and created a stunning trifurcate outline.

Not far from the hamlet of Clashnessie we lowered our eighteen-foot canoe, manhandled it over a farm gate and pulled it a few yards into some heather. We went back for some items of gear – a couple of overloaded rucksacks, a black drybag. Clive climbed the gate, passed them over, climbed back. We lugged the stuff to the abandoned canoe. I had tied two nylon ropes to the bow and put big knots in the middle and at each end. Taking one of the ropes, I wrapped some slack crossways around my torso, once and twice, like a belt of rifle shells, then tugged so it bit into my shoulder. Clive did something similar and we bent forward and started hauling. I was surprised at how easy the canoe slid, though this may have been down to the eagerness of my anticipation blurring any great sense of exertion.

The old rule of portage says that every mile gained requires three of effort. We dragged about a quarter of the first mile and returned for the sacks. As there were three to carry we rotated the drybag, I taking it first. Hefting it on to my shoulder I staggered with its weight and dropped it. Squeezing a little slackness in the middle and wrapping the two ends around the nape of my neck worked better, though the weight had me spread-legged and crabbing to keep balanced.

'Let's just go easy,' I said between breaths, when I reached Clive.

'Fine with me. Where are we headed anyway?'

'See those falls?'

I gestured up and across to where the land arched and broke into a series of small crags. Over one of these was a waterfall, radiant in sunshine, the faint roar of it carried to us despite its sound having to fight through the breeze. It was the outflow of Loch an Easain, one branch of a system of narrow linking waterways that drained a big part of the interior. We dragged in steady relays across a kind of inby; there were no sheep but I kept Holly on a long lead, at least until we reached a fence that I thought marked the open moor. At some point we were in line with the waterfall. We started climbing, steeply, and everything changed. The canoe suddenly took on a dead weight, eighty pounds of it. Clive went to support the stern and we only shifted the thing in small increments, each on the count of three. After some fifteen minutes we fell to the ground breathless. When we retraced our steps to fetch the baggage it took almost as long; and then a few yards from the canoe Clive slipped and dropped the drybag. He watched mute as it pitched and barrel-rolled and came to a rest at a point lower than where we'd started.

'That's walking in wellies for you,' I said. 'No grip.'

Clive was still looking down the slope. 'Can't we do this different?' he said.

'We can try.'

'How about we dump it all in the canoe?'

'You mean drag everything at once?'

'Why not?'

'We tried that on another trip, remember?'

'And . . .?'

'And it damn near killed us.'

'*This'll* kill us.'

The slope levelled, allowing the burn to meander and kink, and although the water ran shallow we used its buoyancy to float the canoe upstream. A last haul over a small lip and we stood by the flat openness of Loch an Easain at its westernmost edge, looking across sun-bright waters only faintly troubled by a breeze. Everything stashed and tied, Clive ready in the bow seat, Holly between rucksacks, I waded and shoved and climbed aboard. The canoe sunk a little and rocked. 'Whoah, steady,' Clive said, clutching both gunwales. Holly whined. Part of the hull had caught so I pushed hard on my paddle; a slight scraping noise and we were free, the shore going backwards and then all the effort of our being here justified in those first moments of being afloat, a serene and easy drift from land and kept going only by occasional paddling. For a few minutes, and save for the odd affirmation, we hardly spoke, almost unbelieving that we were here and floating on this strange loch. Our weightlessness felt sensational. I thought it extraordinary that our progress had climbed by factor of about ten, yet our effort was virtually nil. The lightest of strokes propelled us and our advance was marked by the land on either side. It passed like a smooth pan-shot and there were a lot of different and relative movements; the shoreline seemed in a hurry to get past, the land behind not quite as fast, and the hills beyond not at all, at least not in any way I could measure.

As we were so low on the water the land ahead appeared closer and when I stood up the perspective changed markedly. I could see the shores converging to a small neck, with a boulder midstream presenting an option of channels. It was almost too shallow. We went through, scratching the bottom, and eased into a broad stretch, all the while shadowing the left bank. The sun came out. Clive started to sing an old rock number. Only Holly refused to settle. She twitched and jerked and looked at me and then the land and sniffed the air. At one point she moved towards Clive and made the boat rock alarmingly.

'Hey, keep that hound under control.'

'Sorry. Didn't see that coming. She's just a little nervous.'

I got her back to sit on her haunches and reached in my jacket pocket for a small treat but couldn't find anything. 'Sorry old girl, you'll have to wait.'

When our loch finished at an inflowing burn we took the gear and dragged the canoe a short distance to the next; hard work but we were caught up in the general excitement of another unknown loch, and this one hooked and dog-legged like a river that had outgrown its banks. Not far into it was a tiny island. I am not sure at what point just a gathering of rocks becomes an island, but this place was on the cusp of it, barely the width or depth of water round it for us to scrape past nearside, our paddles catching mud and clouding the water. Square ahead we approached a tiny boot-shaped peninsula on an equally small scale, and opposite that a treeless island which I thought would make an appealing camp. From the heel of the headland we gently pushed our craft across the small reach of about seventy yards.

A few seconds before it happened Holly was leaning over the right side. She had one paw on the gunwale and the other hovering just above the water, as if not quite believing its lack of solidity. In the moment I made to pull her back she slipped and went nose-first into the loch. As I was already moving towards her I continued and everything came with me. I was impressed at how quickly and smoothly the canoe rolled and kept rolling until the hull faced the sky and the two of us and Holly were thrashing about in the freezing water.

The cold went into and through me, and for a couple of seconds clamped around my lungs so I couldn't breathe, but I felt no real panic, just a single-minded desire to reach the shore. I got my breathing under control, reached over to grip part of the upturned canoe, kicked my leaden boots and waved my free arm in a kind of breaststroke. The weightlessness had gone, every action sluggish and horribly tiring and barely gaining me any momentum, and for a minute I thought I was only treading water. Then my boot touched ground and I instantly felt safer, though in fact it was the only the softest mud and offered no support. Worse, it might suck me under, so I kept floating until maybe knee-deep and waded the last yards to the stony shore.

Whether for security or from some instinct to help, Holly had swam alongside and now stood by and shook herself hard and greeted Clive, who allowed himself a wry grin as he clambered ashore, drenched clothes hanging on him and water dripping from his lenses. We emptied the rucksacks and opened the carefully-packed contents to check for leakage. Some clothes were sopping and Clive's sleeping bag had dark patches. One of the food bags ran with water, and from it I dropped three small loaves onto a rock where they exploded. We needed to eat the stir-fry or it would ferment. But that was all the damage.

With our things spread in great disassembly on the rocks to dry, I put up my small tent, Clive unrolled his bivouac sack and we wormed into our sleeping bags in a bid to stop shivering. Later, after supping hot tea we laughed and talked it through and agreed that in a much larger loch it might have been a different story. And we would keep a tighter rein on Holly, we said. She was curled up and steaming in a corner of the tent like a large toffee pudding.

Distance covered may be a crude measure of progress, but bearing in mind how little we'd achieved yesterday we were on the loch not much after first light next morning. Dead calm, a gentle sun through gauzy cloud. I wondered how warm I might get in my buoyancy waistcoat. It felt tight, but if I loosened it too much then it might ride up in the event of another dunking. So I didn't. In any case, our location inspired only the slowest of progress, tracing the curves and indentations from where we'd spent the night, along channels that linked to nowhere, themselves ending in a reedy cul-de-sac or a small bay of black sand. Here was a flooded maze and its unravelling allowed us to forget ourselves, so we cared not when led astray or seduced by the promise of a new shoreline. The still waters gave a double image of everything worth seeing, particularly the fissured surface of a large erratic that seemed ready to topple. Perched at the water's edge, it drew us and we passed so close we were able to stretch to place a palm on its rough grain.

The shorelines came together and there seemed no way through until at the last moment they widened into a new basin, Garbh Loch Beag. We went slowly across and at the far end slid into a tiny reed-filled cove, stepped ashore and hauled everything across a small isthmus to Garbh Loch Mor. Part of this morning's plan was to explore this loch, especially the small archipelago of rocks and isles that nestled at the opposite corner, but I also knew we faced some big hauls later, so we decided to push on. We arrowed across and sought a place to land. The bank came straight down with no easy way onto it, at least that I could see. Clive side-paddled in a manner all of his own to present us broadside and while he kept us there I unloaded and climbed arm over arm to better ground. We hefted and shouldered the dripping canoe and took it grunting to the rucksacks. An eight-foot high deer fence barred our way, a reminder that however wild and beautiful this area seemed to us, it was in fact like so much of the Highlands, far along the road of ecological neglect. The fence protected a square mile of native saplings, planted not long after the crofters' buyout and in a bid to restore at least a part of this moribund region to something of its past richness. If the owners of any estate are unwilling to reduce overall deer numbers then I welcome these intrusions. In the days ahead we thought little of the inconvenience of getting a canoe, dog and ourselves over their barriers.

This fence was of the crosshatched type and easy to climb. First lifting the bow to the top wire, we pushed until the body of the canoe rested midway and in near perfect balance. Clive reached up and supported the stern. I monkeyed over and lowered the bow, then the rest of the canoe. Transporting Holly was a little trickier. With an arm under her belly I climbed slowly up and over, a manoeuvre helped by her remaining calm throughout. I can't imagine she holds specific memories beyond some habitual workaday routines but in the last three years I have lifted and lowered her over countless fences. Once I carried her for a mile across deep snow when her legs gave up.

On the other side the grass and heather had grown so thick it was like walking on a mattress; it certainly helped to ease the effort needed to drag a canoe. Birch, rowan, Scots pine and other saplings were growing in irregular groves. Wind and autumn had stripped much of their foliage and it took an effort of will to imagine a mature woodland in this bleak place; but I have seen Scots pine flourish at 2,000 feet in the Cairngorms, so why not here?

Each loch reached marked a step up the levels, there was a short drop to the next, steep enough for us to load everything into the canoe and hope gravity would slide us down. I turned the bow uphill, lashed a rope around my forearm and nudged the canoe until the slope claimed it. I was jerked forward and began to run, guiding it as best I could, though more than once the craft lumbered broadside and tried to roll. But this was a hundred times better than dragging.

Loch na Creige Loisgte was narrow and may have been only five hundred yards long. Perhaps it was because the loch sat low in its basin, but I thought the waters appeared especially dark, an impression reinforced by a line of overhanging crags that we passed to our left. Huge boulders that once belonged to these crags were set at every angle on the slope below, like some ancient collapse frozen in mid-slide. I imagined mammoth blocks resting on the lochbed beneath us, and it all suggested the waters might be very deep. Only the presence of reed beds indicated otherwise; they made a scouring sound and the seed-pods flicked about as we went by, moving purposely slowly, for we knew what faced us when we reached the little inflow.

There was a straight half mile of rough moor to climb, and to make it manageable we broke it into sections, at least in our heads. At the start of each section there was a moment when we each took a rope and leaned hard into it, and at some point the effort told, the canoe shifted, just a little and very slowly; in fact more slowly than I'd ever walked, but it moved and we made ground, going uphill to the next loch.

Changes in terrain were the problem. Heather going to grass or bare ground, or a minor upturn in gradient, or contrary aspect, all or any could snag the hull and have us stalling. So we read the land and sought some secret thing that might aid our slide or avoid what would trouble it. Like surface water. That was generally good, though not burns and especially not the one we were following. It had worn down and carved spurs and its own small valley, that a number of times crossed our path in its loopings. We should have left it well alone, but it drained the upper loch, the next of the levels on our route.

Hauling and countermarching and relaying, we went on in a slow accepting way. From one rise the blue ridge of Quinag half a dozen miles away wobbled and centred as we set the canoe, then we stood and looked east and west, back the way we had come. Much was already hidden. Of the lochans we'd crossed, only here and there was a sheen of water, still and small and pewter in the moorland scale.

A joyful moment came in the first minute on the new loch, cutting free of land and beginning a slow drift,

caressed by an off-shore breeze. After our claustropho-
bic world of effort there was a lovely sense of space on
Loch an Eich Uidhir. The northern shoreline ran more or
less straight, then about midway a slender promontory
reached some distance into the waters and we paddled
slowly around and considered crossing to the opposite
side where the map marked a tiny isle. We would have to
camp soon, but I wanted to go further. I wanted an island,
a place nobody visited and few had seen, some natural
artefact of the past that was outside of anyone's memory
or at the very least only on its margins. Studying the map
I thought I had found one. A nameless lochan not a mile
away, and on it, as if afloat, a tiny fragment of land. That
was our place.

We headed for the exit, then along a creek so narrow
that in one place we punted at the banks. Large rocks
broke the peaty waters and sloped away at obtuse angles.
It carried us to the smaller Loch na Buidheig, and across
this we came to an even smaller loch with a claw shape
and a far fringe of reeds. A deer fence to negotiate, then a
lochan whose only memorable feature was a dead rowan
that radiated its branches like a starburst.

A paling sky shrunk the day. Soon it would be too
late for anything. We pulled and tugged over land that
was clearly more grazed and wind-shorn, and sometimes
ran threadbare. Mindful of the last big haul, this time we
avoided the burn and instead pulled over clipped grasses
and mosses and attained a little rhythm. The slope dipped
and then there was our loch. Probably less than a quarter-
mile long, shorter across. And its shoreline ran vermicular,
more various than our map could register.

Even in the half-light the island appeared riotously
overgrown. We floated out for a better look, going around

it once. There was no inviting bay or beach, and it seemed well defended by a steepness that itself was packed with pygmy woodland and bushes. Small lichenous outcrops overhung the water, and even in corners where the rock gave out I doubted if we could safely climb the sides. Only in one spot did the shore suck inwards, and when my eyes adjusted to the gloom on this east side I saw a natural rock culvert. I stepped onto it, took the gear from Clive, fought up through tall heather to where the slope tabled. Under my feet was no earth that I could feel, nothing solid at all, the heather so thick and undisturbed it had lost all memory of ground. If there was anything smooth or steady underneath, the surface didn't mirror it. The great bushy ends sagged and folded and were so interwoven a footfall in one place sent a ripple in another, as if a single living organism had colonised the island. Holly moved as she might in deep snow, in big leaps with her hind legs splayed. For us, walking was a matter of balance. When Clive came up, aided by a couple of paddles, he made to jump a few times like a child testing a new trampoline.

'Must be centuries of growth here,' he said. Then something distracted him. 'Where did Holly get to?'

I looked about and shouted. A movement, a head and ears appearing and disappearing. There were no nesting birds but all the same I didn't want her getting stuck.

'Yeah, it's completely ungrazed. I've heard of deer swimming to these islands but I seriously doubt if they could make it up these sides.'

'Has anyone been here? Maybe we're the first,' Clive said.

'A great thought, but I bet bods from one or other of the conservation charities have poked about with their clipboards and survey sheets. They'll have been all over it counting and categorising, you know, doing their science and making a case.'

'For its protection?'

'I reckon so. You can't put a price on this.'

'Then should we even be here?'

Clive had a point. We could appreciate the antiquity of this place without the need to climb its margins and set foot and pass the night on its brow, and part of me couldn't escape the notion that our every step was a trespass and our presence unwanted. Not one creature which lived here knew us, and it's just possible they were holding their combined breaths, waiting for us to go, and for good.

Finding a place for a tent was hopeless. Where the heather seemed level it often concealed hollows and rocks, and in any case our judgement was failing with the light. On a spot that appeared slightly less sloping I laid the inner and tied the corners to the woody stems, the same with the outer, crawled inside and made the whole flimsy structure sink another foot. With my mat inflated I stretched out and went through a series of shufflings until I reached a tolerable position, though my legs were bent and everything canted. If it rained I would get wet; if a wind picked up I would be in the open, no question. Holly as well.

Clive shouted that the heather made a 'bloody fine mattress'. He asked how I was coping and wondered about supper. We had an easy heat-up meal of jalfrezi and rice which I cooked in the vestibule, holding the gas burner with one hand, the pot and contents in the other. In half an hour it had gone dark and there was only a filament of light from Clive's torch as he rustled about. A light breeze came and went and moved something against the fly. I thought it unusual for the air to be so still in such an exposed spot. A bird called from across the water. When this sound ended the world was silent. Everything was still holding its breath.

The quiet that put me to sleep was there when I woke. It was light but not completely. Holly wanted out. When I opened the vestibule she put one paw out, lifted her muzzle, nosed the air. Something told me she hesitated because of the fog that had formed during the night and now ringed the island. Though it may have been a consequence of anabatic breezes rising over the moor and cooling, I had little sense of sea in it and found it hard to imagine the lolling waters of the Minch only a few miles away.

No account of the next section can ever be adequate. In a pattern I could not read the map presented what appeared a random arrangement of small lochs. Unlike the lower systems the lochs here existed largely in isolation, like closed cells, or joined only tenuously through trickle-down or misfit waters. There being no natural line I might sensibly have gone with the shortest land bridges and fewest minutes of portage, but that was never the point. So instead I lined up a route that was cranky, lonely and nondescript, and Clive happily went along with my reasoning. Here were the forgotten places of Assynt, and in the few hours it took to cross their uncharted waters and haul and drag the yards to Loch Crocach, we encountered a rare mixing of conditions and place where, in utter quiet and stillness, I saw the simple beauty of shoreline, scrub island, rock, tree and peat. We followed no trail where folk had come before with their boats, saw no pathways or cairns or quarter-standing shieling or any clue of humankind, and I could fully believe that nature had set everything here in balance and that for every elemental force on the scale there was a counter one.

Unimportant is the precise order of things, but I know our first launch was into the wrong loch – too narrow, which the map confirmed when I bothered to check. We pulled out to the left and beaked into what looked like a flooded crater, waves reaching across the still waters. Fog hid the shores and strengthened a misapprehension that this was a big space. Then a loch so small we crossed slowly in under a minute. Reeds and a mud floor told of its shallowness, and conjoined boulders stood in the middle that I could easily believe were slowly sinking. Over a slight rise and we were into a creek barely wide enough for a paddle. It opened and we kept to a shoreline of stunted willows growing from water like mangroves with their bare branches interlaced. In one corner a soggy ditch drained into a loch where knuckles and inlets faded in the fog and I regretted not seeing how they ended. Loch nan Uidhean Beag was bisected. Then each taking a rope we floated the canoe on a spiralling burn into Loch nan Lion. The south shore made up the lower slopes of a craggy hill, and after a quarter mile their shelter gave a niche for some long-standing rowan and birch, twelve feet high and almost as wide, the largest trees we would see in five days. A tongue of dark water, a rough slide to another level, and we looked about the striking and broad-reaching Loch Crocach. This loch shows a trench-shape of maybe two miles, chiefly north-south in alignment, but its middle broadens out to a large bay filled with many wooded islands, as if the land here had cleaved from beneath and folded and broke and was half-lost in a Pleistocene deluge.

For no other reason than sheer curiosity we paddled the still waters among the islands, through the narrowest of channelways and past small islets that rose sharply to cupolas of heather or gnarly woodland. All we saw above water was twinned on the surface, though a little darker and inverted, and each of the islands echoed the others, yet lochside and close-up they went through every guise of difference. A hanging garden of trees and plants was assembled in a manner no human agency could emulate, or we passed a standing rock face whose cracks housed red and green mosses. The living grew from the dead and there were reasons why it was so, and none of it to do with us.

There was a lot of illusion in our movement in relation to the islands. Especially with the corners. Each island had a corner beyond which we could not see, yet as we rounded it we found only curves and a further corner. Only once and on the largest of the islands did the shore turn back to make two clear sides.

Here we nosed the canoe, scrambled ashore on the sloping side and worked up a ridge to a high point, though it was barely that. Rank heather swallowed each footfall, and it was as hard to move as on this morning's camp. A birch wood undisturbed for hundreds or maybe thousands of years crowded the lee slope, pale and twisted and with all manner of hairy growths hanging on a wickerwork of branches. From our slight vantage the smaller islands hid their separation or grew from each other, and one appeared loaded with trees. But we had no more time. We returned to our craft and cast off and paddled slow-arm for a mile to the farthest end, then into an adjacent cove. In that short time the sky darkened and wind made the loch waters tremble. Rain started to fall as we took the canoe out and began a series of hauls that the map said would get us to Loch an Tuirc.

The lochan-trail led us to a place half-water, half-land, and we had to push against the muddy floor with the paddle blades. The portages refused to ease. I thought the wet ground might aid the canoe, but in fact as the rain came on thicker and the wind stronger we slipped and slowed. On one loch we were made to paddle hard for the first time, then realised we'd reached the wrong outflow, so backpaddled around a small bluff and came out on the east. Two separate lochs nestled in the small basin, but by now the rain and wind drew a damp screen across our world and the remaining daylight hours were pared down to essentials of travel – the paddling and lifting and carrying. We bodily hauled everything up the steepness and above a last nameless lochan, then bent with ropes and emptied our lungs in taking the canoe to the crest of a hill. I studied the way ahead, but cloud and smirr narrowed what I could see. Loch an Tuirc filled a sort of valley below, and farther east and south only muted browns and greys of a crumpled land could be glimpsed. Quinag presented a dim outline; Suilven and her sandstone acolytes were gone.

With everything lashed down and using the ropes as leverage, we ran alongside the canoe as it slid and suddenly accelerated and pulled free and turned onto its belly. Keeping the ropes tighter we marshalled it to some stepping stones and the west terminus of Loch an Tuirc. The running warmed Holly, though now sedentary atop one of the sacks, she whined and shivered. With light fading we went hard into our strokes. We'd seen the fuzz of native woodland from the hilltop on the south shore and hoped it would offer shelter in an otherwise open and barren land. A dinghy rested half-sunken on the shore and there were signs cattle had lately pastured here. It was less wild than the lochans on the plateau, but the trees were long-lived and stately and still retained much of their summer foliage. There was cover here, I said to Clive.

The trees came right to the lochside, their roots growing among the stones and in the water itself. I swung the nose to where the bank curved inward; Clive gripped a root, climbed ashore with a rope. Holly jumped two-footed and I handed over the dripping sacks. Together we shifted the empty canoe onto the bank, then went on small circular scouting trips. Thanks to the cattle there was short grass among the trees and I found a lovely level place for a tent. We were not the first to come here, though probably the first for a while. A ring of fire-stones had grass in its centre and there were a couple of tins so rusted they may have lain there for decades.

Having carried the canoe through the trees close to the chosen site, we faced the hull into the wind, leaning it against two trees so that it protected a space for Clive to lie, then secured the bow and stern lest the wind in the coming night change direction. I snapped together my single tent pole, threaded it, pegged the side and guys and marvelled at the straight lines and taut shape. A showroom tent. I shed my layers, separated the wet from the dry and made an inventory of the food, and got into my sleeping bag. Holly was curled in her favourite corner, the gas firing a pan of loch water. When ready it was easy to fill Clive's cup with tea, twist the lid and lob it over. I did this three times before frying vegetables and chicken for supper. Then I lay back and listened to the rain coming on heavy, larger drops from high boughs clopping on the nylon of the tent and beading the sides.

We gave up on conversation. Wave sounds ran along the shore and in the trees there was a soft thrash of wind, but it was the acoustic of rain that eclipsed all thoughts and carried me to moments ill-remembered, though lingering on in some twilight child memory, of places and camps uprooted from different times that overlapped and came together in a kind of longing.

Though it finally stopped raining, the memory of it was kept alive by sporadic leaf drop and the mist low over the loch, here and there drifting paper-thin to show the brown of heather and bluish of stone outcrop. While Clive slept I got up to stretch and walked a little in the woods. I could see no reason why these trees had survived centuries of overgrazing, when all about the hills and moor were bare. They were well-sheltered and had colonised a north-facing slope that rose steeply to a couple of hundred feet above the loch, but deer, sheep and cattle can and do wander here. There was little young growth and most of trees I noted were aged.

Clive was up and about his morning rituals a little painfully, I thought.

'Slept all cockled and twisted like your Holly, only I don't think I'm made for that sort of thing,' he said, arching his sides and trying to conceal a grimace.

'Reckon it's time you spent some of that pen money on a new bag. Why freeze your balls off for the sake of a few quid?'

'Yeah, maybe, but I love that old sack. It's been half way round the world, and remember it kept me alive in the Karakoram.'

That was an old story and maybe a tall one.

'Methinks you exaggerate. Anyway, have a look at

this. It should warm you up. I thought we might angle for here.' I ran an index finger over some blue, a place called Gorm Loch Mor. Between here and there were lochs and an awful lot of land and contours bunched with shadings of rocks.

'More of the same then?'

'I'm afraid so.'

Loading the canoe, we paddled into the middle of the loch, then bored through the narrows. Close to the islands at the east end were the remains of a croft, Doirean Domhnuill, right by the shore. We didn't stop but could see the green sward from generations of cattle manuring. Further on an old wall marked a place to alight and we pulled to Loch an Tuir, much smaller, like a misfit corrie lochan. More ruins ran in the bracken slopes above the loch and again we chose not to visit, having a long day ahead. For a time we sweated and dragged northeast from the loch on slowly rising ground, grass-covered for the most part. At a featureless watershed where sub-surface burns couldn't decide which way to flow we paused, then went in the wrong direction. Nothing could be seen beyond an encircling of pale outcrops, where the bedrock came through like rashes. I went to the perimeter of our sightline and cast about looking for our lochan. In the land below was an isolated and reedy loch, but the wrong shape. A body of water measuring nearly a quarter mile long should be easy to find. I looked back to Clive who was bent and facing the canoe, as if addressing some beast of burden that refused to move. He still wore his red buoyancy jacket. I veered left or north to a stone crest and here the land swept down to another lochan, pear-shaped with a tiny scrubby island, for all the world tailor-made for its basin. We went down and slowly paddled across.

Considering how lush we'd found much of this land, that downstream of the lochan seemed especially poor, with coarse and short grasses only. Blackened stumps of old heather told a story of a recent burning by local graziers, muirburn. The land had been sterilised, cheated of its richness. Before reaching Loch Beannach we followed the line of a newish sheep or cattle fence. Wire from the old one still lay in tangled coils, rusting slowly along with other agricultural debris.

At the extreme northwestern tip of Loch Beannach we put in. This was a lovely entryway to a loch which compares with Crocach in size, though it is roughly cuneiform in shape. Forested islands abounded at its eastern quarter.

A steady mile of paddling with the breeze on our nose carried us beyond the headlands that clawed from the north shore and small upright boulders to the first of the islands, stretched quite long and thin as if it once formed a land bridge that divided the loch. The sides appeared virtually inaccessible. Rowan, willows and birch grew abundantly to the water's edge, and often a great thicket of branches hung over to skim the surface like some arboreal mutation. Where the island bulged, the weathered and eroded face of rocks carried the most twisted of trees, their bark flaky or mossed in cobwebs, and I couldn't always tell if their frames were alive and would leaf again in another spring or stood as gaunt effigies of a life past.

At the northern tip Clive got onto some angled boulders. He rolled a stone over the rope and took off with Holly to explore. I followed after a little lunch, first over a huge-girthed rowan that had died many years ago yet remained host to secondary growths coming from its base.

I dragged my feet up a slope of tall heather, and ducked and swung under boughs that curled up in great tentacles loaded with all manner of lichen and fern, a woodland so thick I lost all sense of being on an island. I fell in with an uncertain beast trail which hooked and contoured and led nowhere. I suspected deer swam the short channel, but not many and not very often. Other folk will have been here but they'd left no trace I could see.

A swish and crack of something to my left. It was Clive. He must have heard me as well, for only something as large and clumsy as a human could make so much noise. Through a tangle of branches the sheen of the loch ruffled in the breeze. We could see the cape without having to reach it and given how interwoven the growths were I doubt we could even if we'd wanted. Holly listened and smelt the air. I hoped we hadn't unsettled whatever creatures might be living here.

On the water again the larger island drew us, but we didn't attempt a landing, instead going about its base in a slow circumnavigation, then through a small archipelago of scrub-covered rocks. A breeze pushed us broadside and came and went and sighed as we neared a stand of alder and birch. Yellowing foliage fluttered *en masse* and individual leaves drifted about in the air and confettied the dark waters around us.

On the north shore we tied up and I climbed a bracken slope up to a ruin. Walls made from whatever was then found reached only three or four feet high, and under a neutral sky I stood before it as you might an unknown grave. I looked back and down to where our canoe was tied to an old tree and across the quiet loch and wooded isles and low hills, and I was struck by the human scale of it all, even if that was an illusion.

This shieling was known as Ruigh Coinich and was almost certainly part of the Loch Beannach 'township' where a number of families lived and worked throughout the year. I subsequently found through research that these families had names of Kerr, Macleod and Mackascle, and all were evicted in 1821 when the land became part of George Gunn's sheep farm. Of the rest of the interior I found evidence of only one other permanently occupied dwelling, at Poll Tigh a' Charraigein, a couple of miles northeast of here. The inhabitants were subtenants and cleared by Kenneth Scobie in 1812. The other ruins that today dot the empty straths of the lochan interior were likely summer shielings only.

I thought about the poet Norman MacCaig and wondered how many times he'd stood here and looked out over the same view. He liked nothing more than to pass the day fishing on some remote loch five miles from the nearest house or human. Even in Assynt solitude on that scale would be hard to find, but here in the peace of Beannach I knew what he had sought. Would he have minded our presence? Canoeists and fishermen have an old antagonism, but I'll wager in this instance there would have been harmony.

I discovered MacCaig's poetry more than two decades ago when chancing upon the little-known anthology *Poems of the Scottish Hills*, edited by Hamish Brown, for which he also writes the Foreword. I was taken immediately by his quiet observation and brilliant wordcraft. He thought unconventionally about landscape and conveyed it so cleverly in verse. At best he could be spellbinding.

Wagnerian Devil signed the Coigach score;
And God was Mozart when he wrote Cul Mor.

MacCaig spent up to ten weeks every year in Assynt, mostly at Achmelvich by the coast, and from this association grew a deep and lasting affection for the land and its people. By the sea and in the shadow of these low hills he forged lifelong friendships and penned some of his best work. One theme continually revisited is the depth of feeling, described simply as 'love', that he has for the landscape, and nowhere does this better emerge than in his long poem, 'A Man in Assynt' (1969), especially in these lines close to the beginning:

> Who owns this landscape?
> Has owning anything to do with love?
> For it and I have a love affair, so nearly human
> we even have quarrels.

'A Man in Assynt' rolls along in a beauty of rhythm and rich composition that engages both intellect and emotion. It draws me from whatever mood I'm in and enfolds me in its own peculiar enchantment. Beginning as a discussion with open questions thrown to the wind, it thereafter unwinds through the interplay of a geological and human story. MacCaig, the pacifist and humanitarian, shied away from political commentary, but in this poem there is anger about the Clearances: 'men trampled under the hoofs of sheep and driven by deer to the ends of the earth'. The final lines express the hope that people will return like a flood tide to resettle the bays and straths.

MacCaig lived long enough to witness some small reversal of the old injustice when a group of crofters campaigned and subsequently bought the 21,000 acre North Lochinver Estate in 1992. Whatever pleasure this shift to community ownership brought, I don't think he expected a repopulation to match his vision, and perhaps here he betrayed a certain romanticism, the Edinburgh intellectual on a fishing holiday dreamily eying his Pheasant Tail fly on a sultry noonday on Loch Beannach and later tramping home to peat fire and desk to craft verse for townies.

Assynt has experienced a recent small rise in population, but largely as a result of retired folk returning home and the settling here of wealthy newcomers. As in other remote Highland regions, if the young cannot find work they will leave, and beyond seasonal tourism and a cash-strapped local authority who can provide it? The Assynt Crofters Trust is keen to encourage young crofters and has a programme in place, but few are attracted to a tenuous living that without subsidy would cease to be viable. But then I wonder if a solitude-loving MacCaig would really appreciate the crowds, a new Ullapool at Achmelvich, new villages and this old ruin rebuilt into someone's dream home with modern storeys and enclosed garden and satellite dish and vehicle track running a mile and a half to the main road.

We canoed to the far reaches of Beannach, met a small feeder burn and pulled ashore. The lochans from here promised to run fewer and to reach Drumbeg in a day and a half seemed a journey over at least as much land as water. This side was less grazed and our hauling and tramping released the scent of bog myrtle that covered the ground in some profusion. Twice I stumbled in a ditch or unseen burn, and after the ease of Beannach a mile's portage now took the better part of two hours. A small lochan below the pass gave a few minutes respite, but in truth only served as pause before the ensuing effort, particularly as the slope rose and tiredness stole our rhythm. We called on something brute within to carry us to where the ground levelled, keeping on task, tugging with the old emotion of youth until gravity became the third man and the canoe ran of its own accord. We fetched sacks and loaded and eased everything down an angle of maybe forty-five degrees straight to the faintly rippling waters of Loch a' Ghleannain Shalaich.

Our loch was not half a mile in length and we bore slowly northwest. The side we'd come down banked sharply and carried an enormous amount of growth – rowans, yellowing ferns, willows; and rising beyond were rags of gorse and bracken as the land came together and the waters stilled. For a change I occupied the bow seat, Holly just in front, and looked over at my paddle making little whirls and a trail of drops seen clearly in the land-dark of reflection. The water had a fathomless quality right into the shallows. Then the current picked up and all the loch narrowed into a curving helmet, after which the waters ran fast and broken.

We splashed out to guide our craft and floated it some way along the burn. Where it calmed and deepened I stepped back onboard and punted using the bank, though only for a minute. The burn dropped through spurs, and its noise betrayed a run of small falls. It foamed and hooked and the banks grew so rocky we carried the canoe and returned for the gear, and when the flow half-quietened we again stacked everything on board and I resumed my punting.

The current ran more swiftly than Clive could walk, and where a fence crossed the flow I reached for the bank and waited. Here the land showed the ruinous effects of old muirburn; the rich matrix of plants was gone, leaving only black earth and large-bladed grasses. I ran my eyes over the scene and thought there might be some contradiction between an organisation's public aims and actual practice, as on seeing this I could only conclude that the manner of husbandry here was solely to shrink the vegetation to what might thrive and in doing so to homogenise the land. The bludgeoned ground seemed to suck at the canoe. As we failed to drag, so we carried, at first for a minute at a time, then as the contours came together, in short counts or until one of us dropped our end; and in this way we reached the shores of a little loch tucked in a half-amphitheatre of low hills.

Under gloaming skies I went up to a small lookout point and studied the land in an arc from where we had come: folds of dark moor and bedrock and occasionally something perched on a ridgeline, a stone upright like a dolmen. Though we'd crossed it largely on water there was next to nothing of water to be seen. All the lochs and every surface were concealed by the hand of their own cradling. I had an idea where they should or might be, and in a few places I thought ground was missing. I lingered and looked down at the movements of Clive. He was rummaging through his goods and chattels, picking things up and placing them down, working slowly, from weariness and not for precision, I suspected. He unrolled his mat and wrestled off his buoyancy jacket, setting it where his head might lie. For long seconds he just stood there gazing at it, then looked about at his feet and stamped, and moved it to another place.

'What were you doing up there?' he said when I'd come down.

'Oh, just looking.'

'See much?'

'No, not really. It was getting dark. In any case, from where I stood the waters are pretty much blocked from view, as if they're not there at all.'

'They're there all right, and the bits in between. I've got blisters to prove it. That last carry aged me.'

I mumbled agreement and there was a minute when each of us professed the greater fatigue and made mock gestures of sympathy, like some stylised ceremony of companionship.

Clive lifted the lid of his small pan and peered at water slowly coming to boil.

'Well . . .' he said, and paused as if weighing some great pronouncement on the nature of things. 'Let's have one of those teabags.'

I pitched among some bracken a few yards away and settled with a brew, and later after a simple meal drank the last slug of bourbon and shared with Clive the last quarter litre of wine.

In the morning we crossed the lochan in a couple of minutes, then dragged over a low pass to the much larger Gorm Loch Mor. It was still overcast, though where the cloud stretched I thought we might at last feel the sun's warmth. We paddled unhurriedly and I knew we had two easy miles of this if we kept to the indented western side. Holly pricked her ears and I noticed a small wooden rowboat lashed to a little tree. I gestured to Clive. A movement drew our attention upward to a rock bluff. A bespectacled man in army surplus and two dogs was coming down, maybe three hundred yards away. One hand clutched something that hung from his neck, probably a pair of binoculars. Holly sent out regulation barks but I don't remember the man looking over, at least not that I saw, and we shouted no word or greeting. He

stopped and raised his binoculars and studied the opposite shore, and by the time he'd cast off and was rowing
we were well ahead, rounding a headland and creeping
into a small bay.

In keeping with our time on the levels, we went quietly
about our ploy, passing a notable scrub-covered island
and glided through a scattering of boulders and reefs.
Ahead and aslant we could see the waters squeeze into a
neck where the loch made its continuation. The man was
in the middle of the loch and rowing hard and steady to
the north like us, though I calculated he was still behind.
I swung the canoe and went straight for the neck. It was
something subliminal but I found myself working harder,
increasing my paddle rotation and coming down hard on
each stroke, Clive as well. The shoreline passed swiftly
now. I was impressed at the man's rowing technique and
part of me thought he was trying to reach the gap first,
that some male competitiveness was at work or just that
he wanted a guarantee of contact with us. He kept it up
for a straight mile and was not far trailing as we slipped
through the narrows and into a smaller loch. This briefly
yawned in two arms that mirrored each other, then came
around. We nosed ashore and took the sacks to a notch
in some low hills.

The man tied his boat and followed, or appeared
to. On our return for the canoe I held back with Holly
and Clive went to meet him. The man carried his feet
in the same purposeful way that he oared his boat. His
dogs, a spaniel and collie that may have been a cross,
loped beside him and were only moderately interested in
Clive. When I caught up they had been talking for some
minutes. He smoked roll-ups and grinned and moved his
head in greeting. If it were not for the dogs he might have

been a birdwatcher. He was a self-employed stalker and member of the Assynt Crofters Trust, he said, and had a group coming tomorrow. In a disarming tone and betraying no hint of proprietorship he asked if we were aware that this was the stalking season. He offered a phone number for when or if we came again, and talked in a soft lilt for some minutes about the Trust and farming and local deer numbers, and asked a question about our route from here. I unfolded the map and pointed at this and that loch. He mouthed a whistle, pressed a finger to his mouth and said why not just slide down to the road here, at Nedd, only a mile away. I may have been wrong, but I had a sense he wanted us off the land lest we disturb what deer were found between here and Drumbeg. No, I said, we'd come too far to cop out now.

Then, while he peeled off right, we collected the canoe and took it to where we'd dumped the sacks. Below was the jagged shape of Loch a' Bhraighe but the hillocks beyond blocked any views of the smaller lochans before Drumbeg. The slope dropped sharply. At its steepest gravity threatened to take the canoe, but we kept a tight rein and commandeered and lowered it to the rocky shore. There was more wind now, the loch stippled like beach sand after an ebb tide. Coming through a cloud window the sun sent the waters shimmering, the new light in rashes between shadows over the land, paling the rocks to bone and irradiating the dun grasses.

With no cause to rush we went slowly for a half hour, finding the small narrows with a reef barely holding enough water for us to float over and into another loch of about the same length. In an arm that reached furthest west we pulled onto the bank and sat in the sun eating the last of our food. Again there was an impression of being at the centre of some great wild and untrammelled space, despite knowing we were but two miles from a road and the small community of Nedd. Maybe this land with its pockets of richness and pervading illusion is kept alive by miracle, so that the lochs with only one exception remain untarnished, the tracks few and the ride of hills still have their own natural outline. MacCaig was right when he wrote no man can own this land, not the millionaire or poacher or farmer or even he who loves it. To love the land is not to possess it or shake from it some puny return or reduce it to a few species of plant and animal or cross it with roads or alter its water dynamic, making it meet some economic measure. To love it is simply to let it be.

Fresh clouds rolled in as the next portage took us yet lower, and to what was no larger than a park pond with craggy mature trees on one side. We pulled across a peat track, and for most of the next hour faced into a damp wind before reaching the reed-filled Loch Bad an Og. It rained steadily and the wind came all the stronger as we nosed a mass of reeds which nodded three or four feet above the gunwales, finding the burn where it left the loch and deciding to follow it to Loch Drumbeg.

At this stage in our travails we'd reached a level of familiarity with the canoe that made any portage a deal less onerous than in the early days. We could weigh better the outcome of drag or carry, or judge how it might slide over such or such an incline. Its dimensions we knew more fully than an abstract plan and I carried the memory of its deadweight around in my head. Only a quirk of terrain led to a misjudgement. Or maybe it was just plain tiredness. Because I made the mistake of keeping too close to the burn. It had eaten down into its own channel, and in this we managed to wedge the canoe so perfectly

I thought only a spate would ever release it. Sinking to my knees and wrapping both arms about the bow I lifted aggressively, Clive pulling at the yoke, and inch by inch the land surrendered its grip.

A squall arrived as we put into the loch. On the north side, through driving rain we could see smart detached cottages and a place more manicured than anywhere we'd been for five days. A large headland afforded some early shelter, but rounding it we came fully against the wind and paddled hard to make any headway. There is a chain of small wooded islands south to north, and in their lee we hopped across the loch, the squall passing just as we left the last of them, striking the mainland at a small bay by the coast road and a few minutes from Drumbeg. Holly leapt ashore, and for an instant I thought she made to kiss the ground, but there was a different smell here. And whether she thought it good or not I don't know.

Finding Ardnamurchan

On the beach at Sanna with the waves and gulls and a thin chilly breeze and sun beating down I saw no one. If there were any ghosts I couldn't feel them.

I'd been here as a small boy and played among these same rockpools with my brothers, running down the dunes, making patterns in the sand with a driftwood stick. The old go unnoticed to the young, but was there on that day, I wonder, a grey-haired man and woman, one kneeling the other standing, both pawing the water and filling a sack with whatever had been gathered? And on my way to the sands did I pay any mind to the untidy farm, the half dozen cattle and wandering sheep and strip of ripening hay? Some makeshift buildings linked by muddy trails and the waste of beasts? Was there a face at the seaward window of a small cottage, wistful at watching the children play, yet frowning at where my father had parked our aging Jowett?

Alasdair Maclean, who wrote *Night Falls on Ardnamurchan*, rails at tourists who drove their cars onto the precious machair, an ancient raised beach unique to the region. He recalls it from childhood, 'a vast and airy island of grass and wild flowers'. But thanks to the hammering it had received from the vehicles of holidaymakers, by 1970 it had all but gone. Alasdair doesn't just blame the tourist. Overgrazing by crofters' livestock was perhaps in the long-term more culpable, but the disappearance of the Sanna machair, I discovered, was also a metaphor for

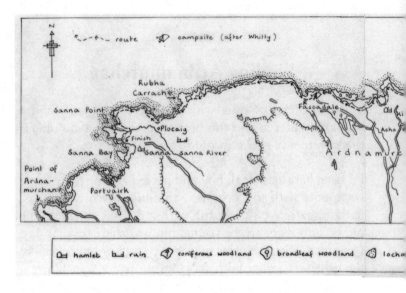

a wider demise, and in particular the passing into history of this once bustling crofting township.

I always knew I'd been to Sanna. To a child the word is like 'sand', which is here in abundance, along with sea and sky. Our family came in ignorance of course, not knowing much beyond what facts were supplied by our cotton-backed Ordnance Survey map. We had no way of accounting for the ruined or empty dwellings, nor knew of a pool in the Sanna River where local crofters drowned unwanted puppies – Toll nan Conn, 'hole of the dogs' – or that the working croft we passed, with its elderly occupants, the Macleans, was the last such in Sanna and was even then in its final painful years.

Alasdair's parents, Iain and Elizabeth, left their native Ardnamurchan in the years after the First World War, and like many Highlanders of that generation, went to seek work in the southern cities. They settled in Glasgow, had

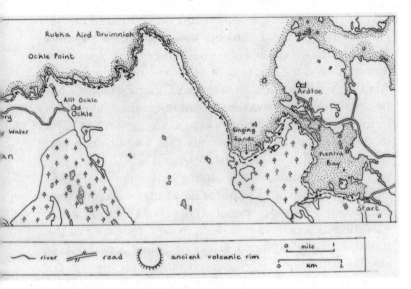

four children, three boys and a girl. Alasdair writes that they were so hard-up his elder brother went to live permanently with their crofting grandparents in Sanna. His father worked for the Clyde Navigation Trust, which ran the Greater Glasgow Docks system, but it was a poorly paid job and eventually in the early 1950s he returned to Ardnamurchan to run the family croft. From what Alasdair writes it is clear his father had no illusions about the crofting life. He was returning to his roots, reconnecting with an old lineage and a tradition of working the land in the way his ancestors had for thousands of years. There was no money in it, he knew that. 'Poverty accompanied him north', Alasdair says. And remained with him until he died.

Night Falls on Ardnamurchan has the story of those years. Largely based on the raw material of his father's journal, it goes way beyond the retelling of a vanished way of life. Here is a meditation on the paradoxes of eking a living from a hard but beautiful land set against the fault-line of a father-son relationship. It is about love and death and the meaning or otherwise of our time here. Alasdair's compulsion to write was motivated by what he calls 'a debt of conscience owed to certain gravestones in the remote townships of Western Ardnamurchan', and in doing so he unearths feelings that for too long had remained hidden – anger, shame, regret.

I have a memory of the author appearing in a television programme after publication of his book sometime in the early 1980s. The detail is gone, but I recall Alasdair narrating as a camera follows him on a foot tour of the tumbled and abandoned crofts of Sanna, one roofless shieling after another. Alasdair shares with his viewers the names of the last occupants and something of their lives, pointing out an overgrown garden, a field gone to grass, old boundaries now unmarked. At around the same time I bought a booklet of his poems in Fort William. But I'd never read his book. Then one day, when researching something in Inverness Library, I came across a hardback first edition. I sat for hour after hour reading.

'A shilling life will give you all the facts and tell you precious little about the man who stands trembling behind them,' Alasdair writes close to the beginning. He wanted to place his late father centre-stage, to speak for himself, and to this end he selects two years from his father's journal, 1960 and 1970, and for each month he faithfully reproduces the same three days, at the beginning, middle and end. At a first glance his father's entries (italicised to distinguish them from Alasdair's much longer parallel commentary) are unremarkable, almost mundane, a brief day-to-day note of the weather and routine work carried out on a small croft. They read like a ship's log, where facts are foremost and any personal reflection merely afterthought. But scratch a little deeper, and beneath this plain account is a picture of a man fighting an unwinnable war – against the elements, an unyielding earth and, latterly, his own failing strength. If we cannot see it, then Alasdair shows us. With great eloquence he decodes his father's words and expounds and lifts the narrative to transcend its own provenance and reach something like a fable, universal in its appeal. Alasdair connects, I think, because he has the language and that rare ability to disclose emotion without allowing it to spill onto the page. He draws us into his world with such disarming honesty that when he writes of his father and mother we see our own parents, when he speaks of regrets we remember ours, when he chronicles the lost harmony between a community and its landscape we grieve because we know it is happening everywhere.

It was only natural, then, to make my return to Ardnamurchan. Though another ten years would pass before I did.

Ardnamurchan is the most westerly point on the British mainland, farther west in fact than a large part of Skye and even Stornoway on the Isle of Lewis. Outlined on the south by the long twisting arm of Loch Sunart, its north side, relatively shorter, looks out across the Minch to Skye and the Small Isles and west to Barra and South Uist, fifty landless miles away. The land is divided into large hunting estates with unknown margins or sheep farms or is lost altogether to forestry. Kilchoan, with a couple of hundred residents, is by far the largest settlement. Ben Hiant, the highest hill, doesn't reach 2,000 feet.

To avoid the long and hazardous drive to reach Ard-namurchan, some residents, I am told, prefer to take the ferry from Oban, up the Sound of Mull to Tobermory and then, weather–permitting, onto Kilchoan. I rather like a hazardous drive, and it would be straightforward enough for me to park up at Sanna, have a stroll and a poke about the coves and bays, Alasdair as my guide. But I knew simply by matching my presence to places and events in the book would not be enough if I wished a deeper understanding. Alasdair's book was a long time in the writing; the least I could do was mark my approach slowly over the course of days, to go on foot and to bring an open mind.

As a peninsula by its nature implies a shortage of land I thought my entry might be along the northern shoreline. On a large-scale map it looked stunning. I ran my finger along the ragged edge as it left Kentra in the east and hooked and jutted for maybe a score of miles till the land ran south, and beyond this last headland was a place of sands. Four days going steady, I thought, would be plenty for a curious traveller to cover this ground.

I was happy to go alone, but a walking buddy, Nick, was in the Highlands. After a week slugging it over the snow-covered Grampians he fancied something a little more restful, and when I presented my plans that included 'strolling empty beaches and wee jaunts along clifftops', he didn't hesitate.

On the Kilchoan-bound bus we spoke to a tall man wearing a South African rugby shirt, a marine biologist by training, he said, in crisp English, but now his obsession was botany. He lived alone in a small cottage close to our start point, and in some depth he described his local backwoods and hill slopes. He knew well the coastal fringe we would follow today, though not beyond the Singing Sands. 'That stretch is a blank,' he said. 'Never been there. I don't know anyone who has.' Years of roaming in search of rare orchids had taken him to the most unlikely and hidden of places, and these he wouldn't divulge. Does he ever meet anyone on these plant hunts, I asked. 'Only the odd forager for mushrooms or berries, and often they are as lost as I am.'

Leaving Salen, the bus detoured to Acharacle and here we and the botanist got off. Our friend collected his small car and kindly drove us a couple of miles across the flats known as Kentra Moss, a strip of land forming a buffer between freshwater Loch Shiel and Kentra Bay, and left us at the road-end at the edge of the bay. A stony track that wound westwards along the coastline beckoned.

A cool spring day and the onshore breeze carried the smell of composting seaweed, a mulched line of it betraying the reach of the last high tide. After a particularly cold and dry winter I thought the hills of Ardgour, seen from the bus, had a dormant appearance as if at the nadir of their cycle. Yet here on the coast among last year's dead herbage were the first small shoots of spring.

The tide was out, revealing a great expanse of muddy sand that in places was patterned by narrow drainage channels. Following the track skirting the bay we passed a small promontory-cum-island clad in birch trees. It was attached to the mainland only by a fine salt turf that looked as though it disappeared with every flood tide. A little further on we left the track and crossed an uneven beach of black rock, and suddenly the going grew rough. The weight of my pack caused my ankle to pinch, and for a short while I needed the support of one of Nick's walking poles.

Kentra Bay was almost completely enclosed, and only for a while we saw across the mud flats to a row of white croft houses on another coast, maybe two miles away. Further inland were the hills of Moidart, the most seaward and distinctive of which I thought must be Roisbheinn, still white around its summit. Blocks of conifers were the greenest thing in the landscape.

On our side the spruce plantations were softened by a fringe of native birch and oak. It pressed right to the coast, and at first we threaded the old stands and made a path over last season's bracken. We puffed rather and soon enough drifted onto the shoreline, footing rocky shelves and hearing the crackle of dried black seaweed. The sludge of neap tides we judiciously avoided. Rank heather reached down as far as salt spray would allow, and from there to the rolling sea was a layering of colours – bluish rock freckled with white and orange lichen, a clean-washed reddish band and below this a covering of millions of alabaster barnacles and tentacles of weed. I could see little sign that folk ever came this way. Of our own passing, beyond some flattened bracken and seaweed, we left no trace.

As the shoreline became harder to reach and rocky bluffs barred our way we were forced to climb inland and take a higher line through the old wood. Amongst the trees the breeze was stilled and wave-sound more muted. In hollows and sheltered places the oaks and birches had become so fattened their limbs broke from the squat trunks and bowed along the ground. One oak grew like a triskelion, in a way I'd never seen, as if some clever arborealist had trained it. And strewn along the ground were decaying remnants and shapes of an older woodland, half-covered in moss and blaeberry, ferns and fungi. Sometimes breaking this skin of understory were outcrops and boulders, and at the base of one we peered into a cavernous place where some animal might be sleeping.

Where at a wooded inlet the slope ran especially steep to rocks on the shore we came upon a small fishing station, half-abandoned it seemed. In the bay a blue-hulled boat pulled at its mooring. Coiled rope, piles of netting, creels, buoys, chains, lay scattered in apparent neglect as suggested by a covering of moss. On the other side of the narrow strait were clumps of reddish woodland and the odd house. The tide was flooding into Kentra Bay, now behind us and largely hidden.

An old high forestry fence that once protected the young spruce from grazing deer now served no purpose. Much of it was broken anyway, pinned to the earth by windfall, or the posts had rotted so the wires ran loose. Escaping the conifers we slugged out to the small headland and looked at a skerry of rocks, each with its apron of surf, to a recumbent Isle of Eigg a dozen or so miles away. Though the going was still rough we could see what lay ahead, a promise of cream-coloured sand and then tomorrow the long arm of coast as it went north again to Rubha Aird Druimnich. All wild land and it gave a tingle of pleasure.

The sun burst through as we left, kicking clear of the rank heather and running down a bank to the first of the Singing Sands, Cul an Croise. An empty, acre-wide beach, and I cried out with joy of it, Nick responding in kind. If it is true the reward of rough travel comes in the stillness when lying at camp, it is also to be gained on a deserted beach. There were some hoof-marks of passing deer, otherwise the sand was blown firm by the winds and this we wandered across, in softer sand by the dunes or close to the small waves as the tide climbed. In the windless calm of evening the sea gave off a muffled sound.

A promontory now blocked our view to the next beach, a smaller one. At the head of the third beach was a salt marsh and a burn, where we collected water. I have never been one for camping on sand, so we pulled above the brash of high tide and pitched in a groove between a dune and small slope of heather, our tents nuzzled together. My preference was to be further apart, so only a raised voice could audibly cross the distance, giving each of us a little moat of privacy. But there was barely any room, and with our flysheets rubbing each other and our guy-strings touching we could converse as if we were seated at the same table.

Night drew down. We ate a large meal and talked much, then a good while later I opened the early pages of Alasdair's book. For a book to work, somehow the author must make a connection between the subject matter and his reader. Why would anyone now be interested in the life of a simple crofting family? So Alasdair begins with his parents, and in writing about them he bridges the gap that so often divides one generation from the next, one culture from another. He shows them as people first. It is the old stumbling block of biographers – given only the blunt tools of language, how do you present the life-essence of a man and woman you can no longer see or touch, and so much harder when the people you wish to show to the world are loved ones of your own flesh and blood? Whether Alasdair succeeds in offering something more than impressions and shadows only the reader can judge, but we are in no doubt he understands the enormity of what he is attempting. 'We see them as hardly human,' he writes. 'These two figures are our father and mother; we say: actors permanently burdened with the parts we have written for them however unwillingly they may tread our boards, however dreadfully miscast they may be.'

He proceeds to sketch his father – intelligent, moody, introverted, 'though capable of great natural charm'. We learn about his sensitivity to criticism, and how he 'often, and violently, lost his temper', one consequence of which was Alasdair's admission of a lifelong fear of angry men. Despite these outbursts he never once struck his children, and looking back on his childhood Alasdair says 'were it given to me to return to those days with a godlike hand, I should tremble to alter a single minute'.

An intensely practical man, he cobbled shoes, fixed watches and radios and could put his hand to all manner of carpentry. He built barns and outhouses for his animals. Cycling and photography were other interests. In the manner of a good biographer Alasdair later enlarges on this with anecdotes that give a more unconventional and rounded picture. Then in a short paragraph he discloses an observation perhaps more telling than any character sketch, a trait in his father that coloured his later life. As the story unravels we are given glimpses of this, and in the end it is the one key to understanding his father.

An overnight frost reminded us that winter had only recently abandoned the northern lands. In the Cairngorms a few days ago Nick found the high plateau under a blanket of snow and deep drifts still choking the high passes. We didn't rush into our walking that morning; instead gave ourselves some time to sit or sally a little and agreed to meet in an hour. I climbed to a small rocky viewpoint where, at my feet in crevices, grew thrift or sea pink, their tiny buds still awaiting the first warm spell. I looked west across the sands. Three figures spread out walking abreast, a dog running between them. Being so early and the public road over five miles away, I reasoned they were staying at one of the cottages I could see by the edge of the wood. Old crofts, I thought, as the map gives them marked out with boundaries. When I got back there was no sign of Nick. I packed and waited. 'Where did you go?' I said when he arrived. 'Nowhere. I've been sitting on the beach reading. Thought I had the place to myself when three folk and a dog showed up.'

At the far end of the beach a burn had spread out in shallow braids that we easily forded and then walked round to a pebble bay. There was a crumbling boathouse and a house further up, but no sign of human life. The roof of the boathouse was nearly eaten through with rust and its concrete base was disappearing with each storm tide. We left and climbed a little and moved slowly along the rough coastline till we reached a spot where the slant of the coast changed direction and we could see some way ahead. Not a hint of softness. The face of the land was all outcrops and shelving, and it bared its teeth where it met the sea, ingrown and convoluted to an extent we couldn't make out but could certainly guess at.

I led down to an uneven beach of black stone, crossed this, climbed a ledge and a small tower and there in the foreground was another strange beach. So it went on. Sometimes our tottering and probing, wanting to discover another untrodden place of Ardnamurchan, was just too risky and we retreated up some loose and mossy gully to easier ground, though returning always to the shore at the first opportunity. I was glad we did. When a little way ahead of Nick I disturbed a couple of otters lounging on a natural jetty. When alarmed I have seen otters plunge from river banks like Olympic swimmers, but this pair showed little fear as they slunk into the ocean, and for a minute swam about with their heads showing, diving just as Nick arrived.

We saw hardly a tree and the only ones we did were wind-crippled and stunted. Then we found a cave. The narrow entrance was almost closed off by a curtain of liverworts. I pushed them to one side, shone my torch and could see that it went down at about forty degrees into the earth, expanding a little as it went. Its floor was covered with rocks, pale and dry-looking. I squeezed in as far as my shoulders would allow and lay there for a minute, the breeze gone and the sound of ocean now distant. The air even smelt fresh. You could make a level place here among the rocks sufficient for a recumbent man, I thought, but why would you? Why move a single stone? When this coast was more peopled, I am sure this cave was known and probably had a name, one passed down and remembered even by those who never tramped here, though forgotten now I'm sure. Which is no bad thing. I probably wouldn't be able to find it again, but it is there for the next person to stumble across.

'What's this?'

Nick showed me something in his palm, a shell, dark-bluish in colour, about the size of a marble.

'A winkle. It's edible. People gather them, but mostly to sell.'

'There's plenty more where this came from.'

'I'm not surprised. This is a remote beach, hard to get to. Can't believe you've not noticed them before.'

I told Nick about a young fellow I once met in a bothy on Skye, a refugee from the city, who picked winkles in the shadow of the Cuillin Hills, partly to earn a few quid but mostly, he said, 'to keep sane'.

Nick thought about that and looked again at the little crustacean in his hand. 'Collecting these critters all day and every day?' he said. 'That would drive me *in*sane.'

Winkle-gathering was and still is a source of income for people living in remote coastal communities, and when one hears today what a 20kg bag of winkles can fetch wholesale, you wonder why more folk aren't out with their buckets and cans scouring the intertidal. Alasdair's parents supplemented their meagre income by gathering but, as he shows us, it was hardly the route to riches. He writes from his own experience when he says, 'I know of no way for a crofter to make money that doesn't carry with it at least one fairly crippling drawback. Gathering winkles has several.' For instance, we learn that the activity is restricted to low tides, so not always possible in winter, unless you wished to gather by torchlight. And poking about an exposed beach in pouring rain or a gale force wind can be no fun, your back arched constantly, the kneeling and stooping, hands in and out of rockpools, which, he notes, was like having 'a snowball stuck on the end of each finger'. Empty sacks were sent up by merchants from London's great fish market, Billingsgate, and were the old hundredweight ones (112lbs, though of course now outlawed in the interests of health and safety). When full they had, he says 'the weight and texture and degree of malleability of a sackful of musket balls'.

Then, as so often is the case with apparently abundant resources, the supply of winkles could, and often did, become scarce. During one winter fierce competition with neighbouring crofters left the nearby Sanna beds exhausted. To find new gathering grounds his parents trawled far and wide, venturing beyond the deserted township of Plocaig and ended up at Carraig Cliffs, the shoreline prickly with boulders. Any shellfish collected here would have to be carried and dragged back for two miles over the roughest of terrain. The picture of his elderly parents stooping, scraping and lifting, all for a slight augmenting of their income, was too much for Alasdair. He lashes out, fuming, 'Sometimes when I think of the system that condemns decent people to a lifetime of such grinding poverty I feel myself shake with rage.'

The cave had a magnificent seaview across the bay to the west-facing Moidart range, and beyond this an outline of higher hills, Knoydart and possibly the jig-saw shape of Sgurr na Ciche. Some coastal hamlets, tiny, were dwarfed by the scale of things around them. On this same land were cities and motorways and people bunched up in their teeming millions, but we couldn't see them. The great overcast sky and breadth of sea lent its own scale and showed up our smallness. The old illusion. A bird with motionless wings hung above, and from there it must be just rock and sea and sky, and the smallest movement of two tiny figures, so slow as they picked their way along the edge of the land.

Nick unfolded the map and studied it. 'See that,' he said, 'that's a decent path. Let's hook up with it for a while. Give these pegs a rest.' I'd noticed it, of course, and wanted to keep to the coast but Nick was right. The afternoon was half gone and we needed to round the headland before nightfall. So we climbed and found the path, which was in fact an old grass-centered track. It ran for an easy mile and lost its modest height gently, finding the shore again, then entered a small enclosed area of woodland.

Our world shrunk to the canopy of an antique wood, centuries old, it seemed, one specimen spreading fang-like branches along the ground for thirty feet before arching them skywards. Not far into it was a clearing and shingle beach and a couple of black-painted buildings, one locked and windowless and probably serving as a boathouse, the other a tiny derelict cottage. Jerry-built in corrugated iron with a redbrick chimney that looked ready to topple.

At its gable end I went gingerly up some rotted steps and found the door, secured only by a piece of string. I untied this and went in. There was an anteroom where someone had left rolls of roof insulation still in their wrappings. The main room was a complete mess. Half the ceiling was on the floor, joists and panel-boards eaten away by damp and woodworm and everywhere a strong whiff of decay. On the shelf of a wall locker was a small jar of Andrew's Liver Salts and Sunray Tips tea, costing 17½ pence, and a china cup with a broken handle. Someone had knifed his or her initials on the wood above the locker, 'J.M.P 1946', and another, 'H.M.P 81'. I picked up a small empty box of blue cardboard. The only words on it were the sender's name and address, and the date it was posted, '1.12.1974'. I looked at it and thought of my life then. Bagging conkers, watching black and white cartoons. Some other memories, a birthday just gone. Nothing specific. Alasdair's parents had both died the previous year, and he had stayed on for a short while to help Jessie, his sister, cut one last rig of hay. It was truly the 'end of an era', for the Macleans and for Sanna.

Alasdair returned some years later for a final time, a spell of a few months, to begin the writing process. His days are given over to editing his father's journals but he finds time for walks, revisiting old childhood haunts, beach-combing, observing wildlife.

Titled *Alasdair's Journal*, it makes up the last third of the book and in some ways is a difficult read, a stream of consciousness with a peculiar Highland flavour. He allows free rein for his thoughts and they tumble out. His parents' absence is felt on every page, as if some previously fixed part of the landscape was no longer there. Gone the periodic hammering of the wind or the tumble of breakers or bird cry. The rain beats soundlessly against the panes. An all-pervasive quiet is broken only by the gentle intake of breath from a man at a chair, the scratch of his pen on a page, the shuffle of leaves of an old journal. Alasdair sits and thinks and recounts times and events now fading. The words come, but not easily, each weighed and re-weighed and arranged with a watchmaker's precision. The book will be a tribute to his father, a lasting one. 'Who will raise a monument if I do not?'

Outside, the bustle of the township is gone. There was a time when visiting one's neighbours was the great social pastime in Sanna, a glue of the community, but now there are no visitors. And no one to visit. From a peak of about a hundred the year-round population had shrunk to six residents. As autumn slips into winter there is hardly even a tourist to be seen on the beach. When Alasdair walks it is alone or with ghosts.

I put the box down and retied the door. Outside, Nick was examining one of two huge rusting anchors that lay on the beach. Anything in there, he asked. No, I said.

At the track's end was a holiday cottage with a simple garden and greenhouse. A pair of red deer hinds stood side by side nibbling what passed as a lawn. They looked up and bolted. We didn't quite reach the true headland of Rubha Aird Druimnich, but saw down to it where the ocean spread, our sea-panorama broader now, with Muck, Eigg, Canna, the mountains of Rum and Skye. Harbingers of weather are always stronger on the coast but I sensed a change. The light was greying by the minute, the tone and detail of things beginning to bleed together. The breeze was almost gone, and when we stopped the air felt chilly and listless.

Leaving the wood we climbed to a foreground ridge and scanned west. Wind-shorn grass and ragged heather was punctuated everywhere by extrusions of pale rock, as if the scant soil had been too much for the earth to bear, appearing so barren it seemed destined to remain fallow for perpetuity.

Our sightline had all the cliffs and outcroppings of the coastline in view together and nothing could be seen of sand-fringed bays, the small debouchments and piedmonts and soft valley-places of Ockle, Kilmory and Fascadale where people lived and still farmed. The bones of the peninsula rose to the sides of an ancient crater, much eroded, which locals have always referred to as the Glendrian Hills, and which on one side look upon the old crofts of Sanna.

I wanted to reach a place italicised on the map as *dun*, but knew now we wouldn't make it. Too far. Instead we settled for the next decent-looking cove. On the map a small river ran through it and down to the sea, and on one of its bends there was sure to be a level and firm place for our tents.

We crossed a nearly-dry burn and gained height until the seashore appeared some distance below, glimpsed now only in snatches due to the cliffs. Going a little inland, away from the grey sea and fuzzy outline of islands, and without at first realising it we began to follow a kind of path, though hardly recognisable as such and maybe used only by a few sheep or goats, or occasionally a shepherd. In fact hardly used at all, but the memory of it still there.

A sea-facing outcrop appeared to block our progress, yet the path continued, vanishing at the next corner. I went to investigate. An easy ledge went around another corner, and from the dead ground below came a hollow boom of waves and sucking noises. One stumble, I thought. I was sure this must be some old forgotten route through the cliffs, never marked on any map and now but rarely travelled. It led us safely around and along, then steeply in wild doglegs to a shingle bay and a small river with high banks. The river had eroded deep into its own bed. Since the last great Ice Age the Scottish west coast, relieved of all that weight, has been slowly rising and this might explain the river's behaviour so close to the sea.

Both of us were tired, Nick especially. This was not the 'wee jaunt' of his imagination. As we put up the tents I said we would have an easy day tomorrow. He didn't believe me.

As night fell the land exaggerated its scale. On every side it seemed to rise higher than it actually was save the narrow opening of sea, its features and detail now became a single dark entity. I felt the press of it as I cooked up supper and refilled Nick's mug with tea, and later while I read, it was still there. Only when I drifted into sleep did the weight of it leave me.

Not far from the bay was a small cottage, painted regulation white and almost hidden among mature stands of conifers.

'That place up there,' Nick said in the morning, 'a holiday cottage, right?'

'Probably. It looks empty to me.'

'But it was once someone's home, lived in all year?'

'Yes, maybe quite recently. In my lifetime. It would have been a croft, a small farm.'

'How?'

'What do you mean?'

'Well, just look at this place. It's all rock. How could anyone make a living here?'

'People did, though probably not much of one. No more than subsistence, I would think. Every crofter kept cows, sheep, poultry, grew hay, some vegetables, cut peat for fuel, and they took what they could from the sea, but it was more a way of life than a purely economic thing.'

'More to do with family and community?'

'Yes, but they wouldn't have thought about it consciously. Whoever lived and died here and elsewhere along this coast were the last in the line of a culture that arguably stretched back to prehistory. Every patch of this coast has a ton of history and human association, and most of it we'll never know. It was lost when the last folk to live here left or died.'

'What pushed the family to sell, I wonder?'

'Don't know, but maybe the kids of that last generation took one good look around them and said, 'No thanks', and they sold up to someone who wanted a little bolthole. How can you blame them?'

'Maybe they just needed the cash.'

'Maybe.'

For a change we turned our back on the sea and went up the track to look at some ruins. Little remained of the dwellings, which I thought must be very old. In time we drifted back to the coast, to the sea that presented a richer face, its detail and sheen returned. Overnight snow had caught the peaks of Rum – Askival and Ainshval – that were fiercely bright when the sun came out from behind a cloud. We trekked to the tip of Ockle Point, sat on the turfland above the rocks, looked west along the coast and saw what was hidden the day before – a green ribbon by the Swordle River, a place farmed and settled for millennia. The softness gave way to more cliffs and the white edge of the ocean in its endless chiselling. Then we dropped from the point and I saw my first blossom of spring, pink thrift on a single stem rocking in the wind. We crossed someone's lawn that ran down and bled onto the beach. Toys lay abandoned, bedsheets draped and billowing on the line. Such a loose idea of property you would never see in the south, or anywhere else for that matter. I rather liked it. The burn behind the house disappeared into a high bank of shingle, as if a bulldozer had pushed it there, though it was probably the result of storm waves.

Where the croftland reached the coast were small stretches of machair, too early for its spring display, and salt turf and irises and stagnant and pungently smelling pools from the last flood tide. It wasn't always easy to see where pasture ended and the sea reach began. A place of transient influences. Scraps of seaweed dried to a crisp were sometime found on fields and I know sheep have a place for it in their diet. Mud-lined ditches and channelways we hopped, sometimes venturing seawards where the still-wet rocks were barnacled and trailed in black weed and green slime, and where the rock platform had been worn away to a great army of distorted shapes frozen to the waves. The tide continued its retreat, leaving us more space to explore, but in places such a jumble of boulders was virtually impossible to negotiate, or the shelving ended in an impossible drop.

Close to a cascading burn we found our way to the soft turf of the cliff edge, and looked back to the rock platform and the spidery shapes of rockpools. In a boyish quest we went to see the caves marked on the map. They weren't really caves. Caves need interior and there wasn't much of that. The height was more than a man standing, but the curved underside didn't go far into the cliff base. Although furthest in the stones were bleached and dry, I expected spring tides to flood here.

The coastline continued its crazy roving, and despite wanting to achieve a certain distance before evening we kept stubbornly to its line, as close to the sea as practicable. Sometimes a half-hour passed with only a couple of hundred yards of gain, such was the manner of obstacles, of barnacled shelves and rock helmets and trenches filled with the creep and suck of the ocean that we might leap at some risk or find an easier way. I minded not a bit. I couldn't remember when I last had so lost myself on the seashore, marvelling at its sheer complexity and beauty, the variety of growths, the luminosity of pools and watery gloss of the rocks. The familiar and ordinary come to life.

A shattered platform that seemed to fit no textbook of geology led us on detours to the waters' edge, where we scanned across the miles of swell to Rum with its peaks in unfamiliar juxtaposition. Around the Ardtoe peninsula was another area of pavement. Bushy willows grew in the small clefts nearby, their branches bare and still weeks away from leaf. But the cliffs had gone now, and the shoreline had a gentler and more open aspect and was easier to track. At some point before Fascadale Bay we found a lovely spot on an oddly human scale. In a miniature cove was a beach of shingle, and facing this a lawn which rabbits and sheep had cropped into such a smooth and man-made appearance I could believe someone came regularly with a mower.

Though the day still held plenty of good walking we chose to pass the night here. We set up our tents leisurely. I'd aligned mine so that later, when reclining inside, I could prop my head up on an elbow and look beyond the gently flapping flysheet to the sea and the Isle of Rum. Wave sound on the shingle was amplified by the sheltering wall of our location, sounding like stones slow-washed in a barrel. For some time, while nursing a brew, I watched that small opening to the outside world, monitoring in a lazy way the random pattern of gulls as they crossed and rode on unseen currents and disappeared. I imagined them dipping a wing and turning, though the points where they came back and reappeared, nearer or further or higher, I never anticipated correctly. If their sky-trails had a language I could not read it, at least not beyond an idea of the grace that is the gift of all birds. On that soft turf I watched these common birds, as I have all my life, and felt I was seeing them for the first time.

Nick read or dozed and I went back along the coast. The wind had dropped. I had seen something earlier. Just above the high tide mark and facing seawards was the remains of a stone-walled structure, almost certainly an old boathouse. It was linked by no track that I could see, though the croft road was not far away. Its construction was one of absolute economy. For the walls, rocks small and large had been gathered and mortared into place and were largely still there, while the fabricated materials of the roof – corrugated iron and square timbers – had collapsed many winters ago. I circled the structure and poked about and stooped to examine a fallen joist. Rust flaked off in my hand. They make them differently these days, I thought. Its abandonment said something about our environment and posed the usual questions on whether it is possible for one or two men running a small operation to make even a modest living from the sea, especially in a place like Ardnamurchan. Today, unlike the decline of the kelp industry two hundred years before, it is not about falling demand, rather a case of too much.

Leaving the horseshoe shape of Fascadale Bay I felt we were now entering a landscape that Alasdair and his family probably knew well. The map told me it was not far to Sanna. There was even a path a little distance from the sea that mirrors the general curve of the coast, and if followed, depending on your ploy, it might get you to the sands in a couple of hours, a distance of only five miles or so.

While Alasdair's story might dwell on the struggle of the crofter in the face of sometimes insurmountable obstacles, the book's magic and final solace comes in his portrayal of that margin of land by the sea, the Ardnamurchan coastline. If I wanted on this last day to carry away some durable impression and prize open a little understanding beyond the merely fleeting sympathy, then I needed to go more into the detail of this land – not just footing Alasdair's turf but finding those unnamed hill-places, the same gullies and coves where he collected winkles and beachcombed and ran ideas through his head. As we walked, places mentioned in the book came to mind. Where was, I wondered 'Butter Creek', named when a case of butter was once found there; or the hill loch where a gamekeeper drowned himself, surrounded by 'a wilderness of grey stone and coarse grass, untainted by man or beast'.

Sheep trails kept us near to the coastline, going gingerly along clifftops two hundred feet or more above the booming sea, and whenever a gully presented or a cove seemed within reach we went down. There was a narrow rocky bay, called Slochd an Bracha, and the rocks here were strewn with yellowed driftwood, old gravel boards with corners robbed of sharpness by relentless batterings. We found a creosoted post splintered at one end that might have held telephone wires. It had been stranded by the last spring tide and overhung the beach so we could sit on it, hang our feet, and look about and take in this near-forgotten place that likely sees no man or woman from one year to the next. Did Alasdair's shadow ever fall here? As a child and young man he loved to beachcomb, an activity known locally as 'going around the beach', never knowing what an hour or day's search would bring. Finds were pulled clear of the high tide-line to indicate ownership and await collection at a later date. It reflects the level of honesty in the Highlands at the time that some finds were left unclaimed, slowly going into the ground, waiting for the finder who had either moved away or died.

There is a story of two seamen washed up and buried at a spot beyond Sanna during the Great War, but with no headstones, and in Alasdair's day the memory of exactly where that was had grown hazy, 'growing from a narrow plot to a wide acre', he writes. The old currency of Gaelic culture was its oral traditions, and as people died or moved, their knowledge went with them. Alasdair refers to this as 'cultural erosion' and it is especially true in relation to placenames. He laments that scores of Ardnamurchan names had disappeared in his own half-century of lifetime. His grandfather, he remembers, had a name for 'every least hillock, every creek and gully', especially in that small orbit around Glendrian and the ghost hamlet of Plocaig: 'He moved through the mansion of his world as a blood relative where I was only a paying guest.'

Giving a physical feature a name confers on it some significance and value, acknowledging its role, however minor, in the unfurling of human history. The Ordnance Survey keeps faith with many of the old names, and there is plenty of continuing scholarship on this subject, but countrywide thousands of place-names have been lost. The land 'set free', Alasdair laments, 'has reverted to hostile wilderness'. But is this true? The Ordnance Survey has fossilised names largely from one culture, the most recent to inhabit these places, and these names no doubt replaced earlier Pictish or Norse ones; they in turn usurping the symbols and memory of even older peoples, those we now refer to as Mesolithic or Palaeolithic, whose language we can only guess at. Names come and go, and I wonder if people find their experience of land any less meaningful because of their lack.

There is a local wood I have been going to now for many years, invariably in the company of our lovely hound, Holly. I doubt that in extent it measures more than a hundred yards by eighty, bordered by a muddy track, a footpath and a large field on two sides. In one corner it extends for a little till reaching the banks of a river. I've come to know that wood so well that in my head I carry a very real and detailed picture of it, knowing the character of individual trees, seeing the places anemones emerge in spring, where the growth of balsam and periwinkle is thickest. Two secret creeks run beneath the leaf mulch, bisecting a Victorian memorial near its centre. Rarely do I meet or see anyone else there, though a beaten path traverses it. I have been there in deep snow, in penetrating frost, in late summer drought, in torrential rain when the fallen leaves turn to porridge. Where it brushes the river, on one day I saw an otter, on another a large half-eaten salmon; and in two tiny hollows among wild raspberry and woodrush I have discovered a bizarre micro-climate that holds snow for weeks after it has fallen, and in a recent year kept the ground frozen there for three winter months. If there are any local names I don't know them, and my map is silent. But every time I cross the threshold of the wood I find something new and understand a little more.

Sometimes we reduce a place, or one aspect or feature of it, by attaching a name. Why should a single episode in history – a battle or massacre or victory of some tribe – define how we feel about a place? Names are too often about possession and ownership, and the overexploitation that often entails. The land doesn't need us. It has being in itself and its dynamic and beauty will always, and hopefully, elude our feeble and clumsy grasp.

The boom and hiss on the clifftop here gave a richer category of sound, and under all that wave-crash was the constant churn at our feet and at the base of the cliffs, coming in with a hollow rush and drawing back in a popping of air bubbles, then the sound of a thousand trickles.

It was impossible to continue at this level so we climbed back to the cliff-edge and, when able to reach the sea again, managed a longer stint along the shoreline. To stay upright we needed to focus hard, using hands on barnacled rock and reaching across water-filled faults at the limit of our hamstrings and going on great loops to find a safe way.

Stumps and egressions of old lavas predominated. The earth has a memory here of a great mountain range and cataclysms that poured magma and showered pyroclastic fragments and which despite the comings and goings of glaciers are manifest even to the unlearned. We were passing slowly around the eroded rim of a long-extinct volcano, a caldera that comprises a large part of Ardnamurchan and is memorable when seen from the air, especially in the shadowed light of a westering sun. More gentle geologic episodes saw the formation of limestone, which in a few places weathered into a soil fertile enough for early farmers.

Climbing up to easier turf I looked inland and across the old crater to the volcanic hills that stretched in an arc for perhaps three miles. They reached little more than a thousand feet, but perhaps because of some combination of naked rock and steepness, appeared much higher. In all the miles I could make out not the smallest patch of green earth nor a single tree, and after a long winter even the coarse hill grasses were washed out, shrunken into themselves. There may have been trees and a richer environment here once, and I know in my lifetime crofters coaxed yields from their small plots, growing hay and vegetables. Now virtually every square foot is roamed over by sheep and deer. They have the run of the land. Holiday cottages in Sanna have strong fences to keep them out. In the richer grazing of the valleys there are still a few cows, and we would see some later that day.

Crofters routinely kept a handful of cows and Alasdair's father was no different. A little money from selling surplus stock was an essential part of his income but, as he shows us, it was a chancy business. The number of stock you kept was limited by how much feeding hay your two and a half acres could produce and the extent of your winter accommodation. When the time came to sell, prices fluctuated and distance to the market, any market, was always a drawback for Sanna crofters. As the author reminds us, no one ever got rich through crofting; at best you survived.

It is here we learn something profound about his father's character, that money in the end wasn't the point of it. Earlier in the book he writes of his father as 'a man constantly gnawed at by insecurity . . . incapable of relaxing or unbending to any noticeable degree. Only with animals was he completely at ease.' Keeping cows did little to alleviate his parents' poverty, but for his father it was the essence of crofting, the point of it. 'Whether it showed a profit or no, it was his road through to pride and manhood.'

Alasdair describes crofting as 'a finely evolved system for extracting the maximum amount of nourishment from the minimum amount of ingredients', and in the case of Sanna it reached its heyday during the turn of the twentieth century. The township then sustained a population of around a hundred. It was 'a late flowering', Alasdair says, 'but while blossom was still opening the rot was creeping up the stem'. The author doesn't attempt to explain what caused the decline, certainly not in any academic way, but decline it did till there was just one man and one croft, then the author himself harvesting a last field of hay, almost as an act of defiance.

Sometimes we came upon an old dyke that ran inland and crossed our line of travel. They seemed to serve no contemporary purpose and certainly didn't contain the sheep in any way. Then a weakness in the cliff face led us down into a gully, steep and crumbly, and once at the bottom, where the ocean's brash had collected, a complete *cul de sac*. I wanted to follow the beach round, but even with an ebbing tide I doubted if the sea would give back sufficient land for us to progress. We climbed up. It was always hard to tell just how close to the cliff face we might safely tread, but the scale of it tempted us, as did our constant seeking of ways to the shore. The small headland of Rubha Carrach was sufficiently high to block our view to Sanna, now only a couple of miles west. The inland moors gave rough, pathless walking, and would look different when the tormentil and bedstraw started to bloom and the ling was a carpet of purple that dusted in the sun at each passing footfall.

Before this headland we had a tricky descent of maybe a hundred feet where we dropped slowly through loose and stony ground. Noting how easily some rocks became unhinged and scuttled loose we each chose different lines. Which was just as well, as when I turned to face the slope a rock thudded past and came to rest at the bank of a small stream. The slope above that was equally steep and we climbed until reaching a grassy ramp that ran below an outcrop. Then we came to a fine viewpoint, looking back to where the old lavas met the sea, ahead to a sand-fringed bay and where a little inland stood the grey and roofless dwellings of Plocaig. The green coastal strip looped around to the low hummocks of Sanna Point, and south of this was a bright wedge of sands where Sanna itself faced the western Atlantic. The mainland retreated as we moved further out onto the peninsula, the coastal hills only shapes in the blue haze. Even without reference to the map we knew the land must either soon run out or change direction. The west held nothing but ocean.

Finding the shoreline we picked a way through the many boulders, relics of the old cliffs, passing and stepping over rock pools where Alasdair's mother and father had gathered winkles. The cliffs and plumb-lines had gone and the land came gently to the sea, but the inter-tidal was as rough as ever. Great wraps of orange weed gave uneven footing and some rocks held a lethal coating of slime. But we explored despite this, surprised at the richness of marine life and the quantity and variety of debris at the high tide line. No one collects winkles here now, and no one beachcombs.

In his day Alasdair allows himself a swipe or two at what he sees as the insular attitude of some locals. For instance he can find no problem with non-natives buying up old cottages. 'Incomers,' he writes, 'are much more vigorous in their defence of traditional values and eco-logical principles than present-day crofters.' Alasdair's attitude comes partly, I suspect, from his own sense of identity, the fact that he was born and brought up in the centre of Glasgow, about as far from the quiet of a West Highland village as you could imagine. At best he was a temporary resident of Sanna, though his roving lifestyle and lack of career meant his stays were sometimes pro-longed. 'Return of the near-native', he says. He certainly displays an ambiguous attachment to a Highland per-spective, especially regarding the much-debated episodes of recent history. 'There is something in the Celtic char-acter,' he writes, 'continually seeking to draw perverted nourishment from dwelling on disaster.' Considering why the Clearances are enshrined in Gaelic legend and not the epidemics and failed harvests, which caused by far the greater suffering, he writes of the latter, 'no doubt they were somewhat less amenable to the folksong treatment. It is harder to make capital out of pustules and diarrhoea.'

There is some truth in this, but it is uncharitable. Alasdair the middle-aged bachelor brings with him his own inventory of burdens. He does not greatly elaborate on these but I sense he carries the disappointment of not reaching his own or his parents' expectations, and he hints at bouts of depression when life was very dark. At times he displays almost a self-loathing, berating himself for a crippling shyness and missed opportunities. When his mother declares she might eventually become a burden on him, rather than embrace her with a few words of comfort, Alasdair confesses, 'I sat silent and terrified, frozen within my own inarticulateness. The moment passes and my heart shrivels a little.'

Perhaps the great existential problems weigh more heavily on those who possess the words to shape their questions, and reading between the lines you find the loneliness of the poet. But there is also a wisdom and truth-seeking quality that can come to a life in its middle epoch, especially one as varied as Alasdair's.

Cloud was away and a fresh brightness squeezed what colours there were from the land and sea. Everywhere the sparkle of contrast. The ocean was transparent enough to the show blurry outlines of reefs and where it came into the shallows turned aquamarine, paling seamlessly till the surf came up the beach. Sounds reached us cleanly: the hollow cries of birds, the unending crack and fizz of waves on sand. Ancient lavas we clambered over had a delusionary look of something frozen yet unfinished, the surfaces fretted, scored, pockmarked. A strange-leaning arch revealed by the ebb tide took us to the water's edge. From one angle it framed the shape of a wine bottle or hands clasped in prayer.

The Carraig Cliffs form one side of a bay more than half a mile across, the last such before the coast swings round at Sanna Point and faces west. At the far end, where it runs closest to Plocaig, there was something I wanted to see. A small wood, the Plocaig Woods so-called. My large-scale map has it as a small sliver of green almost touching the shoreline, so I knew it was still there. The wood was a place of adventure for the young Alasdair. 'A half-hanging thicket – of hazel and oak, in extent perhaps seventy or eighty yards by fifty or sixty . . . You could scarcely force your way into that thicket, so impenetrable it was.' He describes a small mossy rock at its centre where he sometimes lay happily for hours, quite hidden from all-comers. On one occasion he emerged to find the ground around had become a 'tinker' encampment. The thicket was only one of a number that ran for half a mile or so up the creek bottom.

At first I thought I must have misread the map. You can't quite see Plocaig hamlet from the beach, so we gained the cropped turf beyond the high tide mark. There was the gable end of the first ruin. I turned and looked north. Nothing but pasture. We footed over, still believing I'd got the facts muddled. Alasdair had written that the woods were in decline, but that was thirty years ago, and I felt sure some body or group had halted and even reversed that damage. Government subsidies to fence such relics have been around for a long time. But there was barely a tree, and the handful left were clearly dead or dying, stripped of bark to the browse-line or fallen and rotting on the ground. Soon nothing will be here but grass and bracken. Well, so what, you might say, but there is something symbolic here and it makes you think that if we can't do so simple a thing as save a wood here, then what right do we have to pronounce on the great destruction of forest happening in faraway lands?

We truly do not care, in which case maybe there is no hope, and we will drown in apathy before the sea rises up and does it for us. 'How beautiful that little wood was, how dearly I loved it. In my long life as a child I found nowhere else that so generously and fruitfully mingled dreams and plausibilities.'

I was sad because that small collection of trees once evoked for Alasdair the 'spirit of place', and if one thing comes through strongly in the book it is this, what he reluctantly and perhaps clumsily calls the numen, though he gives it no shape beyond that. A long familiarity had drawn him deeper into the landscape, where the past and present seem rolled into one. Inhabiting the coves and hollows and hill lochs and defiles are peculiar tales and castes of the long-dead unrevealed to the casual outsider. With a little knowledge and by entering Ardnamurchan you become privy to a secret landscape and are called into a world of real emotion. When approaching Plocaig as a child he imagined the spirits freezing and blending invisibly with their surroundings. Standing alone among the ruins now he found 'neither hostility nor kinship . . . only the hugeness of departure: a wisp of smoke on the horizon and the bandsmen packing up their instruments on the empty quay.'

Alasdair always insisted his book was to be a 'monument to his father', and it is clear he found some catharsis in the writing process, which he likens to 'crawling out of a pit I had dug with my own horny hands'. But he finds no real peace during his final stay in Sanna. That Sanna was not the one of his childhood. Maybe we have here the old truism that piece of mind is found not in any place but within the confines of our own heart.

In a few minutes we crossed easily the shallow river and now before us and not a few hundred yards distant lay the lovely spread of Sanna beach. Some cars and distant figures on the sands, a small child and dog running, a couple arm in arm walking slowly. A friend had come to meet us and his vehicle was parked up with the others. Under our feet on those last yards was a kind of rough pasture – Iain Maclean's old croft, I was sure. But was this the field where he grew his hay, I wondered? For Alasdair's father haymaking provided winter feed for the animals, and in *Night Falls on Ardnamurchan* we are given its joys and pitfalls, from maintaining a sharp edge on your scythe to the particular way the blade was swung and the field harvested. The harvester was maddened sometimes by midges and clegs, by the sheer unrelenting effort of cutting, spreading, drying and filling the barn to its eaves and then stacking the remainder. When late in the summer of 1973 Alasdair takes on this task it only serves to deepen his admiration for his father and grandfather and the line of crofters preceding them. That solitary field of hay, he says, was the last to be cut in Ardnamurchan and he was the last scythesman.

I conjured it in my mind's eye then and it brought to mind a painting by Van Gogh of a reaper in a wheatfield. Van Gogh describes him as 'a vague figure labouring like the devil in the terrible heat to finish his task . . .' In it he saw the image of death, 'but there is nothing sad in this death,' he writes, 'it takes places in broad daylight under a sun that bathes everything in a fine, golden light.'

Ghost Trail

It seems strange to me now that throughout childhood and adolescence I never read *Seal Morning* by Rowena Farre. During that time and scarcely known to me a red hardback edition nestled on our bookshelf, alongside tomes on history, horticulture, sailing adventures and novels of many genres. I suppose there was just too much else to read. My parents loved books and every room had its repository, including masses of old hardbacks with gold inlay that had been inherited from my maternal grandparents. On rainy days I would tilt my head to read the spines and probably pulled Farre's book down more than once, noting the dust and yellowing pages and line drawings, but it lacked photos and was not specifically about 'mountains'. My parents retired and moved to a small cottage close by the sea, shedding much of their library in the process. For some reason *Seal Morning* escaped the cull, and visiting them in the late nineties I finally sat down to read it.

When *Seal Morning* was first published in 1957 Britain was still emerging from the long reach of the Second World War. Memories of rationing and austerity were fresh, as was the barbarity of what had occurred during the years of conflict, humanity trawling new depths in its ways of killing. Yet the insecurity of nation and race still prevailed as east and west aimed their missiles at each other, providing the only certainty in an uncertain world, that of mutually assured annihilation. Just two years before, William Golding's *The Lord of the Flies* shocked its readers with a raw examination of how a group of children stranded on an uninhabited island resort to savagery. The launch of Sputnik prised open the door of space and on a different scale Bernard Crick began unraveling the double helix, the DNA of life, reducing everything to cell reproduction and protein synthesis.

Perhaps amid this change was a hankering for old truths, a dimly-perceived nostalgia for a gentler world either real or imagined. To a generation weaned on classics such as *The Wind in the Willows* and *Black Beauty*, Farre's tale of growing up on a remote Sutherland croft with a menagerie of animals that included a pair of otters and a seal named Lora must have been deeply appealing. A reviewer of the time called it 'an astonishing book, a gem of purest ray', another described it as a work of 'real and rare enchantment'. For its publishers *Seal Morning* was a dazzling success, selling out in its first month and going through five reprints in its first year.

Farre was a child of the British Empire. She was born and passed her early years in India, then when aged eleven was sent 'home' to complete her education. Unlike her contemporaries who were shuttled off to boarding school, Farre went to live with her Aunt Miriam, a teacher of some twenty years standing and who had, she writes, 'decided to give up her career and return to her native Scotland'. Miriam secured the tenancy of a croft in the wilds of Sutherland. The nearest village was nine miles away. 'A path, little better than a sheep track, wound from our door over the moors. It gradually merged into an unsurfaced road, and for the last four miles before entering the clachan (village) there was actually a coating of tarmac on it.' No one else lived within a radius of four miles around the croft and all supplies were brought in using a pony and trap. In winter snowdrifts often cut them off, sometimes for months at a time. They were utterly on their own.

Struggling to survive such isolation is a story in itself, but the primary focus of *Seal Morning* and the reason for its popularity is the animals, especially Lora the seal. Inquisitive and affectionate, Lora's almost human personality draws in the reader. Tales of her antics tumble from the pages. We learn how she was coached to be useful, for instance by fetching different objects and collecting mail from the postman. She could prepare a picnic by unrolling and spreading the table cloth and dropping a plastic cup in front of Rowena and Miriam. One trait that begun endearingly and became in due course less welcome was her habit of falling asleep on the author's lap. As a fully grown adult weighing something over three hundredweight she would clamber onto the laps of visitors to leave them 'breathless and terrified'. The problem of how to feed an adult seal was solved by allowing her to hunt fish in the nearby loch.

Lora's chief quality is undoubtedly her talent for music. Early during their stay Farre noticed that Lora would attempt to sing along to the piano, and very soon the seal was having 'practice sessions'. 'Within a week she was able to get through *Baa-baa Black Sheep* and *Danny Boy* without a break and was beginning to learn *Where my Caravan has Rested*.' After a fashion Lora learned to play the mouth organ and could bash out tunes on the toy trumpet. One tale involves Lora being taken to Aberdeen to sing at a ceilidh. Farre notes that she 'raised her head and roared her way from a deep bass to a seal top C', and later entertained the gathering with the xylophone by holding the beater with her mouth and thumping it down on the bars. Somehow we are not surprised when told she outperformed everyone and stole the show.

The other creatures inhabiting the croft have rather less of a presence. Shortly after their arrival in Sutherland their far-flung neighbour, Mr McNairn, presented Aunt Miriam with a pair of otter cubs, later named Hansel and Gretel. I was probably not the only reader disappointed that the otters didn't feature more strongly. These intelligent creatures have always fascinated me, and along with millions of readers I loved Gavin Maxwell's *Ring of Bright Water*, an intensely personal account of the author's relationship with an otter called Mij. Farre's pair of otters dip in and out of the text. We are never furnished with much detail and they remain shadowy, bit-part players in a drama whose star was a singing seal and the narrator herself. When Hansel dies after being caught in a gin trap, Gretel disappears and is never seen again. Oddly, another of the animals, Rodney the rat, often surfaces in the narrative. We learn of his habit of attaching himself to one of the goat's teats in an attempt to suckle, and how he became inordinately fond of Sara, one of a pair of grey squirrels. He was fastidious in his washing habits, licking his paw and sweeping it behind and over his ear. Running the gauntlet of stoats and buzzards and surviving so long in what for them must have been an alien environment, Rodney and Sara were there when the croft was finally abandoned and were taken abroad by Miriam, no doubt to begin a new life of rodent adventures.

Living so far from conveniences and in such isolation, you might expect Farre to paint a stark picture of their struggles; in fact we read of their embracing the wild and delighting in it. While most of their food was bought from the local village store and carted in using the pony and trap, around the cottage they cultivated a small garden and from the stony soil raised 'greens' and soft fruit, having predictable run-ins with marauding deer and hungry rabbits. They sourced wild herbs, fungi and edible plants such as nettle and dandelion from the moors and river banks. Two goats gave a supply of fresh milk and any surplus was stored and made into cheese. There is a brief mention of a small field where they grew hay, scything it in high summer, leaving it to dry in rigs and storing it in the byre for animal feed over the winter. By far the most laborious job was peat-cutting. 'The cutting and stacking went on throughout the summer, a seemingly endless task,' she writes. There was also plenty of digging when winter blizzards dumped heavy falls of snow. 'Sometimes,' she says, 'when it had been snowing for several days on end and the snow level reached eight or nine feet – up to the roof of the croft – we would dig in shifts from morning to late at night.' When the loch froze Lora and the otters fashioned plunge holes and helped themselves to the sleepy trout.

Though she does not say so I had a sense that Farre was not especially interested in other humans. Relatives and friends come to stay from time to time, but their presence is noted only fleetingly and usually as the pretext for an anecdote about Lora or the other animals. Two Indian friends of their parents arrived one day unannounced and families of tinkers sometimes camped nearby and called in. Even Aunt Miriam remains slightly mysterious. We are told she has 'many talents', is resourceful and has a special way with animals, but learn little else about her. Mr McNairn, their closest neighbour, is described as a bachelor shepherd in his mid-sixties, and by Farre's pen we are presented with a portrait of an intelligent rational man of eclectic interests who, he told the adolescent Farre, had no time for 'aery faery talk'. The only other neighbours to appear are the Frasers, and by a strange contrast Mr Fraser has a reputation as a healer and seer. 'People came long distances to seek his advice or ask him to put a spell on a sick animal,' she says. Curiously there is no mention of any dealings with the laird or his agent, and not once in seven years do they meet a stalker or ghillie or even a tweed-clothed gentleman with rod and line, despite the loch being plentiful in brown trout.

The book's ending is abrupt and a little strange. Farre had turned seventeen and knew she would soon have to leave her Highland idyll and 'join the ranks of the earners' as she put it. Miriam intended to remain at the croft. Then quite suddenly Lora vanished. Last seen sitting in some shallow water in the lochan, she never returned home. Farre called her disappearance a 'mystery', and lamented, 'with her going I lost the closest and most intelligent animal friend I have ever had.'

The other tragedy that summer was the trashing of the garden and vegetable patch by a herd of deer. In the aftermath Farre persuaded her aunt to take a holiday, and it was when Miriam was staying with friends in the south that she met and fell in love with a Canadian. Miriam came home and announced to the astonished Farre that she and the Canadian planned to marry. The croft was abandoned and their time in the wilderness came to an end. The final paragraphs describe how, after the passing of five years, Farre makes a kind of pilgrimage to her old home and then wishes she hadn't. The roof was down, nettles grew among the fallen masonry and amid this wreckage was a rusted toy trumpet that had once belonged to Lora.

Seal Morning may not be on a literary par with Max-well's books or the nature writing of John Lister-Kaye, but it is passionate and unsentimental and I could on one level relate to the author. A kindred spirit, she loves wild land and cares deeply for its creatures, which she brings so vividly to the page. If at times the text appears to have been bolted together and her descriptions are some-times generic, there are also fine passages that capture a moment and evoke place. In the midst of a wind-storm on the open moor she writes, 'For several miles the only trees in view were a few scattered birch which bowed and rose at the touch of the wind, like swimmers breasting huge waves.'

I finished the book, though with mixed feelings. The tales about Lora seemed far-fetched and embellished. Even if we put to one side doubts over Lora's musical abilities, I struggled to believe how a single small loch could have supplied her food needs over seven years. There is a simple imbalance here involving the quantity of fish needed to sustain an adult seal and the carrying capacity of a small Highland loch. A seal would clear the loch of anything edible in a matter of weeks. It is well-documented that many Scottish lochs have been so over-exploited it is now rare to find any sizeable fish in them.

Was Lora no more than a figment of the author's imagination, dreamed up to add spice to a matter-of-fact account of life on a remote Highland croft? And if Lora was fiction, what of the other stories? Some of them, especially those about the harsh weather, have the ring of exaggeration.

One of the first things I did when finishing the book was to attempt to locate the Farre's croft. I pulled out and spread the relevant Ordnance Survey sheets and placed a couple of steins at their corners so I could match the grid lines. I gasped at the emptiness. The joined maps showed an immense tract of largely treeless moorland, the peaks of Ben Armine and Creag Mhor at its centre. Bordered by Strath Tirry and Kildonan and the Lairg to Helmsdale road was an interior I thought might be some four hundred square miles, a huge area. It was a place I'd never crossed, although I had skirted some of its margins. Somewhere in all that vastness was Rowena Farre's croft. Although the author doesn't pinpoint its location she does offer clues. 'To the west,' she tells us, 'was the mountainous district of the Ben Armine range . . . To the east were the Knockfin Heights and Cnoc Coire Fearna.' That sketched the general area and interestingly I noticed a building marked 'ruin' in the Skinsdale Valley, which lay perhaps nine miles from the village of Kinbrace. What I couldn't find was a loch. In fact there were hardly any lochs in the area. Those I could see were either too remote or too small or too close to the road. But if, as I suspected, Lora was an invention then so probably was the loch.

From Lairg a small tarmac road beckoned, lifting us above the morning mist and fogs of the valley. Looking back after a short while we could see a landscape enclosed by rough fields, and a scattering of farms and hamlets and dark bands of conifers. Smoke drifted skywards from some chimneys. The odd car had passed on the main road, but now all was quiet, save the *tap-tap* of Nick's walking poles and random birdsong.

It was cold but not especially so for a middle week in February. The night had escaped a frost, though field sedge and gorse were heavy with dew. Climbing slowly, we joined a track, passed a farmyard with uninterested sheep, then crossed over a low fence onto some moorland. We went easily to the brow of a hill. From this vantage point and through a mist window we glimpsed corries and snowfields of the Assynt peaks over in the northwest. The land was changing, though. Since my last visit to these parts wind turbines have popped up, and now haunt the crests of local hills, wandering blades on an army of stilts. Painted white just to make them really stand out, even in the mist.

I recall one of the arguments against a windfarm proposal on the hills above Dunbeath in Caithness was that it would despoil scenery featured in Neil Gunn's classic book, *Highland River*. What would Rowena Farre have made of these giant turbines, I wonder? Her words had inspired me to undertake a series of treks through this remote region, and I'd discovered wild land unsung and largely unvisited, though as fine as any in Scotland. But it was changing. The proliferation of wind farms in East Sutherland had hastened what for me might be a last journey. I also wanted a last look at Farre's work in the context of its setting. Were these hills and moors really the haunting backdrop of her adolescent years, and if so where was the croft?

A very gentle descent led us to a wizened birchwood, some specimens with their arching limbs hooked into the ground. The heavy snows of December had largely gone, at this level at least, but the ground was mostly still frozen after a fortnight of frost, and beneath an inch of melt-water our feet found the hardness. Climbing over a fence to gain a track we came to some commercial forestry, though the trees were set back from the track. Frost had softened the growth down the middle of our path and the tyres of a vehicle had left deep ruts in places. The luminous quality of the mist enhanced every pigment in the vegetation – a verdant green of spruce and Scots pine, the yellow sacking of moss and rich umber of heather.

I thought I knew the way, but somehow when a firebreak presented we turned a blind eye and drifted west when north had been our intention. The track terminated. More firebreaks. Each time I came to this forest I found a different way through it. The trees needlessly corral you. If they were planted at wider intervals you could, with some effort and relying on compass, wander at will and make your own route. Instead we were shoved this way and that and herded along gloomy corridors. As always when entangled in a man-grown jungle I imagined the land before trees, not so long ago, then a more distant age when birch and rowan grew naturally in this place. Beasts had been here and we followed their desultory pathway through the tall grass. For most of the time great stands of conifers pressed in on us and our only views were of miles of trees, ranked like the formations of an army set in a tableau.

Eventually we came to an opening of tussocky and flaky grass and a swiftly flowing burn. Choosing to head upstream, we found that the going worsened to quagmires and sinks, where only the frozen sub-surface prevented us from sinking in deep. A kink in the burn led to an ice-covered loch, and to avoid the rough shoreline I tried walking on ice by the shallows, but it cracked and splintered and gave way, so I joined Nick at the forestry edge. Some of the hills now were of moorland and to these we headed.

Plenty of trees had failed in their efforts in flourish in such waterlogged conditions. They stood without needles or bark like piscine skeletons. Or they had been tossed aside by storms or felled by weight of snow. Almost all were brown-tipped, bitten by the great frost of December last, the coldest twelfth month in Scotland on record. The brash line surrounding the loch was considerably higher than the present water-level and that suggested this loch must be a gathering place for all local rainfall, and the burn we passed would at such times be a torrent of note.

By first going along a small creek we began to escape the forest. Conifers pressed right to the banks but the burn was a delight, cloudy at times, slow and dark, then an amber-tinted transparency revealing the pebble bed and rock strata crossing its path more than once and causing a gentle rush. At a small clearing were piled stones of a shieling, a place that was old when the last residents of a nearby croft regularly passed this way. Beyond the forestry fence the land evinced all the signs of being heavily trampled and eaten by the cloven-footed beasts, but it was open and we were glad of that

A ruin hereabouts is worth a visit, and I always make a point of stopping. If all ruins share a poignancy, it is especially so when the casual visitor has some knowledge of those whose passed their time here. A step beyond the shadowy facts of a generalised history narrows to the particulars of a place, provides individuals with names and dates and small details of their everyday lives. Coming to this old house a decade ago I stood at its crumbling threshold in ignorance. It was a deserted croft of the type you find dotted all over the Highlands, this one forsaken in quite recent times for reasons economic and even social. Like the empty houses on Stroma there was no tyranny in its abandonment. Over the years I have always wondered about it, then one day when on a research errand at my local library I came across a book which told of the last families to live here. Within these walls towards the end of the nineteenth century Edward and Anne Macleod brought up their eleven children. The youngsters walked to Lairg every day to attend school, a round trip of some eight miles. The last tenants were a shepherding family, Archibald and Mari Clark and their daughter Lily. They had two cows, some hens, grew vegetables in their small walled garden at the rear of the croft. Lily remembers a peat fire constantly aglow and a large pot of soup always on the simmer. I read that, returning home from school in her little tackety boots, she would greet the cow by swinging on its neck. The croft was deserted for good sometime before the Second World War.

I thought of this young family as I brushed aside the surround of dead nettles that in the summer months would virtually bar entry. I walked through where the door had been. The slate roof looked in fair condition, but now as I stood inside and looked up I could see that the lead ridge was missing. A simple act of greed but it had condemned the place and now decay was sweeping through. The wall plaster was gone and the floor piled with animal droppings. No stairway and no partition and no rooms any more. Rotting and fallen rafters. Stains of algae creeping up the walls to a virtually non-existent upper floor, the joists and boards covered in mould and moss and ferns. At a corner the boards were still intact and I noticed a plastic water bottle. Someone had passed the night up there, but how? I could see no means of climbing up. Crumbled mortar filled the fireplaces, and in one still hung a rusted hook on a chain, probably the same one that held the soup pot.

A single small opening for a window faced north and gazed out to an inbyre or garden squared off by a dyke. Vegetables would have flourished here unmolested by deer or rabbits. At the west end the byre was heaped with fallen masonry, though the walls still stood and a window retained a wooden lintel above it. The opening was high enough for Lily's beloved cows to pass through. A kind of saxifrage was growing in a crevice. Lily married and settled in Lairg, and I believe she sometimes visited her old home. She died in 1996.

From the side of the hill away from the ruin we looked back in the direction of Lairg, now unseen in its valley. Only the odd hamlet and distant wind turbines broke the regularity of moor. It was easier going now on the much trampled ground. A muddy beast trail led in our general direction and it took us around the hill to more moorland vistas and turbines miles away on a hill above Rogart. A small group of deer caught our scent and scarpered.

Signs of past habitation everywhere. Outlines of shielings and tumbled dykes, some so old a layer of peat had grown on their crests. Here and there the moor gave way to a splash of pasture, faded green in the wan sunlight, and on one someone had raised a rough four-sided stone to stand in an unnatural manner. A marker of some sort, a grave, a shrine? Curiously the map had no mention of it. I made a show of studying the stone, but as an amateur and with no real knowledge of how to read the clues, of this or even any of the history that lay thinly around us.

For a good while we crossed the moor and kicked out each stride and relished the open easy nature of the terrain. Our light sacks certainly added much to our enjoyment. I'd probably never before carried so little on a four-day walk, making do without a tent and any spare clothing, and packing only basic food.

At some point we dropped into a dell with a small burn and stopped to drink. On a rising island of sheep pasture we came upon the old farm and steading. For many years this place was known as the Priest's Bothy, so named because a Catholic priest, a hermit, had lived here on and off from 1971 to 1987. I know his name but little else about him, and that gleaned only from what he left behind in the house. The farm was never a bothy, but for many years after he died folk who came this way found the building unlocked and the interior cared for. A visitors' book was prefaced with a message imploring users to say nothing to any living soul. Keep a vow of silence, it said, if you wanted this place to survive and its casual use tolerated by the owners. I only knew of the Priest's Bothy because someone had broken that code, and while I was deeply grateful, perhaps a loose tongue led to its eventual passing.

I tingle remembering my first visit. It was a warm spring day more than a decade ago when I pushed open the door on its rusting hinges. The ground-floor rooms were pretty bare, though tidy. In an alcove at the back, a small crucifix had been set on the wall and an offertory lamp hung from a long brass chain. It hardly prepared me for what awaited in an upstairs room. A theological library. Hundreds of books on shelves that began on the floor and went to the ceiling. Not just of theology; here were tomes on science and history and mysticism. *Piers Plowman* and the works of John Berger and other renowned thinkers rubbed shoulders with books on music and French and one on clocks. As the breeze rattled the old slates I sat in an armchair and read. What plateau of ecstasy had the hermit reached within these walls? There was belief here, but also a quest, a journey.

It's all gone now. The basement was used periodically as a shelter for animals, it seemed, given the quantity of straw and dung. In the alcove where the offertory lamp once hung were coils of rusted wire and empty plastic containers. The upstairs room that once held the library was completely bare. Not one page of one book, not a stick of furniture. Even the old newspapers that lined the ceiling rafters had been ripped off or hung like rags at a wishing well. Bird droppings marked the floor and the boards creaked as I went from the empty room to landing to empty room, then slowly down the rickety stairwell.

The attached byre was missing a wall and on the earthen floor I noted rotting fence posts and an ancient piece of farm equipment, a roller shaped like a furrow. Some detritus from the cottage was dumped here. A rusted kettle, cooking pots, cutlery, strangely-shaped glass bottles. Wrapped in brown paper was a large, two-foot high candle. I also found a *Catholic Directory* and a periodical from the sixties, some old stationery and, oddly, a small wedge of newspaper cuttings. One had a picture of two elderly but sprightly men and was titled 'The Monk and the Soldier' – Dom Columban Mulcahy, Abbot of Nunraw Cistercian monastery, and his brother, General Richard Mulcahy, 'one of Ireland's best known political figures'. Covered in bird dung was part of a dog-eared bible. Scraps of someone's life. You can build up a picture but it tells you little. What do we really know of anyone? What can we know?

Outside I blinked at the sudden brightness and looked about. I have thought about this and believe I know why a mystic might choose to spend the last years of his life here. The hills rode gently away in a great arc to the south, the outline of each going behind the other serenely. There was nothing dramatic for the eye and nothing to distract, and the rows of distant mountains in the west are hardly seen. The nights here, I remember, are unbroken and seamless in their star-sweep or darkness. No sound of plane, the road far away. Wild and lonely if you like, yet there is no real sense of isolation, just a kind of peace and I feel it every time.

We left the house feeling a little deflated. The path leading away was too wet to follow, so we went along on either side, coming soon to a large deer fence where beyond and for some distance the land had been planted with native woodland species – rowan, hazel, birch, Scots pine. I hoped they would take root and flourish on this waterlogged hillside, which probably hadn't seen a tree in centuries. The presence of these saplings lifted my mood. In the fading light of a winter's afternoon we sided up a rough hill and hopped and skipped over a morass of bog where the land levelled, moving with some haste as we still had a good mile to cover. At the crest we could see up-country to a knot of hills half-obscured by cloud, among them Creag Mhor. The thaw had broken up the snowfields and gave a splotchy effect. Across the valley was the distorted outline of a lochan and the air above it was now cool enough for mist to be forming. The valley floor was all pasture, through which coiled a broad river. A little past the far bank and where the moor began its climb was a building, though because the walls and roof had taken on the colour of the land I could barely make it out. Age and neglect had softened it.

Nick was slowing. As I waited I rummaged for a little dead wood in some pines planted long ago as a windbreak. Everything was soaked, but I went through the motions of breaking a few pieces and strapping them to my rucksack. When Nick arrived he did the same. We splashed across the valley flats, easily forded the river and approached the darkening outline of the croft. I remembered the rusted wire that kept fast the double doors from my last visit. It was apparent then we were entering what was once someone's home, maybe not so many years ago. The place had been in limbo ever since the last residents left; no longer a house, it is now sometimes a bothy or a make-do barn or just forlorn and empty and unvisited, at least by humans.

We followed our torch beams and went inside, turned right to the only habitable room. It was as if not a soul had crossed the threshold in the three years since I'd last been there. In the corner was the same pile of kindling and chopped logs that some generous soul had left before. I was astonished.

A crude bench and a table were pressed into the corner, and on it were bird droppings and a few pages from a Gaelic bible. There was a rusting firegrate, curved at the top and flaky to touch. On an inbuilt shelf by the fireplace were two white bird's eggs, each about an inch in length and almost certainly belonging to a house martin. White feathers and lots of dry sedge for nesting material lay scattered about. The other downstairs room was a complete mess, floor littered with farm rubbish and crumbled mortar and an old range half-covered in ash. A rusted Singer sewing machine was set on a side table in the small middle room, the black and gold inlay still visible. Hanging above it and attached to the ceiling like some huge growth of fungi was an abandoned house martin's nest.

I trailed Nick up a stairwell covered in mould. Flowery wallpaper hung in sheets and tears, and I ran the torch over copies of the *People's Journal*, dated 11 January 1902. The curious news and odd items. An advert said 'James Doan's Great Discovery, Doan's backache kidney pills', apparently endorsed by prominent Edinburgh citizens.

'Look at this. Some animal has been living up here.' Nick was tiptoeing about in an upstairs room. A meat-eater, I guessed, when I saw the piles of scat, dark and rich in protein. When Nick sliced open a piece it contained many animal hairs. Here were the winter quarters of a fox or maybe even a feral or wild cat. One of the sky-lights was missing and the invading elements were slowly rotting away the floorboards, but it had allowed in the wildlife and for me there was something comforting in the thought that local creatures had filled the vacuum of an empty house and squatted and procreated and fashioned lives here.

We lit the single candle stub and swept the floor of droppings and cleared the rubbish and moved the bench. I filled a pan and fired the cooker as Nick fetched more water. When he got back he fussed over something while I sat on an upturned box and waited for the water to boil. Only then did I feel the weeks of frost come into the room from the stone walls, a cold dampness that went right to my core. I got to work on the fire. No paper, so I took a handful of dry sedge from the former nest and weaved it about shards of wood and put a flame to it. It flickered slowly. I watched it grow, adding more kindling to the flames until I placed on them a piece of split log. If this took then the fire was 'in', I thought, and silently thanked whoever had left the wood.

Had the hearth felt no warmth in three years? I thought that extraordinary. But then few walkers come this way. If one's calling is to be among dramatic scenery then it might be hard to justify an exploration of the quiet moors of Ben Armine. And given some folk do from time to time stravaig up this forgotten valley, why choose to pass a night in such a decrepit place, crumbling and damp, home to beasts and haunted over by an atmosphere of the past? For me, and probably for Nick, it was just right. We'd caught it at the cusp, where it might in a decade be reduced to ruin or perhaps go the other way and be cleaned and reworked as a locked lodge with bars on the windows or run as an open bothy with a smoke alarm and a Norwegian woodburner. Sometimes an apparent improvement is not that. If I could freeze it like this I would, keep it so, with damp and trash and scat and traces of memories. Tonight it was a haven transformed by fire and the company we gave it. Would the original occupants, a couple who were perhaps born at the height of Queen Victoria's reign and had a taste for flowery wallpaper and the *People's Journal*, be pleased their old home gave two strangers rest for a night? I hope so.

Our nest-making was but temporary, and by morning cold and damp had come into the room again, which looked shabby in the wintry light. An overnight frost and my shoes left marks across the pasture when I went to get water. We packed, and after a last look about secured the wire on the door and followed the stream up the slope behind the house. North from here was some of the emptiest land I know, empty of people, that is, when the next inhabited house or hamlet might be two or more days away. Small pools were glazed in ice, and as we climbed the valley began to open up. In the first hour we saw neither bird nor beast, and there was no movement save for a slow drift of cloud or fall of a burn. I thought the moorland held a lovely blend of colour – crimson mosses, grasses and heather and greenish lichen and growing in between, small fern-like plants. When the sun came briefly out it deepened those shades and threw even the smallest grass-blade into relief. We saw further down the valley to a loch still with its ceiling of mist, and then turning caught glimpses of a higher loch, for which we were heading, this one with scrub-covered islands. Footing over a burn we stopped to drink, then continued upwards, the near-hard ground easing our progress. When we reached it, the loch was completely frozen. The thaw of the last few days had smeared the surface, and reflecting a wan sun it seemed like a sandy beach lately wet from an ebbing tide. Snowy corries of a hill-range appeared through a cloud to the west, almost certainly Ben More Assynt and the peak of Conival about thirty miles away.

We were forced to pick our way rather, as the ground underfoot was all tussocky grass growing in odd clumps. By now the first inch or so of ground had softened, but below that it was frozen and unforgiving, and some of the bogs were still fixed in translucent ice. At least they were safe to step on. The closer rising moors where the bedrock came through had hollows and gullies, some snow-filled. Beyond these the hills showed more rock and were darker in tone, and clouds blocked out or rode just below their summits or crowns. We came to a pair of smaller lochs, reed-covered and frozen. They seemed shallow and I wondered if the ice might hold us, but when I put a foot on its surface it sagged and began to split. Nick was already going around. The burn which ran into the lochs guided us north and was a joy, at times flowing nosily among small boulders, then later dark and sluggish in a corridor of sedge and by banks of faded pasture. Though it meandered it was easier to trace than a route over the moor.

At some point it brought us to the wreck of an old pony stable. The corrugated walls had collapsed, but in such a way that there was still a gap for you to crawl into, as a pal and I did one summer's day during a thunderburst. We'd reached a kind of plateau, and on this high tract there appeared less colour, a brown-grey scene with a more distant skyline and a space like the moor of Rannoch. A nagging cold wind was blowing and the cloud base had lifted just for Ben Armine and Creag Mhor to raise snowy arms. I pulled on my gloves and put up my hood and bent into the wind, footing a path of sorts, winding or straight, but no longer worked by the estate and now fading into the moor. Probably a good thing. As the turbines go up at least the land was taking something back.

For a time we moved with some ease, though the land about us refused to change and our progress went unregistered by far-away moors, as if this path was in fact a treadmill that rolled beneath us. In the wild lands of the west I am always encouraged at how each step brings a change in the arrangement of nearby peaks, but not here. The face of the land after five minutes, after ten, was much the same, or so it appeared. The thought was forgotten as soon as we lost the path and were at once among a snare of ditches. They seemed to appear from nowhere. The ground opened up and most were just too wide to safely leap and too deep and wet to negotiate, so we backtracked and sought land bridges and went wildly astray. The roughness only let up when we found the banks of a narrow gushing river. We forded it by an aged rowan that grew sideways from a boulder, the first tree we had seen all day.

Here was another little-used route, though well graded, and for an hour we went along almost without effort, climbing high to the flank of a hill. Before our eyes was now a great spread of moorland, brassy and varnished with passing sunshine. A few lochans gleamed like polished coins, bright on dark, but nothing in the wider land was dominant enough especially to draw in the eye or hold it for long, just bowls and shoulders and tangents. It was the small details at my feet I really noticed – opaque ice in a trough, the dark peat and ruby red moss and fibrous lichen. Nick pointed at some deer on the skyline and we watched a herd of about ten lift their heads and strike away uphill.

A steep-sided valley was the first noteworthy feature we reached for a while and we heard the lively river at its base before actually seeing it. Hemmed in and running fairly straight, its bed was dashed with rocks and boulders. It wasn't in any kind of spate and when crossing it we were surprised at how clear the waters ran, given their provenance in the peatbeds of Armine. We followed its right bank. In one place rock sinews squeezed the channel into a small gorge, the rock here smoothed and hollowed by the water-action. Higher up, the river spread itself over shoals and shingle banks and ran thinly with a lighter sound. At some fifteen hundred feet we were in the zone of snowdrifts and frozen spillways. The land increasingly had a desolate feel to it. There was no shelter of any kind if the wind got up. Afternoon was drawing on, and ahead lay miles of rising and desolate moor that only finished at the crown of a hill, the highest in these parts.

Too cold to stop for more than a few minutes, we forged on until ahead, in the curve of the valley, was a small building. Not a house – it was so far from any road no one could ever live there. It was a hut for ponies and built by the estate in the days when ponies were employed in the transporting of deer carcasses to the larder or head of a vehicle track. Hundreds of such shelters were scattered throughout the Highlands, but most estates stopped using ponies decades ago and it is now rare to find one in a half-habitable state. It is a rude shelter only, offering accommodation somewhere between a bothy and a simple stone howff, and I have sometimes used it over the years, though never before in winter. Stepping inside and slipping off my rucksack I realised why. The wind came through the drystane gable, the cold stones giving it an added edge. A tent would provide better shelter but I hadn't brought one, so we settled and brewed, and in the grey light read the old graffiti penciled on the sides of the partitions where the ponies were once tethered. It reached back a hundred years. There were names of estate workers and passing hikers. George Elphinston from Rogart was here on 1 May 1912, not long before Scott's ship, the *Terra Nova*, returned from the Antarctic. Hugh Mackay scratched his name on 2 August 1944, at the height of the Allied Campaign in Europe. Twenty years later Robert W. Brown from Liverpool perhaps hadn't planned to spend the night as he adds, 'Lost the way home'. At least he had a roof. At the top of a partition and carved with a sharp knife at 3 am one morning was a message, or maybe a plea, 'looking for lost hill-walkers'. It was signed by the keeper and wife of the remote Ben Armine Lodge. The older inscriptions, neatly pencilled and little flowery even, were fading and year by year the names slip from view.

There's one name you won't find here – Rowena Farre. Living in the general vicinity for so long, she would surely have known of the stable, but marking a wall with her name was perhaps not a habit of her class. But then Rowena Farre was not her real name. It was Daphne Lois Macready.

That fact was only generally known after her death in 1979. While it is fairly common for authors to publish under pseudonyms, it is perhaps unusual for someone to conceal their identity entirely. When *Seal Morning* was reprinted by Mercat Press in 2001, Maurice Fleming wrote an investigative piece for the *Scots Magazine* which appeared in modified form as an Afterword in the new edition. He describes the phenomenal success of *Seal Morning* when it was first appeared and notes that when a curious press made requests to interview Farre, her London publishers, Hutchinson, admitted they were unable to contact her. Hutchinson later put out a press release saying, 'Farre has disappeared and is thought to be living with a tribe of Romany gypsies'. When the author finally surfaced years later, she was able to collect some £10,000 in unpaid royalties, a tidy sum in the 1960s. It may have been that Farre was an intensely private individual who shirked self-promotion and had no interest in book signings or receiving accolades from her readers, which might explain why she wrote under a pseudonym. Or maybe there is a more obvious reason, that her entire tale was a fabrication, a fiction cooked up by her imagination.

While Fleming casts doubt on the some of the stories in *Seal Morning* he stops short of denying that Farre might have once lived in a remote Sutherland croft. I think that is generous. I believe the key to *Seal Morning*, its truth or otherwise, lay in what she actually wrote and whether her narrative chimes with the land, this land. Tomorrow we entered Farre's country, where she claimed to have spent seven years of her life. Here were the hills and corries and dubh lochans of her milieu, and the intimacy drawn from such a long association would have generated in her writing some truth about these places, especially given Farre's ability with the pen. Is this so? Do we have something beyond the generic, and does the picture painted on the page capture some essence of the land?

Overnight, a band of rain driven by a gale had passed through and I was woken twice by its relentless drumming on the metal roof. I felt a cold draught and the river's sound was cleaner and louder. A little later, as a grey dawn gathered, I went outside and filled a pan and gazed about to get a sense of place. It was a high shallow valley, at the centre of a wheel at whose rim were moorland crests a mile or so away that rose or fell depending in which quadrant I looked. Ragged white clouds drifted right to left. Most of the river stones you could see yesterday were gone or now shown by helmets of water with short trailing stoppers, but the rain had eased and the wind blew a little calmer.

With no stepping stones I removed my shoes, endured the freezing water and crossed to the far bank. Nick, with better gaiters and less patience, hopped and waded. We pushed eastwards, the land rising steadily at first, and we couldn't see much ahead beyond shifting clouds. The old path, fashioned by cheap labour for the hooves of ponies and the purposes of stalking, I will admit saved us some effort, and bore us on its raised walkway above a great morass of snow-filled ditches. It had an easy angle that kept your gait right and our walking developed a comfortable rhythm. But it was not an ease I sought.

Knowing how local folk and itinerants were exploited in the making of these ways, something in me resented their presence. Our following them was incidental. They were scant luxuries on this trip, at any rate.

It was not a day for the summits, so we kept to the bealach area and found the river's headwaters, crossing a burn-gully where the snow had drifted ten feet or more. At another the snow-bridge almost collapsed and my foot hung in a void above the rushing meltwater. Ours were the only prints. The land opened up to the east, a vast country whose perimeter was bounded by the Knockfin Heights and the hills above Helmsdale and Brora, of which Morven rose the highest. The middle ground revealed an expanse of moorland first evoked by my map more than a decade ago, tens of square miles and engraved by the headwaters of various rivers and burn courses, their alluvial fringes showing as a lighter brown against the predominant dun and grey of the moor. The land lay in shadow, but during our descent a pallid sunlight brought out loops of silver and the glint from dubh lochs.

With the crash of water in our ears, we dropped and swung south. The wind had picked up and it now gusted and knocked our balance and the moor trembled. Cold katabatic winds came straight from the hill. In among a boulderfield and at the base of Creag Mhor we found a little shelter and took some lunch. Propped up against his rucksack, Nick dozed. I looked up a thousand feet to the corniced rim of Creag Mhor where clouds were streaming. A frozen waterfall had glued itself to a series of crags and emerged from old snow that was layered and dirty in places. Only a few yards from us, the surface of a small pool was puckered with small waves, furiously throwing themselves at the shore.

I had to rouse Nick and we edged around the wave-filled Gorm Loch Mor. To our right the land was broken with tilting boulders and small crags, and growing about them and along the lochshore was a relict woodland – bare-branched rowans and stately birch wrapped in mossy growths and others skeletal and dying. By the loch a large tree was down, its roots upright and trunk lapped over by waves, yet it will live for another summer or two at least.

It's rare for Farre to detail much in the way of place-names, but on one occasion she describes leaving Strath na Seilge for a day's walk and 'was climbing in the direction of Creag Mhor'. Strath na Seilge is also known as the Black Water, a river which drains the great peaty hinterland to the west and south of Armine and Creag Mhor. From this we can establish that she was heading more or less north, and this is confirmed a few lines later when she notes 'the azure loch, Gorm Loch Mor, as it is called in Gaelic, lay to my right'. Then, quite out of character, she reveals something of the whereabouts of her croft, one of only a handful of passages in the book which offers the reader a clue to its location. 'I stood on the open hillside,' she says, 'and noted the River Skinsdale far off in the valley below, the croft to the right . . .' The Skinsdale drains the moors to the east of Creag Mhor and runs pretty much due south until meeting the Black Water some half a dozen miles further on. That would put the croft at the confluence and in the vicinity of Pollie Hill, some eight miles south of Ben Armine.

If that was the case, then where was Lora's loch? And why does Farre never mention that they lived by a river? Nor does this location tally with an earlier description, that when looking out from their home they could see

Ben Armine to the west and Knockfin Heights to the east. Armine, Creag Mhor and Knockfin are dominant features in this landscape, and after seven years I cannot believe you would not know precisely their arrangement in relation to your home. This is loose writing and I am surprised that no reviewer, perhaps one whose credulity was stretched by some of the animal tales, spotted it.

Her tales of winter can also puzzle hill folk. She describes a three-day blizzard at the end of October one year which left a blanket of snow so deep it reached the eaves of their cottage. Weather events can be verified, of course. Farre was born in 1921 and lived with Aunt Miriam for seven years, leaving when she was seventeen, which would make her years of residence from 1931 to 1938. What struck me when researching weather records for that part of Scotland was just how benign were winters in the 1930s. Farre claims the 'our third winter at the croft was the worse we experienced', yet the records show 1934/35 was in fact one of the mildest winters of the century. Interestingly snow did fall across Scotland in October 1934, but only a few inches were recorded, not the nine feet dreamed up by Farre.

Once it becomes apparent a writer has embellished the truth with one or two stories you begin to question them all. Did Farre really experience a hill mist so dense that when she reached out a hand she 'was just able to see the tips of my finger'. Was she nearly caught in a sudden spate on a nearby river, 'a great mass of water, like a brown avalanche, coming towards me'. On one winter's night she claimed to have witnessed a pack of yelping stoats chase a mountain hare to its death. And I wondered why she has no anecdotes of the Highland midge? Not one appears, yet they are the scourge of every summer visitor and colour my own memories of childhood holidays to Sutherland. Did Farre really observe wildcats in a tract of native pinewoods? Which tract? These lands are some of the most barren and treeless in Scotland.

I cannot accept that Farre's work is what some have called an 'autobiographical novel'. It is presented as truth, as an actual depiction of events and places. That the story itself is harmless and people wanted to believe it doesn't excuse what this actually amounts to – a fraud, a fairy-tale from start to finish. No Lora, no Aunt Miriam, no croft in the wilderness. The truth was probably much more mundane. In the process of researching his piece Maurice Fleming was contacted by Margaret Allen, who had roomed with Farre when working at an RAF station in Wales during the Second World War. She recalls a 'complex character' and something of a 'loner'. But they got on well, perhaps because they shared similar backgrounds. Both their fathers were doctors in the Royal Army Medical Corps and they had both been to boarding school. Margaret Allen had no recollection of her friend ever reminiscing about a childhood spent on a Sutherland croft. So Farre went to a mainstream school and sat in rows of desk and did her sums like everyone else.

Having immersed myself in the classics of outdoor literature from an early age, I find Farre's fiction presented as fact deeply unsettling. When we read Shipton and Tilman we trust them. Their reputation and integrity are grounded in the truth of their writings. We believe Shipton's account of the first epic ascent of the Rishi Gorge, not just the fact that he and Tilman reached the Sanctuary but the small details of their ascent. The details matter. How important it was for Apsley Cherry-Garrard to note that on their 1911 winter trek to Cape Crozier in the Antarctic the temperature dipped to -61C. Cherry was a master of understatement, but the reader knows at that temperature trees explode and your breath reaches the ground in a tinkle of frost crystals.

The Long Walk by Polish soldier Slavomir Rawicz was once a favourite book. It chronicles how he and a handful of fellow prisoners escape incarceration in the Russian Gulag in 1942 and trek some four thousand miles through forests, deserts and finally the Himalayas to reach safety in India. The story is brilliantly ghostwritten by journalist Ronald Downing. When I first read Rawicz's book I was unaware of the scepticism to which some had received it, including Eric Shipton, who noted inconsistencies about the distances Rawicz claimed to have walked. Rawicz, who moved to Britain after the war, stuck to his story, and it was a few years after his death in 2004 that an American researcher, Linda Wills, found a document signed by Rawicz himself. It revealed that he had been released from the Gulag as part of a general amnesty for Polish prisoners in 1942. No escape and no heroic walk to freedom, only a lie nurtured by Rawicz and lifelong plaudits that were entirely unwarranted.

Farre and Rawicz to my mind have broken the assumption of trust between reader and author. They have committed a kind of theft, such that we can no longer approach a non-fiction account as an innocent narrative and must be on our guard for fraudsters and charlatans. Their actions diminish the written word everywhere.

We needed a bearing to find our way across the great moor. At first we were able to fix on some small feature – the sheen of a dubh loch, a standing boulder, the crown of a small rise – though later there appeared almost nothing to aim for and we moved across land that was unchang-

Springtime at the Sluie Gorge, River Findhorn.

In the forests near Daltulich Bridge, River Findhorn.

Looking down on the Streens in the Findhorn's middle reaches.

Portaging to Loch a' Bhraighe, Assynt.

North Ardnamurchan coastline looking east to the hills of Moidart.

The beach at Sanna.

Descending east from Ben Armine, with Knockfin Heights and Morven on the skyline.

Eilan Cro Balair, the last wildwood on Lewis.

Clive at daybreak, Eilan Cro Balair.

Nameless loch in the heart of Lewis's wetlands.

Looking north from a midsummer bivouac on the summit ridge of Creag a' Choire Aird.

Ascending Sgurr nan Ceathreamhnan via its northerly ridge.

Gavin on the summit of Lurg Mhor looking north to the Torridon Hills.

Dropping from Lurg Mhor with the hills of Torridon in the distance.

A view looking up Glen Geusachan to Monadh Mor in the heart of the Cairngorms.

ing. When the sun came through to stain the moor russet and gold, we looked back to the snow-rimmed hills and I wondered if there was anywhere a setting more lovely and lonely. That didn't make the going any easier. We could achieve no regular pace. The mires and troughs were unseen until we stood at their threshold and considered whether to jump or scramble down into their labyrinths or somehow go around. A still-frozen layer just below the surface helped, but the peat banks, owing to their colour, had all but thawed and were soft and cloying. Real progress was hard to measure, and after climbing from one trough we rested at the beginnings of a small brook.

This was the one, I thought. It went between grassy banks, and for the best part of a mile we followed its course as it sunk gently into the moor. An anonymous burn when seen on the map, but on the ground an unfolding delight, a winding low-way over banks of free-draining silts and shoals and braids and divided by islands of rock, and with a brash-line that reached to where the heather and moor began. In places gravel and sand from the riverbed and clods of peat from the moor had been left on the grass as a signature of winter floods. A dipper pulled itself onto a midstream rock and took off and played 'follow me down'. Then the burn turned a sharp corner. We edged beneath a small cleft where the rock was layered and friable. The water disappeared from view and there came the crash of a waterfall. For about ten feet it ran white as it belted over a sloping platform and brought up a small mist.

On our bank and within stepping distant of the pool was something I'd stumbled across years before and wondered if I would ever find again. It was a small stone-built structure set hard into the bank, and completely hidden unless you were standing right over it. No question a great deal of thought and energy had gone into its creation – with stone walls about five feet in height and almost half in width, and a large lintel stone, now fallen, that probably once framed the entrance. The downstream wall curved over in a slight overhang and at its base was a gully of some kind. Moss and ferns and clumps of heather colonised the wall crests but didn't hide the unusual outline. The whole structure was oddly partitioned. Why such tiny rooms? If this was some hermit hideaway or poacher's hole, why build so close to a burn that invariably flooded? More likely this old place once functioned as an illicit whisky still, which would explain its proximity to water. And its concealment. The 'gully' was probably the old lade, that in its heyday siphoned water from the burn to the distilling room. With my back against the lintel I could see that the siting was almost perfect. There was a glimpse of the summit of Creag Mhor and some distant hills to the south, but Ben Armine and all surrounding land was unseen behind high banks. Illegal whisky distilling more or less came to an end with the passing of the 1823 Excise Act, which sanctioned whisky production on payment of a license fee. That would make the building some two hundred years old.

A compass bearing led us from the gully and across the moor, near-featureless and gently sloping and a repetition of the same mires and sinks. Sometimes a grouse rose and punctured the quiet with its startled cries, but away from the burn only the sighing wind, now much quietened, lent any sound, that and our footfalls over wet ground. The horizon hills were now sharper in outline and the land was at ease with itself. Only the wind turbines of Gordonbush added a note of incongruity. We walked towards them for a while, then swung more northerly so they were out of view. At a grass-fringed burn I rested and waited. After a few minutes I turned to see silver-edged clouds piled high above the hill-shapes and the wide blank of the moor and a small figure working slowly across the foreground, coming towards me.

In late afternoon we climbed the slope to almost flat terrain where some tiny lochs lay clogged with algae. Now we could see something – the broken walls of a ruin not much more than a mile away. As we lost ground our world began to shrink. One by one the turbines went, then the hills above Helmsdale and Brora, though we could still see the summit crown of Morven a dozen miles away to the northeast. Now we were in a broad and shallow valley. The ruin was fixed on a great terrace raised above a bend in the river and on a small island of pasture. East and west the river looped away out of sight. The wind still came stiffly, so we sought the shelter of an outside wall and near to where the front door would have been. Nick put up his small tent. I unrolled my bivouac sack, then fixed a small piece of corrugated iron to act as a further windbreak and shelter for my cooker.

In the dimming light I poked about the building. At the entrance was one part of a cast-iron treadle that once held a manual sewing machine. Between the supports the iron had been forged into a kind of wreath and on it were the words 'Sing . . . N.Y'. The hometown of Singer and Co is still New York. The croft was dominated by two large rooms, one of which would still provide fairly decent shelter for someone without a tent. The small room in between was probably a kitchen or pantry. Upstairs, of which nothing remained, would have held the bedrooms.

Since I was last here a large part of a wall had collapsed, revealing some internal timbers and at the same time burying the iron bedstead. The remaining walls were some six feet high though the gable end reached to about twice that height, which is what we had seen at such distance on the moor. I ran my palm over a coating of orange and grey lichen that covered the stonework inside and out, and I reckoned this place had been open to the skies for many decades. But did someone live here in the years before the war? I thought that likely, given the treadle table was probably a Class 66 and first made by Singer in the early 1920s. Evidence of cultivation surrounded the building, an inbyre, tumbled dykes and probably some outbuildings.

After filling pans and water containers I climbed into my sleeping bag and settled, listening to the purr of a gas stove working on a pan of water, a wonderful sound after a long day on the moor. Nick crawled into his tent and was asleep before the water boiled. He roused himself later for a little conversation and tea, and we watched the night gather around us, the light fading until the land presented only shapes and the river-sound grew stronger in the background.

Throughout her life Farre was a compulsive traveller, visiting and living in various countries and continents. I believe after the war when still a young woman she came here to Sutherland and found this deserted croft, which perhaps back then was still habitable. She stood and witnessed the same view, the moor riding up for miles to the twin peaks of Creag Mhor and Ben Armine, then behind to Knockfin Heights and the summit cone of Morven probing the sky. Below her the broad river on a big meander curled away out of sight and reappeared and vanished at each interlocking spur. The peace and beauty here are heart-rending. I believe she tarried here and the seeds of an idea were sown. In other writings she let slip something of her troubled relationship with her father and mother. 'There were few ties of affection between my parents and myself,' she says, 'They were parents to me in name only'. Having not seen her father for many years she even admits to struggling to remember what he looked like. An unhappy childhood, and then, we presume, she was sent to boarding school. Was *Seal Morning* a heartfelt attempt by Farre to fill an emotional vacuum by reinventing her childhood, with animals replacing humans as objects of her affection?

Something about Farre compels me to sympathise with her imaginings. *Seal Morning* is harmless enough and it has given pleasure to many thousands of readers, and I daresay still does. Writing it was part of her journey. She briefly paraded her emotions on a public stage before covering her ears and running back into the shadows. A restless, questing soul, she could not embrace the habitual routine of a career ladder or the commitment of a family. The purpose of work was solely to raise funds for her next journey. In her third and last book, *The Beckoning Land*, these journeys are increasingly inward. The book describes her travelling across Asia and ending in the shadow of a high mountain in the Himalayas where she lives for a time with a mystic. Farre came to realise that happiness and fulfilment are not found in any one place or country but in our innermost selves. 'Within and transcending the self lies an undiscovered country,' she writes, 'an invisible, boundless and nameless realm not subject to change.' And later, 'There is a call. The traveller listens and turns within. He has taken that first step towards that bright land in comparison to which the countries of this world appear as fleeting shadows.'

We packed up for a last time in the half-light of a cheerless morning, grey and cold, the peaks barely seen through the murk and their presence indicated only by their snows. Alluvial flats by the river gave easy walking and in a short while we crossed the shallow waters and worked up a sodden slope of brown grasses. The going remained easy, if a little soft, and with want of any feature to hold my attention my mind slipped away. Each step demanded but little care, and on this, day four, my feet found their own way in any case.

At some point we stopped climbing and began an unending contour, for an hour at least. The ruin haunting its perch now slipped away behind us, seeming impossibly remote and soon just an inconsequential mark on the land. There were long miles to anywhere, the moor rising or falling in increments and often not even that, though there was always water and it always flowed. We looked over to the river valley, so lately followed. It turned in on itself and was engulfed by the moor and the shadow of the hill crests, now lost to the eye. A big land and huge sky and its truth greater than any story penned.

Gradually there were signs that the place was used more frequently – some heather burnt, a strip of sheep pasture, a walled enclosure for livestock. A cairn from antiquity. After an age we came upon a rough beast trail, this in time curling round to the headwaters of another broad valley. We lost ground and picked up a landrover track and this led to what was once a farming hamlet of two houses; one a ruin, the other of more recent abandonment. The scattering of outbuildings was now used by a grazier who commuted by four-wheel drive. It was a sheep station only. The burn coming off the hill to join the river was shored up with wooden butts that I thought looked very old. A clump of planted pines and spruces stood sentry by the former dwellings and we sat among them and out of the wind and ate the last of our snacks. We studied the remains of a red-brick house. Only the lower walls were *in situ* and a clay chimney-stack retained any height. The stone-built end still remained, the older part, two rooms with a fireplace on either side. A corrugated iron roof, probably added later, carried a layer of turf and moss and the limbs of spruce trees. Years ago one of the trees had fallen, and in doing so its roots had pulled up a length of clay drainage pipes. This slow vandalism I thought astonishing; tentacles around the terracotta like the slow judgment of nature – though maybe not judgment, only indifference. Trees planted as saplings by the occupants of this house, presumably to shelter the structure, were now playing a hand in its passing. Here was an image of a post-human world, like the ancient temples of Angkor Wat lost to an invading jungle. I noticed the fallen tree had not died but re-rooted itself by its side branches and now grew as tall and straight as its predecessor.

There were shelterbeds and fenced native woodland, willows I think, then we left the track and crossed the wide valley flats and a field of wintering sheep. The river was easily forded and we went up the side of a burn in an opposite valley, though it could hardly be called a valley as the land here rose only slowly, the burn quiet in its sunken channels. Drifting over a broad pass we fronted a cold drizzle carried by a north wind. The final hurdle was Helmsdale River and its three feet depth of fast-flowing water. Nick went in barefoot and yelped. I kept my shoes on.

Although I was concentrating hard on placing my feet, as I neared the far bank I noticed some movement, a fox caught in a snare and darting about. Rowena Farre would have hated that. In an effort to escape it had excavated a trench around its anchor and dug down into the bank. Then something extraordinary. At my approach it went into an absolute frenzy. It managed to shrug off the wire noose and shot away in the direction of Kinbrace.

Secret Waters

Leaving the stone circle at Calanais you could walk south and west for days and not see a house or cross a road, in a journey of lochs and low hills and peatlands that ends, if you so choose, at some raised beach by the Atlantic. Human echoes are found in placenames – Norse overlapping with Gaelic – in moss-covered cairns and dolmen stones and where old causeways cross loch and channel. I remember the moment I first saw this land for myself. Our boat moored at Tarbert, we'd gone up Clisham to escape the sultry air of that rare phenomenon, a Hebridean heatwave. From the summit we surveyed the aquamarine waters and white sands of the Sound of Taransay, swinging our gaze over the hills of Teileasbhal and Stulabhal to the curving finger of Loch Langabhat. At its tip the land opened to a strange piedmont half drowned in lochs and with gnarly hillocks among them like old magma come to the surface. Naturally I wanted to go there, but how? There was so much water.

The lochans of the Outer Hebrides were the first to interest me in the use of a canoe to explore such places and initially, with the map spread, I conceived an east-west route, effectively a crossing of Lewis by canoe. It was something of a grand gesture and a younger self would have left it at that and made preparations; but increasingly I saw the land-locked waters northeast of Langabhat as a world in itself.

I'd never before seen a system like it, an almost bewildering arrangement and I struggled to see a beginning.

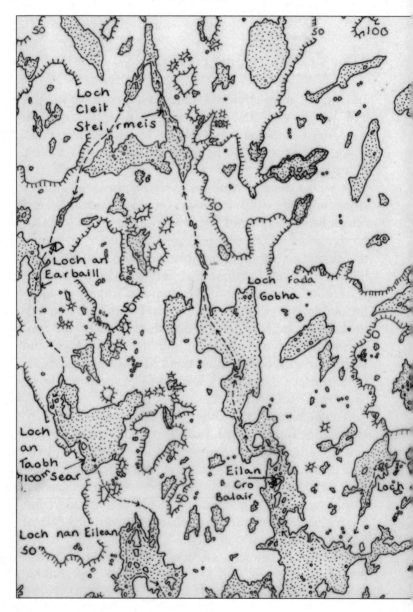

Isle of Lewis

Loch Trealabhal

Loch an Drunga

Bhroma

110

Trealabhal

Loch Trealabhal

Eilean Mòr Dubh Loch Trealaval

Loch nam

At first it seemed I was looking at a random scattering of lochs where natural dips and hollows in the gneiss bedrock had flooded after the last glaciation, but it was more that my map failed to present a deeper truth. Maybe the scale was wrong. It is strange to be able to cover a crooked mile of loch shore with your thumb, yet know nothing of its reality on the ground. Maps struggle to reveal more. They show composites – a hill but not a single rock, a burn though not its eddies or pools or where it runs deep or thinly over boiler plates. They caption a place, no more. I often think that I might one day do without maps altogether, finding my way from memory and the old clues of nature. How much more magical and fresh would places then appear.

But then I have always loved maps for themselves, as a window to the world and often the first trigger of inspiration. Here are conjured up possibilities and a hope that even in my middle years there are new lands and waters to reach, pockets of blue where I might drag my canoe and launch and undertake a quiet tour of unimagined shorelines.

If I realised anything from my map gazing, it was that the old creed of haste is redundant here. I would go slowly and burden myself only with the necessities of survival and a small ambition to see these places in all their revealed detail before they are gone.

At the second attempt we found the rough peat track which dropped away from the main Stornoway to Tarbert road and for a few hundred yards led us across the moor. A concrete ramp full of holes lifted it over a burn, the going worsened and before we got stuck we parked up, not far from the rusting hulk of a long-abandoned camper. It took only a minute to carry the canoe to the muddy edge of Loch Stranndabhat, then a couple of shuttles to collect and stow and strap in our camping gear and a few days' provisions. I held both gunwales as Clive clambered in and went aft to his preferred spot at the bow. Floating the canoe a little further out, I stepped aboard and we both used our paddles as poles to reach open water. As the shore receded I looked at the three large sacks that lay at our feet like ballast, and my only thought was that we'd taken too much. My long-held practice of travelling light didn't apply to canoe journeys, it seemed. It was too late now at any rate.

We bore north along the left shoreline, away from the busy road, vehicle noise replaced by paddle-splash and the rustle of the canoe through water. A light wind played over the loch's surface making bath-sized waves, and these tinkled past with each stroke. Slow, unhurried progress, our effort hardly matching the chill air of late autumn. I looked around. There were tiny islands of fading bracken with the odd tree, half-grown and bare. Sheep dotted some of the slopes ahead, and beyond them, about a mile away, the land rose nearly a thousand feet to Roineabhal.

The loch was narrow in character. When studying the map for a water route to the interior I was taken by how curious was the outline of Stranndabhat, evoking something bestial, I thought, a quadruped with a long neck and carnivorous jaw. As we approached its end, some mile and a half from our put-in, I saw an old sheepfold, angled the bow east and in a short while we reached the nose of this strange creature, the waters here draining into a rushing burn. We landed with a scraping noise. Clive jumped out and with both hands hefted the bow ashore. From the map I knew this burn reached the sea two miles away at Loch Eireasort, not where we were heading, but at least we could follow it for a time. Considering our weight of gear, for the first day at least everything would have to be relayed, and this initial portage of a mile or so was pretty long. After some rocks and an early drop the burn grew sluggish and deep, and so with a rope each and walking on opposite banks we guided the canoe a little way, as better than having to carry or drag. Though I was slightly ahead Clive was still in my peripheral vision when suddenly he dropped from it. A loud splash followed, then cries and curses. I swung round to see him standing in about three feet of water, still holding the rope. 'Don't worry,' I said, as he kneed back onto the turf, 'nobody else saw that.'

The burn widened enough for me to board the canoe and navigate solo its coiling path for a couple of hundred yards. In the distance was the road again and the back of some grey-walled houses. Turning from these we relayed everything steeply up a track, then dragged it all on a long slow decline to Loch Cuthaig, a slab of blue that only very slowly grew in size. The loch parodied the land, which had a flattened and restful quality, broken only occasionally by random boulders and rock warts. A low sun brought out golds and russets and brightened a few splashes of verdant pasture.

Perhaps it was no coincidence that our put-in on Loch Stranndabhat was only a few miles from Leurbost, home village of the writer and environmental campaigner, Alastair McIntosh. I'd only just finished reading his seminal work *Soil and Soul,* and which is subtitled *People versus Corporate Power.* If the measure of a great book is one that upsets and challenges long-held preconceptions, then *Soil and Soul* achieves this. McIntosh claims that only by changing the way we think can we begin to heal, both at a cultural and individual level. 'The great disease of our time is meaninglessness,' he writes. 'We are materially richer than ever before and yet suffer a spiritual poverty that is difficult to pin down.' These are bold statements and the efficacy of much of what follows hinges on their essential truth.

Soil and Soul feels like an outpouring of ideas, a polemic that threatens to drown the timid reader, but at its heart is a search for meaning in the face of globalisation and indifferent corporate power. Drawing on memories of his childhood on the Isle of Lewis, in the first half he presents the reader with a deep and lucid analysis of how a greater part of humanity has lost its connection with the earth and, more crucially, with itself. He then chronicles two important campaigns seen through the lens of his own activism – the successful opposition to the Harris superquarry and the community buy-out of the Isle of Eigg.

Before leaving for Lewis I'd thought deeply about some of the issues and events McIntosh discusses, and I wondered if his words would add anything to our experience of these backwaters.

A shout from behind. A man on a quad bike with two dogs was rounding up a small group of sheep. The dogs ran in overlapping circles, marshalling the sheep this way and that, though broadly in one direction. They headed back and the land was silent again, just our grunts and sloshing footfalls as we pulled ever harder, the ground levelling and softening with the loch shore coming closer. Reaching it was a joy. Loch Cuthaig is quite substantial, but we only needed to paddle its easternmost fringe. At the outflow we dragged over the short land bridge and entered one of the tentacles of Loch Trealabhal, the most extensive loch system in the Outer Hebrides and whose great labyrinth we hoped to explore in some detail.

The lag from an overly wet summer ensured water levels were high and the shoreline inundated in places. A good sign I thought. Sunshine revealed fur-covered shallows and orange sediment kicked up by our paddles as we went slowly into deeper water. The sky suddenly darkened and from nowhere came a squall. It raked the waters and spun us sideways. With no wish to be caught in the open we pulled hard for the nearest bank, and there Clive hung on to a rag of heather and we cowered beneath our hoods, watching the rain bounce from our sacks and pepper the loch. The shower passed, and in the sudden brightness a huge rainbow arched over the flatlands to the north.

Stepping stones shown by the map where the loch narrowed lay feet underwater and we drifted over these into an open sound, the banks peeling away. With all the portaging the day had slipped away somewhat, and I reckoned there was now little more than an hour of daylight left. We chewed over some options. Although our itinerary was loose, I had a notion to see if we might discover some tangible evidence of the old Lewis, places little-known that have somehow escaped the human influence. Islands for instance. Would we find here any clues to the way Lewis looked a thousand years ago? Eilean Mor Dubh, 'large black island', with its woodland relic, was only a short paddle away. We swung the canoe and headed across the loch.

As we neared what I judged to be suitable landing spot, a small group of deer moved briskly away, their pale rumps disappearing over the brow of the island. We never saw them again and assumed they must have swum the narrow channel on the far side to reach the mainland. Their presence was not a good sign and even before we touched land I could see the place was run-down. The land was well into its seasonal dip, but there seemed here something of a long slow decline – what trees remained were going, a few aged and half-dead rowans, last of their line and end of a continuum that stretched unbroken perhaps to the last periglacial era. They were being replaced now by a blanket covering of bracken.

We beached and pulled up the canoe and rolled it so the hull faced skywards; in its shelter we placed what was not needed at camp, then scouted about for a spot to pass the night. On such trampled and grazed ground there were many.

In a small clearing and on a bed of woodrush, sorrel and tormentil we fixed our small camp; then in the fading light I went to the island's modest high point, a place simply marked as 'cairn' on the map. Some rocks were piled by human hands to about three feet and almost entirely concealed by coarse grass. I looked to the southeast quarter. There was low-slung moor to the bundle of hills of the Pairc Peninsula, a dozen miles away and soon to be marked at intervals with the white stilts of wind turbines. Beyond the land of unseen lochs was an outline of peaks, Clisham and her neighbours, Teileasbhal and maybe Oireabhal. I watched clouds roll in, smudging the land and hastening the onset of night, and after a few minutes made back along the faint path through dead bracken to our small encampment. Clive was tucked up in his bivvy, reading by torchlight. He'd not taken off his hat. A long evening lay ahead and nothing for it but to crawl into my tent and while away the hours. I boiled water for the first of many brews and cooked a large stir-fry to share. Later we sipped whisky and reminisced on mutual friends and laughed and offered thoughts on some issue and our plans for the morrow.

If childhood is rarely wholly idyllic, after reading about Alistair McIntosh's early years you feel his came close. Growing up in the village of Leurbost with his parents and sister he recalls that for a short time they lived in a 'little croft cottage'. Water for washing was piped from a well, drinking water collected from the roof. When it rained he heard it trickle into a large tar-caulked barrel, and every day his father would fill a bucket and leave it in the kitchen. The surrounding moorland was his playground, and with his pals he hunted rabbits and caught brown trout in the nearby river. In Leurbost, as in almost every village on Lewis, most people spoke Gaelic as well as English. It was a tight-knit, deeply rooted community where folk looked out for each other and shared a degree of familiarity that today would be unusual. Crime was virtually non-existent. Doors and windows were left unlocked and McIntosh mentions how 'you were in and out of other people's houses as if they were extensions of your own'.

His father, a community doctor, was well-liked by everyone, 'a friend of the great and the good', the author tells us, one of whom was Lady Thorneycroft, who owned the 27,500 acre Eisken Estate, a vast roadless tract of lochs, hills and moorland which lay to the south of Leurbost. Today it is usually referred to as Pairc. The young Alastair adored it. Sometimes the family were invited for lunch at the old Victorian lodge and he remembers the huge drawing room with its billiard table and rows of stuffed stags' heads. His father was an accomplished fisherman and revelled in pitting his wits against the salmon of Eisken. Despite his father's highbrow occupation and friends among the gentry, the young Alastair had little sense of being different from his neighbours, though he remembers one local family washing their clothes in the same river he and his pals fished.

Looking back on his childhood in the 1960s, McIntosh recalls that at the time he did not question the disparity between the lords and ladies of Eisken Lodge and subsistence crofters eking a living from a sour hillside. Pretty much all his neighbours were crofters, but because crofting could supply only a portion of family income most also held down other jobs, often in fishing or the merchant navy, or worked in the island's thriving tweed industry. It was an era when unquestioned respect was accorded to anyone of status, whether a laird, policeman, teacher, church minister or village elder, but at the same time there was also a sense of belonging shared by almost everyone. People's notion of equality transcended, on the surface at least, any difference in income. They thought nothing of helping one another. When McIntosh was taken fishing by his old mentor, Finlay Montgomery, any surplus fish caught, which was nearly always, would be given to folk as he cycled home. Sometimes he received eggs in return.

McIntosh describes an incident from those times that demonstrates clearly how people felt towards each other. It happened during the long seamen's strike in 1966. One of the strikers, a family friend called Nellie, was having a new bungalow built. McIntosh asked the builders how Nellie, being on strike, could afford the bungalow. In fact they were not being paid, they said, at least not with money. Nellie had helped them in the past and now they were returning the favour. McIntosh notes sadly that the bungalow was probably the last communally built house in the village.

Like most islanders, if you wanted to 'get on', then you had to leave and McIntosh went to study at Aberdeen and Edinburgh Universities, eventually becoming a well-known academic, broadcaster and writer. It was only then he came to see that his giving away of fish and receiving of eggs, perfectly normal for the times, was actually the last flowering of a system and way of life that had remained unchanged for centuries. Here in fact were the economic principles of *mutuality*, *reciprocity* and *exchange*, practised to a greater or lesser extent, though always in tandem with the cash economy. It underpinned Hebridean society and the benefits were obvious. Not only was everyone provided for, but the very act of giving, receiving and exchanging drew folk together and created a strong sense of community. McIntosh saw similar practices when working with indigenous communities in southeast Asia and the Pacific Islands. It was not exploitative and did not show up in any audit. Government statistics showed the Hebrides at that time to be a deprived region, yet its educational standards were the highest in Britain and the incidence of tooth decay by far the lowest. According to McIntosh, what the Isle of Lewis experienced was not poverty but a 'dignified frugality'. He writes, 'sufficiency not GNP is the real measure of prosperity'.

But Lewis was changing, ushered along, one suspects, by aspiring individuals who, like McIntosh, wanted to 'get on'. The author struggles to explain fully why this happened, if indeed such an explanation is possible, but he witnessed it and in fact admits to being part of it. The effects of these changes on the local environment were tragic and unforeseen.

It rained during the night, but when I peeked outside frost whitened the ground and clung rigidly to the bracken. In the lingering pre-dawn a rosy hue gathered behind the hills of Pairc and stained faintly the crown of Roineabhal. Elsewhere the clouds were silver-lined or layered in blue or metallic grey. Only the smallest breath of wind marked the loch. I pulled on my boots, and in a few minutes was back at the cairn. From all points the land unrolled its emptiness, spreading in muted tones of heather and paler grasses and grey bedrock. In the distance was an amphitheatre of hills and just across the loch and rising some 300 feet was Trealabhal and its skyline cairn, watching like the cold eye of a reptile.

Our aim was to seek the western reaches of this loch system of which Loch Trealabhal was the centre, then to work north and east with an idea to have a night among the groves of one of the last native woods on Lewis, the island of Eilan Cro Balair.

By the time we'd broken camp, a biting wind was coming across the open water. Casting off we paddled hard for a few minutes to get our blood moving and unstiffen muscles, heading for a gap in an old causeway and entering Loch nam Faoileag. A short way in I nosed the bow onto a small boulder-fringed isle that seemed to bulge from the loch. Spidery trees perhaps twice my height, loaded with all manner of moss and lichen, were growing from mounds of untrampled heather. Not the slightest sign that anyone had ever been here before.

Crossing the channel we began a slow shadowing of the shoreline, past a stonebuilt boathouse and the sound of water falling over a small weir. From what I could make out this was the loch's sole overspill, though we could see nothing of it or where it went from our level. The land about barely rose and what didn't rise remained unseen. When the loch thinned to a slit of water between two low ridges, we scraped the bottom and got through only by some hard punting. Next we went over an isthmus a few yards in width, around a dogleg promontory and re-entered Trealabhal, now feeling our way into its northern reaches.

We spoke little, occasional words about keeping it steady or some detail of shoreline, like where the bedrock had split to reveal a section of bedding plane all twisted from some unknowable and ancient upheaval. Hairy lichen, the colour of sage, had colonised every weakness in the rock. The water appeared dark and without visible depth, but from the lie of the land I sensed its shallowness and many yards from the bank my paddle touched a soft peat bottom or recoiled from a rock or rattled over some gravel. It was so quiet and so far from any road. The fishing season was over and it was unlikely anyone would be on these waters before next spring, maybe not even then. Beneath a grey sky and in the play of breezes we went about our exploration in quiet reverence, ears cocked for any sound that wasn't us, and there wasn't much – faint cry of bird, tinny echo of some burn. A pair of deer hinds stood on the far bank unmoving. They watched and we watched and the silent land waited for the onslaught of the dark and cold of the coming season, hunkering down for what lay ahead. There was nothing we could see, yet I knew every creature of this half-flooded land, hardwired to survive, was already long into its preparations.

The breeze swirled a little. Opposite shorelines came

together where the loch turned a corner, then it opened out and again we saw a scattering of bald islands. They called us but we drifted past, swung left and found a tiny inlet and burn with a languid flow. Here was our take-out. The half mile of haulage we managed in two relays, and for most of the first leg we were able to float everything and line the canoe by its painter. We pulled out at the remains of a dead sheep half in the burn. Nearby, a large solitary rowan grew from an outcrop, the only tree we'd seen not anchored to an island.

Trealabhal now presented a more imposing aspect, so that its mass and steepness stole a quarter of our sky, dimming the land over which we pulled. Loch an Drunga, not quite a mile in length, comprised three distinct tongues that reached all the way to the first ground of Trealabhal, and each we explored, hardly paddling as the breeze was with us.

Today's portages promised to be quite short and not especially hard owing to the remarkably level and soft ground, though everything still had to be relayed, and I think would have to be for a day or two yet. One benefit of relaying was that we saw the same ground three times, the heather, mosses, grasses, bog-loving flora, pools, peat-sinks, boulders and bedrock. I said as much to Clive, but he wasn't convinced.

Trealabhal was now behind and drifted away as we made west, the land resolving itself into knolls and gently rising moorland. After paddling a reedy and nameless loch we pulled over flat country and canoed Loch à Bhroma. On the buoyancy of a following wind we crossed from one end to the other in just a few minutes. Hauling across the wetland to reach Loch Fada Gobha, we rejoined the maze of lochs and waterways on which we began this morning.

In a kind of arc we steered northwest, and as we neared Eilan Cro Balair a late sun came through, intensifying the blue of the water and casting the moor in terracotta. The island was unlike anything we'd seen on Lewis. Perhaps two hundred yards in length, much less in width, it was shaped like an hourglass and almost wholly covered in bare-branched rowan and birch twenty to thirty feet high. I had known of this place, but how strange to see it for real, a small piece of Eden in the desert. It spoke clearly the last words of a lost manuscript which once inventoried the wildwood of Lewis.

At a small bay on the west side a finger of rock came into the water. Clive slipped as he clambered ashore. Steadying himself, he shifted the bow clear and we unloaded everything, raised the canoe and turned it over on some bracken. A grassy place was found for my small tent beneath a fan of branches, pegs sinking easily into leafmould, then after some tea it was time to explore.

Given constant exposure to damp winds, every upright thing on the island was coated in lichenous growths. At first it was hard to tell a young tree from an old wizened one, then it dawned on us there were no young trees. The first impression of the island as having somehow escaped the attention of grazing beasts was wrong. There was no balance, no healthy age structure. To a specimen the trees were old, and some were dead, their brittle and lifeless canopies still reaching skywards, the boughs of others among the rank heather. Pathways through the groves were in fact animal trails and I had no doubt hungry deer were frequent visitors to the island. Who can blame them?

If sheer remoteness had a hand in saving this remnant, it may now be its death-knell, because unless some landowner or government agency can be bothered to fence the shoreline and prevent its casual invasion then I fear these trees will soon be gone. Another acre of emptiness to add to the thousands we already have. The ignorance of the traveller who feels no sadness at the present treeless state of Lewis is matched only by the idle incompetence of those who could, but choose not to, save this last fragment. That is a tragedy.

In the last of the light we took the canoe unladed for a quiet circumnavigation, marveling at the rock gardens of juniper and downy willow and wild flowers gone to seed. A few minutes of the slowest paddling. How small and precious a thing this island was.

Ecology is one of the great themes of *Soil and Soul*, and perhaps its message first struck home for McIntosh in around 1970 when he was still an adolescent. He'd gone fishing offshore with Finlay in the usual place, a spot where for years they'd always pulled in a plentiful supply. On this occasion they caught nothing. They tried at a different time but again their hooks came back empty. The fish had mysteriously disappeared. It was about this time, he says, that he noticed a new type of fishing vessel at the quayside in Stornoway Harbour. With the help of government grants and loans the fishing fleet was being modernised, a new generation of supertrawlers with powerful engines and fish-seeking sonar devices. Then came reports of trawlers breaking the unwritten law by fishing in coastal waters, usually at night and with their lights off. Not foreign trawlers, as first suspected, but local fishermen, fathers and sons of the Western Isles. In a matter of months an easily accessible resource that for generations had supplemented the diet of islanders was no longer available, wiped out by over-fishing.

The same thing happened to scallops. McIntosh would spend many a Saturday helping to gather them on Loch Eireasort. He worked at the oars while a pair of divers went under to harvest the seabed. Diving for scallops was a relatively new thing and the pickings were good, 'there always seemed to be plenty of scallops when we went out', he writes. The divers made good money. In fact they were being over-exploited and by the early seventies some inshore beds had already vanished. These days most scallops on a restaurant menu have been dredged, of course, with metal spikes that plough the seabed and throw everything into a huge trailing bag. The areas dredged are far out to sea. They would be wasting their time by the coast.

The tale of the collapse of fisheries around the shores of the Hebrides is one repeated in islands and coastal communities the world over, part of a much greater and unfolding tragedy that even today the world has hardly woken up to. It's a well-worn mantra for those that bang the environmental drum, and in our busy, self-obsessed lives we grow weary of it. But the facts speak for themselves – from the poisoned wastes around a shrinking Aral Sea to the toxic presence of PCBs and fire-retardants in the blubber of Arctic wildlife. McIntosh presents a startling figure of 74 species becoming extinct every day as compared to one per year in a human-free world. How did we arrive here? Where did this profound disconnect with nature come from? It's an important question, and if we could answer it, even partially, then perhaps we could begin to heal. Focusing largely on a Scottish context, *Soil and Soul* embarks on an intriguing historical quest to find out.

McIntosh draws much inspiration from what he calls 'Celtic Ecology', a mindset especially prevalent among

Celtic peoples in pre-Reformation Britain and quite unlike the rational, empirical modes of thinking that underlie modern western society. He argues, and produces many sources to back this claim, that the ancient Celts had a deep reverence for nature, a veneration found in prayers, blessings and songs from the time. It is a worldview shared by many indigenous peoples and at the heart of it is the construction of reality from story. Crucial to this understanding of the world was the role of the bard or shaman who articulated his people's story through the medium of poetry and myth.

This way of thinking goes to the heart of McIntosh's beliefs, and he explains this more fully in a later chapter when he compares Hellenic, or *logos*, thought with what he calls Hebriac, or *mythos*. The first is rational and empirical, the second mythic and poetic. He also argues for a third, *eros*, which is essentially knowledge through experience. McIntosh demonstrates the differences by posing the eternal question – 'What is love?' A scientific materialist might answer, 'Love is a biologically evolved neurochemical stimulus'. But in terms of eros it is simply, 'love and you will know'. The modern western world, he believes, is too wedded to rationalistic modes of thinking.

He attempts to show how this shift in the way we think fashioned historical periods such as the Scottish Enlightenment where the capitalist ideas of Adam Smith and Francis Bacon were taught as mainstream. It was the beginning of the end for the Celtic Highlands. In 1597 the Scottish Parliament ordered everyone who claimed land to produce title deeds. In Gaelic regions, McIntosh argues, 'the traditional tenure system of heritable trusteeship known in Gaelic as "duthchas", was usually oral – spoken but not written down.' What passed for title deeds was held only in the bard's memory. King James VI and I, with an eye on the agricultural wealth of the Hebrides, granted a charter to English-speaking men from Fife to establish Protestant communities on Lewis and in parts of Skye, one cog in an overall strategy which McIntosh simply refers to as 'colonisation from the inside of the culture'. He writes, 'James clearly understood that if he was to control people politically, he had to take control of their indigenous religious and poetic structures and replace them with his own worldview.' Another plank of this policy of 'pacification' was the infamous Statutes of Iona in 1609, which among other things called for the eldest child of every chief to be educated in English, and to cement this further a law banning anyone who couldn't speak English from owning any land was also passed.

A frost made the moss by the shore cloying to step across as we loaded the canoe. With gloved hands we secured the rucksacks and pushed off into the open, blue sky beginning to haze over, a breeze from the south, light but steady, easing us along to where opposite shorelines drew together. They were so close you could stand on one bank and lob a stone to the other. On some of the islets we noticed small cages just above the waterline – mink traps, we discovered later, part of an ongoing and concerted effort to rid the Outer Hebrides of this aggressive intruder. As we kept left the loch swelled out and we looked across a wide sound to levels of burnished moorland, broken only by isolated outcroppings of pale stone.

I think an hour had passed when the sun dimmed and we noticed a grey bank of cloud building above the Pairc Hills. After maybe a mile and a half of gentle paddling the loch tapered until we slid along a channel pointing north.

We dragged to a small slim lochan. The ice on its surface cracked and pinged as we forced our way across. Two very small lochans at the wide col were even more firmly iced, and this time we broke a pathway with our paddles. Leaving everything in the canoe we hauled it over the stiff ground and down to the gravelly shore of Loch Cleit Steirmeis.

One last drift of milky light and the sun was gone, lost behind a cloud wall. A little ominous that, I thought. A rising breeze now, and away from the shore it hurried us northwards, my paddle in the water only to guide. Old rowans swaddled in moss grew by the water's edge at the base of small clefts and boulders, their leggy boughs skimming the loch surface in an inverted arch. After less than a mile the loch virtually came to an end at some narrows and I thought I might have to step out and pull, but there was enough water, just, to see us through.

The loch opened again, though barely, and never lost its hemmed-in feeling, especially as rough ground came steeply down on the right. Waves of about two feet now rolled under and urged us forward in quiet momentum. I felt the wind on my back and noted how quickly the rocks and heather of the shore were hurrying by. This was easy – just keep a line perpendicular to the building waves – but I watched the land on our left and knew we needed to change direction and trace an offshoot of the loch to the southeast. Ahead I could see a small planting of native woodland on the side of a hill called Neapabhal, the very last we saw in that direction. I gave the word. We swung the canoe into the wind and only then did we appreciate its strength. It caught the bow and pushed us back and for some seconds we fought with everything to straighten, shouting to each other over the roar. Owing to its length and shape a canoe will naturally sit broadside to any wind and roll with the waves, just about the worst situation you can get yourself into in the middle of a loch. We wore no wetsuits and a capsize was unthinkable. Clive rotated his paddle, hard in one side then the other, as surprised as I was at the rapid deterioration in conditions. Clouds thickened to blot out the Clisham. Our world was shrinking. As much for morsels of shelter as for the security in the event of a spill we ran tight by the shoreline, so our paddles banged against rocks and the hull twice caught the lochbed. We nosed into the bank, dumped the gear and dragged across an area of quaking grassland and bog, heads bowed to a wind that appeared to be ratcheting up with every passing minute.

Our intention had been to sound out the western portion of Loch Cleit Steirmeis, reached via a short portage, but worsening conditions pared down our options. Still, once we'd gathered our sacks we attempted to launch in a narrow cove facing the wind. Small white-crested waves steamrolled ashore. We pointed the bow out, and while I steadied the canoe Clive stepped over to his seat, snatched his paddle and began to punt, leaning on the grip as if trying to crowbar something from the water. Breakers fizzed over the gunwales and I shoved the stern, but the moment we were afloat a gust caught and dumped us sideways and ran us back into the shallows as if we were made of polystyrene. Twice more we tried. On our third attempt a wave larger than the others lifted and almost rolled us. Time to concede. We took the gear a few hundred yards along the shoreline to the point furthest west, then returned for the canoe. At first we made a futile gesture to float it round and walk with the ropes, but gave up soon enough. As the land was too steep for us to drag we carried, and there in a hollow away from the main force of the gale we chewed on some lunch and pondered what to do next.

During his long summer break from school and university McIntosh often worked as a ponyman and ghillie for nearby Eisken Estate. When out on the hill he couldn't help but notice broken stone walls of old dwellings, and nearby the telltale signs of ridge and furrow. Folk once lived here, but who, and why had they left? The estate's keeper and good friend, Tommy MacRae, was evasive. It was only much later when he began to delve, in particular reading Jim Hunter's work, *The Making of the Crofting Community*, did McIntosh appreciate what had really happened. The Clearances were not a subject ever taught at his local school, though the evidence of this largely forced migration from the land was everywhere on Lewis. It explains to a great extent why so much of the land today is deserted and most communities are strung out along coastal strips. His investigation uncovered the story of Pairc, which he knew as the Eisken Estate. By 1817 the entirety of Lewis came into the ownership of Lord Seaforth, that is Stewart Mackenzie, and soon after he began clearing large tracts of the resident population to make way for sheep, which the laird hoped would produce a better return. Simple as that. Some of the crofters emigrated to Canada, others resettled along the Lewis coastline, including at McIntosh's home village of Leurbost.

The author's take on Highland history is far removed from the cool revisionist stance of some historians, Michael Fry for instance, whose pessimistic work *Wild Scots* somehow reduces it all to economics. Some scholars have argued that a good many of the Clearances were motivated by benevolence, crofters being moved to the coast so they might benefit from the burgeoning herring and kelp industries. If that was the case at Pairc then the resettlement failed. In 1887 some of the grandsons of those cleared a generation before and now living at Leurbost and Balallan were so hungry they embarked on a mass deer hunt, and for three days gathered what meat they could, reportedly killing some 200 beasts. It was an act of 'theft' considered so serious that a detachment of Royal Scots and Marines arrived by gunboat and arrested six of the ringleaders. All were later acquitted.

For McIntosh the Highland Clearances are just another episode of dispossession or what he terms 'cultural genocide', and part of a process that had been happening across Europe since Roman times. From the Tudor age successive Enclosure Acts, until recently a much neglected field of study, caused mass evictions of small-scale farmers and closure of age-old common grazings. The hordes of newly poor adrift from the land became fodder for the factories. 'Larceny' is what he calls it, and it concentrated landownership into the hands of a small number of very wealthy individuals. By 1876 the process was so complete that less than one percent of the English population owned some 98% of agricultural land. There is an untold and toxic history lurking behind the manicured parklands and sandstone colonnades of our stately homes, many of which are now in the hands of the National Trust. In the Highlands today a thousand individuals control nearly two-thirds of private land.

Our plan of reaching a small island on Loch an Taobh Sear, about two miles away via a circuitous lochan route, now appeared beyond us. Conditions on the water had deteriorated to such an extent even small lochs were probably out of bounds. Safer to stick to land, yet I doubted we would get far against this wind relaying an 80lb canoe and three weighty sacks.

Climbing the rough slopes we struggled to get everything to what on the map showed as nothing more than a scratch, a blue vein that bulged slightly at one end. Wind scoured and whistled the length of it, though the waters were not churning in the manner of a large loch and I thought we should take a closer look. Its first yards were shallow enough for me to lead the canoe and cargo by the painter. Then the waters deepened and our side became rock-strewn. I looked at Clive. How about it, I said. The wind came in squalls and made small dancing waves rebound from shore boulders and spread transverse across the loch. Not sure, he said. Come on, it's only a hundred yards. Has to be better than dragging. Clive gave a nod. OK, he said, and while I held fast he climbed over the sacks and took up his customary seat, paddle raised. Standing in two foot of water I shoved off and stepped in just as a gust caught us and we careened to one side. To counter we threw our weight opposite, but rather too much so and the gunwale went under; water spilled over to slosh about our feet, though somehow the canoe righted before we were swamped. For a moment we had no control and just let the wind sweep us from the bank, the canoe wheeling as if on a pivot at a mooring. I dug in my blade and got the bow round; we paddled like fury to keep head to wind, not letting up until land was reached.

We beached and emptied and took stock. Clive parked himself on his soaking rucksack and bit onto some chocolate. I didn't think there was much left of afternoon, daylight now visibly shrinking as if a great awning had unrolled over the land. The hill crests had gone and a vanguard of rain rapped at our jackets.

A slight descent to our next target, Loch an Earbaill, and to save time Clive carried two of the sacks and I dragged the canoe with the third. A much larger loch, we could see its troubled surface long before arriving at its shoreline, the spume trails and wind scour as waters piled north and out of sight as if towed along by some tide rip. We needed to progress to one of its south-reaching fingers, but the shoreline offered no protection and I could only imagine a continual struggle to stay afloat and avoid being swept into the middle of the loch with its three foot rollers. And now it was so grey we couldn't see more than a mile or so ahead. Let's camp, I said to Clive.

We'd reached a small thumb-shaped inlet on the east side of the loch, its half-sheltered waters accounted for by the presence of a low hill that climbed straight from the peaty bank. Hoping that somewhere on its slopes might be a shelter of sorts I set off to investigate, Clive watching from the beached canoe. I kept to a line where the wind was least strong and strolled up, light at heel for once. I'd seen something from the shore, a corner or hollow where for a handful of yards the land levelled. A single bite taken from the hill. There was no burn or spring, so perhaps here in the last periglacial era some ice or snow had gathered and lingered through the cool northern summers. It was nothing anyone would have noticed, an anonymous and forgettable facet on the side of a nameless hill, and yet its small signature might provide our warrant.

I waved to Clive. What do you think, I said when he reached me, adding, it's the best room in the joint. He paced about and studied the ground thoughtfully, as if he'd lost something. The land was sloping, uneven. Do we have any choice? he said, not expecting an answer.

After we'd yanked the canoe up I tilted it on its side so the arc of the bow rested against the concave of the hill, creating something of a wind-break should the gale veer during the night. Clive unrolled his bivvy and went inside and watched as I fussed over where to site my modest shelter, trying it first this way, then that, fixing some of the guys with rocks prised from the slope. I pushed the pegs in deep and on each I placed a rock, then I went round checking and prodding like some officious scoutmaster.

When I ducked inside it was practically dark. I pulled off my wellingtons, shed my dripping outer layers and zipped myself in. For a minute I lay in the gloom, steam rising, and listened to the battling elements. Rain clattered, but the storm largely thundered past a small distance away, a deeper and more general sound. We settled for a long and troubled evening.

Clive was plugged into his tiny radio and at five minutes to six relayed the shipping forecast: 'Storm force ten,' he said, 'rising to violent force eleven in East Hebrides at first.' Tonight or sometime in the morning gusts of sixty or seventy miles an hour would sweep this land. It might swing or veer a little, but in essence it was against us. Given the miles to cover and a hill pass still to cross, dragging a canoe and all the gear into such a wind might just be impossible. So I took the map from its casing and spread it and searched for another way out, trying to visualise the nature of the land from the contours and markings. So many lochs, and for us to enter even the smallest of these would be risky. We would be flotsam in this gale. I believed if the forecast came to pass we would have no choice but to retreat north, and then it was still three miles of hard pulling to the road.

All night the rain came in pulses and the tent flapped madly, defying the tautness at which I'd set the guys. We communicated only during lulls and even then had to shout. After a while we largely gave up and retreated into our separate worlds. I had a book, Sara Wheeler's *The Magnetic North*, Clive his radio. At some point I shut out my small light and just lay there in darkness. However much the tent shook I knew by some strange geometry it was receiving only the dregs from the main wind. Rogue draughts. The real storm raged beyond in the pitch black just a few yards away.

If *Soil and Soul* at times seems like an enigma, the reader unsure how the various threads come together, if indeed they do, I think McIntosh is establishing links, as he says in the book's introduction, 'by showing the particular to illustrate the general'. So when we read of Matheson, a previous owner of Lewis who grew rich from the Chinese Opium Wars, and Thompson, a one-time laird of the Isle of Eigg who made his money as an international arms dealer, this is of a piece with a mindset that places acquisition of wealth above all else, even the ethical.

Eigg is one of the four islands that make up the Small Isles, the others being Rum, Muck and Canna, and all lying between Skye and the mainland. It measures barely two miles by three and in many ways its story echoes that of the Highlands in general, though with this difference – Eigg today is a model of community ownership, thriving, outward-looking, confident that whatever its future, every islander will have a say in shaping it. The story of how it achieved this status forms a large part of the second half of *Soil and Soul*.

In the north of the island are the ruins of St Donnan's Monastery, which scholars believe was an important missionary centre of the Celtic Church. The Gospel replaced the pagan gods but it failed to quell old hatreds. After the Gaels wrested control of the Hebrides from the Norse there followed centuries of internecine rivalry between the various clans, and the people of Eigg, belonging to the Clanranald, probably suffered more than most. Every visitor to Eigg these days will be told of the 'Cave of Massacre' or Uamh Fhraing, when in the late sixteenth century some 395 islanders, virtually the entire population, were smoked to death by a contingent of Macleods from Skye as they hid in the cave.

Perhaps due to its isolation Eigg escaped the Protestant Reformation and stubbornly remained Roman Catholic. Its natural sympathies were with the exiled Stewart Pretenders and as a consequence of its support for the Jacobite cause in 1745 Hanoverian militia sailed in and scooped up some participants in the rising, who were never to return. Amid the disastrous harvests later that century, some 176 people, almost half the population, left the island. In 1828 Ranald MacDonald, the ancestral head of Clanranald, finally sold Eigg, apparently to clear a gambling debt. The buyer was Hugh Macpherson, a professor of Hebrew and Theology at Aberdeen University.

Either the professor was a poor judge of character or he lacked a Christian conscience because he leased some of the arable land to a sheep farmer from the Scottish Borders, who promptly evicted fourteen families. Land that for millennia had been tended by plough was now converted to rough sheep pasture. A remnant of the indigenous population tenaciously clung to coastal strips, only receiving security of tenure with the passing of the 1886 Crofting Act. Not only did the Act fail to alleviate their poverty, for both Eigg and the Highlands the measure was about a hundred years too late.

One notable owner of Eigg was the historian Sir Steven Runciman, author of the influential three-volume, *A History of the Crusades*, who inherited the island from his father. According to McIntosh the Runcimans 'ushered in a golden age during which staff were looked after, houses improved and agriculture flourished.' Runciman sold Eigg in 1966 for £82,000. By the time Keith Schellenberg bought the island nine years later the purchase price, fuelled by land speculators, had more than tripled to £274,000. Schellenberg later admitted to buying Eigg specifically to prevent the Highlands and Islands Development Board from bringing the island into 'experimental public ownership'.

In some respects Schellenberg was not in the usual mould of Highland laird. His vegetarianism led him to ban hunting; and he invited incomers, raising Eigg's population from thirty-nine to sixty. McIntosh writes that 'many islanders experienced him as an idiosyncratic autocrat'. Outwith the crofting areas, protected by the 1886 Act, Schellenberg could do as he pleased, handing out and withdrawing leases as he saw fit. When folk he'd invited in wanted more independence, relationships broke down, leases were terminated and eviction orders filed. Some islanders spoke of an 'in-group and an out-group', even to the extent that residents would ignore each other when passing.

Alastair McIntosh became part of the campaign for a community buy-out of Eigg in 1990, and a year later was instrumental in launching the charitable Isle of Eigg Trust, whose sole objective was to raise funds for the purchase of the island. He presents an interesting portrait of Schellenberg. 'He tried to be kind and wanted to be popular. The only problem was he never recognised how the spectacles of wealth and power tinted his vision.'

Critics of *Soil and Soul* have claimed the author has a rigid anti-landlord stance and this last sentence rather supports their view. Later in his book McIntosh writes, 'I do not believe people like Schellenberg are conscious of constructing reality to legitimise their power. The process is inevitable in a ruling class who, since childhood, have generally been emptied out from within and are desperate for a world to fill the emptiness.' Yet when McIntosh worked for his local estate during college holidays he counted as friends some of the rich clients who came to fish and shoot, saying, 'a majority of them held a strong and at times unexpected personal sense of honour'.

Meanwhile, in 1995 Schellenberg sold Eigg to a bankrupt German artist, Professor Maruma, for £1.6 million, banking a handsome profit. Maruma's tenancy was farcical. He rarely visited the island, had no money for investment and couldn't even afford to pay his staff's wages.

By now the ownership of Eigg had become a national story, a 'soap-opera', and donations to the Trust flooded in, a total of £600,000 from ten thousand small donations, including two pounds from an unemployed Londoner. Eigg was again on the open market, and McIntosh felt they would need at least £1.6 million. It was a contribution of £1,000,000 from a 'mystery English woman' that clinched the deal. A millionaire purchasing the island for its people may not have sat comfortably with McIntosh, especially given his disquiet about the trappings of wealth, but in the end that was not the point. On 12 June 1997, the day of the hand-over, a friend and Eigg resident, Fiona

Cherry, said to him, 'Yesterday I had a house. Today I have a home.'

The early night had me awake early, and I dozed and waited for the coming of dawn. In the vague yellow light of the interior, shapes began to materialise. I could see the sagging walls of the tent, the map unfolded by my side. The booming wind had miraculously halved in strength and when I looked outside a grey sodden world stared back, like a place viewed through some screen and more desolate than I could have imagined. Throughout the night I'd been aware of a distant splashing of falling water. I couldn't see where it came from, but the sound was cleaner and louder. Another good sign, I reckoned. The loch rolled in a grey swell but the white caps had gone, and that fact alone lent me hope we might yet make our way south and arrive back at our start point.

We skipped breakfast and in the gloom loaded the canoe and slid it over wet ground to the inlet. A strong wind came at our nose as we rounded the main body of loch, and only a frenzy of paddle strokes prevented it from casting us against the shore rocks. The burn draining into the loch brimmed with overnight rain, though it was also sluggish enough to allow us to float the canoe upstream. When it narrowed and there were just too many rocks we began to portage. Tattered edges of clouds lifted from some of the hills. The rain stopped. Roineabhal was clear. A wedge of sky above the hills of Pairc had filled with lurid light and seemed to speak of portents. From somewhere a hidden sun drew what pigments the land would release, a spectrum that reached a kind of apotheosis this week before winter, not the fine-drawn outline of a distant ridge and new snow on Clisham, but rather the slow register of what passed underfoot that renewed an old vision of beauty – tiny yellow bronchi of lichen, clumps of copper-tipped grasses, mosses in collage and a last pink bloom of bell heather.

I knew the burn would lead to Loch an Taobh Sear, but at some point and in the absence of any landmark to aim at a different burn led us astray, and we needlessly veered from our target. At the bank of a much smaller loch we could at least fix our position, and in another quarter hour found the loch we were looking for. Though distances between lochs were often short, with a lack of distinctive features the terrain was sometimes hard to read. Solitary cairns stared down from surrounding hill crests, the only human features we'd seen in days. These were not the rock piles found on the busy mountain summits of the mainland but raised long ago, a legacy of our ancestors who first peopled this land. Though it was impossible to date them accurately or know their purpose, somehow that morning being in their vicinity was strangely evocative. The stones could not speak, yet I guessed that this was an old trail for hunters and I liked the thought that our short journey was but one of many in the land's chronicle.

Our chosen shoreline was well-protected by the rocky slopes of Ciorabhal and in this relative calm we made progress, keeping away from an island whose heather shook wildly. On it was a handful of dwarf trees as bent as any we'd seen. I was rather sorry we'd not managed to pass the night there, though I could see there was not the slightest protection for a tent.

Concerns about the hazards of paddling in these conditions were now tempered by a joy and engagement with the lochs; and now, on our fourth morning, there could be nothing more beautiful than the setting before us. We'd dragged to a point where Loch nan Eilean unravelled, the waters decorated with pygmy-treed islands and its surface puckered by wind scour, and it seemed to epitomise what wildness remained on Lewis. It is reasonable to believe that six thousand years ago a man standing here clothed in animal hides and carrying stone tools would have witnessed more or less the same.

I thought the wind had grown by the time we found the shoreline and attempted to launch, waves slapping against the hull and onto the rocks. The inlet was completely exposed, so with Clive at the bow I waded and arrowed the canoe towards open water, stepped aboard and we paddled with some venom, fighting the gusts which did their best to roll us back, then around a hook of land to marginally calmer water, though shallow. This was betrayed at every headland, where half-sunk rocks and shoals forced us out into rougher open water, though the gusting wind never reached last night's strength. Still, we went about our business with every caution, precise with our strokes and coaxing our craft along a safe and as trouble-free route as we could judge. We resisted the shortcuts. Where we might have crossed a large bay at its narrowest point, instead we chose to bank-crawl, in no mood to tackle the waves and fickle winds of the centre.

Now into our rhythm we felt safer. Gusts troubled us less. And they advertised their approach. At first the loch seemed to contract, then sent out a spasm of disturbed water which ran towards us. We turned the bow to face it and braced and held the canoe straight with our paddles until the danger passed. Wind-rush filled our ears and it added a thrill and tension to our time on the loch.

If we were not so concerned about a worsening of conditions we might have landed on one or more of the wooded isles. They had an age-worn maturity, the trees as a single canopy and so interlaced and wind-clipped they mimicked the curve of the land.

Loch nan Eilean is naturally linked to Loch Roineabhal by a small channel which folk will have crossed via a causeway, probably for thousands of years. Today this was submerged and we could hardly see its line. The wind funnelled straight down the channel; we struggled to a small headland and found the calmer waters by the shore. With the immediate threat of a capsize over, we could relax a little and admire the setting more. We beached on a crescent of sand where Roineabhal threw up its bulk to block half the sky, and tried not to think too much about the 300-foot pass and two miles of canoe-dragging that awaited.

There is another hill named Roineabhal in the Hebrides, a fifteen-hundred foot hill on the southern tip of Harris by Leverburgh. Alastair McIntosh knew all about this hill.

Like every child I'd grown up believing mountains to be timeless and immovable. When later I learned of their origins and how they evolved it served only to deepen my love for them, an appreciation that here was something immeasurably old, having come about by heat and pressure and the collision of continents, worn by an unending cycle of water and ice. A geologist once told me she was not concerned with footpath erosion as it was a mere scratch on a mountain that for millions of years had withstood the bulldozing of glaciers and the attrition of wind and rain. I didn't believe human beings could harm mountains, not seriously at any rate. Then in the late eighties I read about a plan for a superquarry on the Isle of Harris. They wanted take away fifteen-hundred foot Roineabhal, every last stone of it.

The numbers involved were staggering. Put simply, to extract the million tons of rock it would require an amount of dynamite equivalent to the power of six atomic bombs of the size dropped on Hiroshima. The hole left would possibly be the largest man-made excavation anywhere in the world. Roineabhal was a key part of the South Harris National Scenic Area, but the plan to reduce it to rubble was fine because, according to Ian Wilson, the Scottish businessman behind the plans, the area 'already looks like a moonscape'. The hole would eventually be flooded to create a 'new sea loch, and a man-made marina for passing yachts'. A tourist attraction. As a fillip to potential detractors Wilson promised the barren and stony land surrounding the new loch would be 'remineralised', that is dust from the quarry would be mixed with silt dredged up from the River Elbe in Germany, resulting in a rich soil for crofting and forestry. On the face of it the scheme was impressive. Here was a promise of long-term employment for local people and a sustainable future for a relatively poor region of Britain.

By this time McIntosh was working at the University of Edinburgh's Centre for Human Ecology, a research body that among other things was exploring ways of bringing industry and environmental agencies together, to work as partners and not always as adversaries. But for McIntosh there was something fundamentally wrong with the logic underlying the quarry proposals. At its heart this was much more than a hole in the ground; as McIntosh writes, 'It was about a deadlock between an industrial society that makes things over and over again, and a natural world that was made only once'.

That a mountain millions of years in the making could be destroyed in a couple of generations was not just a depressing thought but another case of corporate greed, greed that while raising living standards for some was also pulling the earth inexorably towards environmental disaster. The chief use for the rock was to be hardcore for roads. An increase in motor transport was hardly compatible with any claim of 'sustainability'. Here was yet another grand scheme imposed from outside, whose only benefit to Harris, when really boiled down, was the provision of low-paid quarrying jobs.

Initially the promise of jobs had persuaded most local people to support the scheme, at least tacitly. McIntosh was in a small minority who opposed it, and this group began campaigning for a public inquiry. By 1992 and in the wake of the Earth Summit in Rio, cracks began appearing in Wilson's vision. Some commentators widened the debate, as McIntosh hoped, and asked pertinent questions. For instance, *The Scotsman* wrote, 'Quarrying is moving to Scotland because it is finished elsewhere. So where does it end?' A public inquiry was indeed called, and it became the longest in Scotland's history.

As the date of the inquiry loomed, McIntosh and a small number of islanders vociferously opposed to the quarry engaged the help of an unlikely sympathiser, Sulian Herney, or 'Stone Eagle', a well-known and somewhat controversial figure who'd campaigned for the land rights of native people in Canada. With no formal introduction, McIntosh phoned Stone Eagle and persuaded him to come to Scotland. Another prominent individual he asked to testify was Professor Donald Macleod, an outspoken theologian of the Free Church of Scotland. On the face of it these were unusual allies to bring to the public inquiry. Perhaps an environmental lawyer would have been more suitable, but after much reflection McIntosh felt the real objection to the quarry was cultural and theological. Such a hole in the earth would compromise the 'integrity of Creation', he writes, 'the basis of using natural resources should be reverence: profound respect for Creation.'

At the inquiry Dr Macleod stressed the Judeo-Christian tradition of an intimate link between man and the soil. 'Man,' he said, 'is taken from the ground; his food is derived from it; he is commanded to till and keep it; and he returns to it.' The superquarry represented a crime against the earth, which is in essence a crime against man.

Usually in a public inquiry witnesses are required to read from written statements, but in the tradition of his people Stone Eagle spoke from his heart. To damage the earth in one place was to damage it everywhere. 'Your mountain, your shorelines, your rivers and your air are just as much mine and my grandchildren's as ours is yours,' he said.

Another motive McIntosh had for inviting Stone Eagle to testify at the inquiry was the knowledge that Scots Highlanders cleared from their land in the early nineteenth century were partially responsible for the suppression and disenfranchisement of native peoples in Canada. It was the old lesson of history – the oppressed had become oppressors. On one level he saw the invitation as an attempt to heal an old and largely unspoken wound that had been festering for nearly two centuries. It was only a gesture, maybe, but an important one. When McIntosh took Stone Eagle to community projects in Glasgow, to Iona Abbey, and the Isle of Eigg, whose people were campaigning to purchase the island, he was asked 'How come these are the same Gaelic people that came over and did terrible things to us?'

As locals on Lewis became better informed of the true impact of the quarry many experienced a change of heart. While in the early days a majority supported the development, by 1995, and after the inquiry, the tide of opinion had changed and now over two-thirds opposed the development. The Western Isles Council reversed their earlier support and unanimously voted against. Despite the now overwhelming opposition, the 'director' of the inquiry, Miss Gillian Pain, recommended that the application be approved. In the end democracy and good sense prevailed. On 3 November 2000, the Scottish Labour Government refused the application.

Reckoning our sacks were sufficiently light after four days, we left everything in the canoe and started hauling. In minutes we had worked ourselves to a standstill, so we began relaying again. At some point there began to unfurl behind us the patchwork of lochs and channelways we'd explored, and their interlocking nature was seen for the first time as a whole. How generously the land held the water, smooth facets among the knots and warps of bedrock. The sun was out and the waters china-blue and the land portioned into light and shade. It was a scene as yet without the scar of wind turbines or superquarries, near treeless but still beautiful for lack of human interference. I thought that from this vantage point and on such a day you would never more clearly see the incongruity of imposing industrial scale turbines on such a naturally inclined landscape. The mast at Eitseal could be seen about seven miles away but that was all.

At the broad and boggy col we looked southeast to the uplands of the Pairc region, the hills crested in rock and giving the impression they rose higher than their modest map heights. We rolled the canoe onto its side as part wind-shelter and lunched, then set off downslope in high spirits. The road appeared in the distance with its tiny moving vehicles and the land by it a deeper green and numbered over with sheep. The canoe slid under its own weight. For a while the slope eased and the effort grew and Loch Stranndabhat appeared not to be getting any nearer. A winding burn was deep and its current strong enough for me to float the canoe and guide it to the loch. Four mornings ago we idled across these waters to begin our journey, now we had to fight our way back. There was a slow option to wade and lead the boat around the shallow shore fringe, but we were determined to canoe. The wind never let up. A number of times it threatened to either dump us ashore or sweep us mid-loch; it was the hardest and most sustained paddling of the trip, but now we oozed confidence, reinforced by familiar surroundings. We made our way beneath electricity transmission wires and past old peat cuttings and shadow tracks of some vehicle; and there was the friendly rusting carcass of the camper, and my van parked just where I'd left it.

Sanctuary

As a boy I remember an old cotton-backed map unfolded on a table, the colours strengthening as the land rose from palest green to browns to narrow strips and islands of purple. An area, if you included its margins as Loch Ness in the south and Strathcarron to the north, that enclosed eight hundred miles square, give or take. So large it stretched pretty much across Scotland. At its heart were three twisting lochs – Monar, Mullardoch and Affric – but my eyes were drawn to the serpentine pattern of mountain peaks and ridges that marched east-west across the map. You could fashion real adventures here, I thought.

A long time later I slipped down-country from Achnashellach with a schoolmate, Eugene Coyle. After a soggy and midgy camp by a ruin we went around the bulk of Maoile Lunndaidh, over a pass and down to the grey waters of Loch Monar, where draw-down from the dam showed naked bedrock and the tangled roots of an ancient forest. Roaming west we came to a land that was empty but for looming hill-crests and bare and gullied slopes pressing against our narrow trail. In the shadow of Sgurr na Lapaich we set up our tent, brewed tea, cooked a meal of rice and slept uneasily. Perhaps the desolation weighed more heavily on Eugene, because in the morning and in a rising wind he took one look at the mountain and elected to walk a lower path and meet later. On a page in my notebook I sketched his route, and climbed into the mist. Passing squalls had me bent or hunkering in the

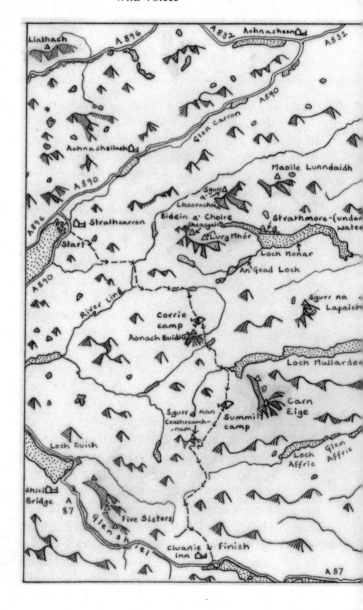

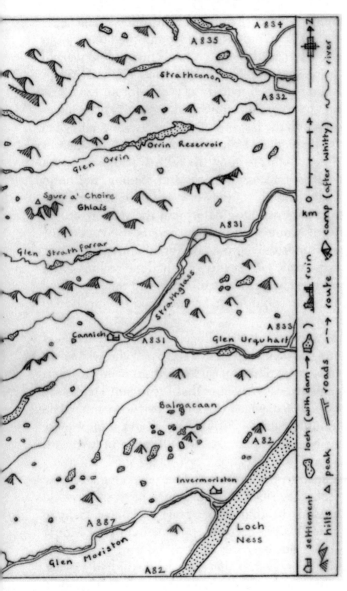

lee of boulders. When I came to rain-sodden clearings I studied the waste of moor far below and tried to pick out the figure of my friend, as if to console myself that we had been right to separate. I never saw him. The mist swept in again and wrapped me so thick and for so long, this time I thought it would endure. I was about to drop lower down and climb the last hill of the day, An Socach, when a window opened and the late sun flooded the mountain in peachy light, turning the hill's scaffolding into a maze of gullies and bright rock, and daubing the basin so its lochans were like pools of some molten alloy. Just across from me rose Lurg Mhor and the shapely crown of Bidean a' Choire Sheasgaich, and beyond were the quartz and sandstone cutouts of Torridon. After so long in clouds the scale and beauty of it had me reeling, and I knew then there were things of the world that remained beyond us, that could never be conveyed or imprisoned by our words.

For the record I did see Eugene again, and the next day, running low on supplies, we crossed the watershed to Morvich, so making my first north-to-south traverse of this region. It was only later that I read Iain Thomson's *Isolation Shepherd*, which chronicles five years in the late 1950s the author spent at Strathmore, a croft at the remote west end of Loch Monar. By then I'd fallen in love with the area, and Thomson's book cast such a spell that in my mind I came to see Strathmore and the unspoilt marshes he so beautifully describes as the drowned heart of this wild mountain land. Strathmore has gone, of course, covered over by rising waters after the construction of the Monar Dam in 1960, but over the years and during many visits I have often wondered if this great land still had a heart, a centre, some inner place narrowed to a plot and known to but a handful of souls and seen by each only once. I thought it might. I also thought I might try to find it.

Soon we looked down on glistening mudflats at the head of Loch Carron. There were quartz and scree-bleeding hills just across the glen – Fuar Tholl, An Ruadh-stac and Maol Chean Dearg, one minute starchy in sunshine, the next deep in shadow as more rain moved in. Stopping to pull on waterproofs, Nick looked over in some discomfort. It had been fine and warm for so long. The wind snapped at Aaron's flimsy jacket before he could thread his arms and zip himself in.

The path twisted south again and climbed and ran level. Every minute it seemed we stepped over burns and around flooded stretches. Passing reedy lochans we reached a kind of plateau. Like knuckles on a withered hand the low and wooded hills of Attadale ranged off westwards, and presented a forefinger to the mountains of Skye, seen today in hazy outline or not at all. For a couple of miles we contoured and gained height only marginally, to a small pass, the wind now in our faces as the narrow way dog-legged and went steeply down and melted into the moor.

At our feet was Bearneas Basin, whose empty miles are interrupted only by Bendronaig Lodge, a small unimposing structure used for holiday lets. A four-wheeled vehicle track comes here from Attadale, seven or eight miles away. We made along it for some minutes, turning off a mile or so before the lodge at a bridge above a toffee-coloured river. Its waters dropped over a small shelf and ran churning and chaotic into a gorge. The Uisge Dubh or Blackwater is a major artery, and part of a network of rivers and burns that drain a huge western tranche of this region.

Aaron was Nick's half-brother, and this counted as only his third trip into the wild, the other two being in the Cairngorms. Tall and lean, he moved well, and if the rough and unfamiliar ground sapped him he didn't show it, drawing from the energy of youth, I suppose. Nick grunted away at the rear, lugging his customary heavy rucksack. Most of what he owned in the world seemed to have found its way in there. Aaron, for all his inexperience, was much more savvy and carried less than either of us.

'How about some lunch? This is a lovely spot . . . don't you think?' Nick was keen for a good rest, and had already slipped the load from his back.

'Agree. I had this in mind. I first came here twenty-odd years ago. It was roasting hot and I think we sat in the shade of those birches over there. We'd come in from the east and had pretty much run out of food,' I said, peeling open a tin of fish.

'Reach for your hard-hat, Aaron', Nick warned, 'here comes another epic tale of survival against the odds.'

I smiled. 'It wasn't quite like that, but this place has a knack of catching you out. It's the sheer distance to anywhere once you have reached the middle of it. Anyway, I recall we were a little hungry by the end.'

'So what's the mission this time? We *are* on some kind of mission, aren't we?'

'No, not especially. It's like I said to Aaron. A good old romp in the hills.'

'Ha, don't believe that. There's always something up with you. Some ploy. Where are you taking us this time?'

'Ok, then, there's a ridge. I've only been up there once before, and never from this approach. It's somewhere I'd like to see.'

'A place in the middle of nowhere, perhaps?'

'No, in the middle of here, the centre.'

'Dress it up if you want, but what you mean is that we're going about as far from civilisation as we can get. Remember, I've been knocking about with you for a while. But how will we know when we get there?' Nick asked, feigning interest.

'Well, I hope there's not a sign or anything. I think we'll just know. It will feel right.'

Nick was silent for a minute, then said, 'You know how I am going to feel when I get there? Same as I always do – bloody knackered.'

Despite the wind the air felt warm, and after lunch we climbed the slope behind the bridge, gained some height on Beinn Dronaig and began a long contour. From here there were no paths, at least not where we were heading. The going was tough. Summer growth on the hill was reaching its peak, heather was at the cusp of blooming and grasses were lush and spongy and cushioning each footfall.

As we rounded the shoulder of Dronaig the land squared up, higher and wilder. Ben Killilan and Faochaig threw down muscular arms traced by thin white burns, all making for the River Ling which ran below on a drunken course, late for the sea. Climbing to a high shoulder we were able to look almost directly onto the river, and saw that it was only a few miles from its lochan-studded headwaters. Across the valley and from a watery basin rose the three prows of Aonach Buidhe, each hiding a corrie. The prows propped up a fast-moving cloud base like hands beneath a great grey sheet. Our line crossed the rough slopes and more than a dozen burns, each cascading brimful to the Ling; in another hour we stood by its bank and contemplated the torrent. Every boulder was betrayed by a helmet of peaty water, and every wave crest sent a trail of spume coiling in the eddies. The river didn't bar our way south exactly, but at some point we needed to ford it to access the remote ground of Aonach Buidhe. For an hour or so we followed its winding bank until reaching the mouth of Loch Cruoshie. I knew the Ling and its crossing places well, and had waded it here before in spate. We slipped off our sacks and loitered for a longish break. Nick and Aaron wanted a good look. Though wide and deep at this juncture, the flow is usually less strong, even languid, and in high water it's the only vaguely safe place to cross. Sometimes it's too powerful, even here, and once I was trapped on the other side.

It happened like this. After some winter climbing in the Torridon area I'd set off alone from Strathcarron on a Friday morning, aiming to reach Morvich on the Glen Shiel road by Saturday evening. Around a foot of snow had fallen overnight, but the day dawned bright and windless and the prospect of trekking the snowbound lands I found deeply appealing. It was a romantic dream of sorts, an image of a small figure and a staggering line of footprints on a pristine land. This was something dimly perceived and I'd held onto it and idealised it, though of course in reality the hours of toil it took to reach this point by the Ling left me spent. I splashed easily across and settled into a nearby bothy. By this time I'd decided the snow was just too deep for any further probing south. Instead I would cut my losses, retrace some of today's route, then follow the landrover track to Attadale. Not quite what I'd sought, but in the circumstances a decent enough adventure.

After a freezing night a soft light filtered through the room's only window. Not a sound came from outside, as if the large burn close by had ceased to flow. I opened the door to a perfect white-out. Heavy snow was falling and had been doing so, it appeared, for most of the night. I boiled water and slid back into my sleeping bag. By about noon the snow eased and the sky began to clear, but it was too late in any case to make my escape, so instead I struggled some miles through drifts to a northern corrie of Aonach Buidhe. I picked my way over jumbled blocks from a small avalanche and stood and gazed in an arc across white miles, the sole beholder of a desolate land that stretched away north, the beauty of it holding me for a while. Only the ice-free Gead Lochs broke the uniformity and appeared as muddy stains on an otherwise virgin world.

I turned and followed my old trail, reaching the bothy by nightfall. It was empty and there was no audience for my tale. I wrote in my journal, ate my last evening meal and read to all hours by the light of a solitary candle. It was a great adventure but tomorrow I needed to get out.

The elements troubled my dreams, and woke me. There was a hollow draw of wind over the roof and around the gable and rain like a fine spray of pebbles on the small window. Over and above this was a kind of vibration, the crash of water-sound. When I opened the door it was to a different place. Half the snow had gone, most of it into the nearby burn which bristled and churned and whose standing-waves were caught by crosswinds and flung beyond the bank and over the flattened heather. A great invisible weight seemed on the land. Every hill was stitched with white and all the waters were meeting at the Ling which had spread itself over the basin like an incoming tide, its banks and low country all flooded. The wind strength was shocking. As I ventured out a few yards to fill my bottle, a gust put me on my side. It was Sunday morning and I was due home that evening, at work tomorrow. On the wax-stained table I laid out my remaining food. Two eggs, a little porridge, a small bag of rice someone had left in a tin on the table. No date on it. I also had three bars of chocolate I was saving for the walk out. With the map spread to its margins I thumbed the miles and weighed options. Encircled by hills and rivers and pathless ground, it would be harder to find a remoter spot anywhere in the country, I thought. Five miles away and on the south side of Loch Monar was Pait Lodge. But if I survived the burns and reached it, would they have a phone and would anyone be there? And if no, then what?

All day I watched the snow retreat and the burns rise and the storm rack itself up to a pitch I'd never heard or seen before and have witnessed only a couple of times since. It blew through the night and into the next morning, but by then at least it seemed the water-levels had fallen. I hatched a plan to trace the Ling westwards to the hamlet of Killilan, where the map promised a phone and a minor public road, a journey of about eleven miles. With an iron stake salvaged from the redundant deer fence, I went thigh-deep into the bothy burn and could barely stand for gusts. A few hundred yards on was another and more torrential burn, this one draining the northern corries of Faochaig and Aonach Buidhe, still largely covered in thawing snow. It looked wild but I had no choice. Taking the iron stake, I jammed it into the bed and entered the stream, and was almost upended. I felt weightless and for a minute fought with everything just to keep anchored. I turned and kicked my way back and bow-footed over the ground and was twice floored before reaching the bothy.

Sitting against the wall I thought back to my arriving here weary-legged on Friday, cupolas of snow on a trickling burn, a sun-bright bothy with an icicle hanging from each corrugation of roof. Now it was damp and gloomy and the interior walls like a kind of solitary confinement. Another day marooned here with the deadweight of time. No food but for half a cup of porridge, and not a lot to do. Except read. On the wax-smeared mantelpiece above the hearth was a copy of *Annapurna* by the French climber Maurice Herzog. I'd read it before but had half-forgotten how beautifully conveyed was this account of the first ascent in the world of an 8,000-metre peak. Frostbitten and snow-blinded, Herzog's escape from the summit and the subsequent painful journey through the Asian monsoon to Kathmandu reads like a literary thriller. The author and his summit companion, Larchenal, had to be carried due to their frozen toes and fingers, and we are spared no details, particularly of the treatment they endured for their frostbite. An almost daily round of painful injections administered by Oudut, the expedition's doctor, has Herzog weeping like a child. Reading his narrative, the grey world of the basin dissolved to a vision of the snow and ice of Himalaya and a line of bedraggled Frenchmen and porters, and Herzog screaming as the syringe searched again for a vein. The author's suffering lent a kind of perspective to my own small plight – a little hungry, a tad windy and wet outside. That was all.

On Tuesday morning, the wind halved but the burns still high, I went over the pass to the south, and walked twenty miles to the main road and the shores of Loch Duich and later got a lift in a farmer's pick-up to Inverness.

Nick looked over the dark waters to the far bank. 'What d'you reckon?'

'I reckon we should go for it.' I'd seen and tackled much worse.

'I'm not sure. It looks tricky, a little dangerous. Aaron's new to this, remember.'

'Well, if you don't fancy a wetting here we could go around the loch, which will mean miles of bog and then we cross a different burn. Either way we get wet.'

'Shame there's no bridge,' Nick said.

'You want a bridge, just to keep your feet dry?'

'Not only that, but to make the crossing safe.'

'If you build a bridge you have to maintain it, then you make a track to reach the bridge, and so it goes on. Why tame this place? For me the fact there are no bridges is the whole point of it. And let's not kid ourselves that by putting a bridge here it makes this place any easier to reach.'

Aaron, sitting some yards away, was half-listening.

'I'm with Mike on this one,' he said. 'Who needs a bridge? Come on, let's get wet.'

Pulling off my boots, I tied the laces together and slung them across one shoulder. Then, for what it was worth, rolled my trousers up and stepped in. After weeks of sunshine the water felt pleasantly lukewarm. As expected the current was pretty benign, and though it came up to my waist and I got soaked, I waded across with some ease. Nick and Aaron also.

At the limit of the flood plain, and just as the ground begins to rise, there is a tiny enclosure of native trees planted by volunteers – juvenile birch, rowan and alder.

Bent to the prevailing wind, it is an embryonic forest that I hope one day will spread its green tentacles to every corner of this land. It's a hiding place for a pair of merlins, and from maybe only fifty yards I watched the birds ride the breeze, loitering while Nick and Aaron pushed on up the hill ahead of me.

A few miles away to the northeast and rising from the zone of watershed was the hunched form of Lurg Mhor, the hill taking its name from the spur that extends south from the summit. The hill marks the termination of a great horseshoe of peaks that fills the land north of Loch Monar – Bidean a' Choire Sheasgaich, Sgurr a' Chaorachain, Maoile Lunndaidh, the arching crests of the Farrar summits above the glen of that name.

This land was the fabric of Iain Thomson's book, *Isolation Shepherd*, published in 1982. Thomson reminds us, if we needed reminding, that people once lived and worked and thrived in the wildest and hardest-to-reach corners of the Highlands, where distance to a neighbour was measured in time, when no road came to your door and the only sounds were wind and rain and birdsong and silence. The author's writing revisits an era and events that were shaped over a quarter of a century before, and his words at times carry faintly the nostalgia of a man in middle age casting back to his twenties and to a simpler life. A familiar tale in some ways, yet it manages to pull free of the standard countryside memoir. Behind the stories of sheep rearing and remote living and all the fun and life-enhancement is a thread of sadness. Like grief he cannot hide it, nor perhaps does he want to. It seeps onto every page. Thomson's book is a lament, because the beginning knows the ending. *Isolation Shepherd* is part autobiography, part elegy for a lost land.

In 1956 Thomson took a shepherding job at the west end of Loch Monar, a place called Strathmore. In the opening chapter he describes how he and his family battled through a storm on the loch to reach their new home. While Thomson steers the small estate launch, the *Spray*, Betty, his wife, cradles in her arms their new-born baby, Hector, and crouching nearby was his two-year-old sister, Alison. Thomson shields his eyes and looks around at the scene. 'White rolling tops stretched away to the grey in-distinction of storm-swept hills,' he writes. 'Our world shrank to simple elements, raging or shrieking . . . gone the false world of human progress. I felt the first thrill of wild isolation.' Accompanying them in their 'flitting' were the MacKays, their only neighbours, who lived at the isolated Pait Lodge a mile or so away and across the loch. When they arrived, the small wooded pier was flooded and they had to wade to reach firm ground. Thomson described their new home as 'small but comfortable . . . two downstairs rooms and a bath-room. Upstairs, the two attic bedrooms were lit only by skylight windows.'

The author had taken his young family to live between a marsh and a loch and at the centre of an empty region of mountain and glen. They were completely cut off from the outside world. In a crisis the only practical way out was by boat or a six-mile slog along the lochside to reach the private road at the head of Glen Strathfarrar. North and west were barred by an encircling arm of high hills. An old cattle droving route led southwest past the Gead Lochs and around Aonach Buidhe, but they would need to cover twelve rough miles before reaching Alistair and Flora MacRae at Iron Lodge. It would have to be some emergency.

The reader of *Isolation Shepherd* is left in no doubt that Thomson willingly sought this wild posting and relished the prospect of living and working there. It was almost a calling. He hoped to discover something, to unearth some truth, as he writes 'for those prepared to live simply, intimately in trust with those testing elements, might not such country slowly yield of forgotten pathways?'

From the flood plain the land climbed steadily towards Aonach Buidhe and I made for the point where I'd last seen the lads. The slope eased to an area of peat troughs and bog. Sometimes the grasses of an alluvial terrace or bank gave easier going. I scanned the waste of mountain ahead but could see no sign of them, though otherwise there was plenty of movement, heather pushed about by the wind, grasses rolled flat with each passing gust. A flash of water was the burn tumbling from the closer of the two corries in a waterfall, its noise rising and fading. I had the map and hoped they knew which of the corries to make for, 'the one with the falls,' I'd said. Surely they wouldn't go wrong.

Somewhere among this wild morass I found the walls of a long-deserted shieling. I'd been here before. In winter a great shadow is cast by the high ridge of Aonach Buidhe and then I'd imagine this old dwelling to be a gloomy place, but in spring new warmth rekindles the grasses by the lochan and I know that folk once passed the summers here. It was quiet now. No path reaches it and we were on no sensible route to climb this hill. In the shelter of a lee wall I sat for a minute and listened to the wind and drew breath. Cloud shadows dragged over the land, and at my feet yellow tormentil were flowering their little heads off.

When I studied the falls about a quarter of a mile away I noticed two figures. They were working up the steep ground to the left, the tall one leading the other. Shouting was no use, so I got going and put in a spurt and caught them and together we followed the burn over the lip onto gentler ground leading to the corrie. In its innermost recess was a small lochan which we rounded until finding its feeder burn. Here on a small shelf, where all those winters ago I'd picked my way over the debris of an avalanche, Nick and Aaron placed their bivouac sacks and I set up my tiny hooped tent. There was something intimate and cradling about this natural arena, though that was maybe an illusion, as the corrie sides rose nearly a thousand feet.

Rogue winds came and went with little warning. They smothered our small camp, drowned our chat and ran with a whistle through a nearby boulderfield. A wild night was in the making and the creatures of the day would be hunkering down in what shelter they might find.

Thomson's main occupation at Strathmore was shepherding, and he details the yearly routines with some relish. Crucial to his success as shepherd was the skill with which he managed his dogs, and unsurprisingly he devotes plenty of space to extolling their intelligence and companionship. One dog, Nancy, could with little instruction assemble and corral a flock of some 150 sheep and marshal them seven miles along the lochside to Strathmore. Thomson enjoys making the reader squirm and rather overstresses how he would stone to death an injured or diseased ewe or castrate newly-born lambs. For the latter he and the MacKays employed the 'old method of knife and teeth'. With a sharp blade they exposed the testicles, then pulled them out using their teeth. 'The testicles came away quite freely,' Thomson writes, 'taking a long length of cord with it.' What the shepherds spat out, the waiting dogs gobbled up.

The sheer physicality of his life as shepherd and crofter comes across strongly in the early chapters. One essential task was rounding up his flock so they could be dipped and sheared. Most of the sheep were easily gathered, but a few always roamed far and wide, and so armed with dogs and a telescope Thomson scouted the high corries and ventured sometimes onto the crest of a summit to search for strays. Sheep nibbling grasses on remote ledges had sometimes to be flushed out by boulders being rolled onto them.

He delights in being on the hill and at times I sense Thomson's role as shepherd and searcher of lost sheep was almost incidental – the sheep gathering was just an excuse for forays in the mountains. The chapter finishes with an exciting account of a gather on the slopes of Bidean an Eoin Deirg. In many ways this is Thomson's best writing, immediate beyond the generic and words that convey the raw truth of the moment. I know this hill and I see myself with Thomson on the crest of it, '. . . fine and fresh was the day, filling the lungs with pure mountain air . . . the great bond between man and environment never felt more real.' He describes the Bowman's Pass as 'slashed across the ridge like a giant hatchet blow.' The author in his prime probably had the fitness of a modern athlete and perhaps when he spoke of the MacKay brothers walking and running thirty or thirty-five miles in a day shod only in plimsolls he might have been speaking of himself.

A flexible work schedule suited the author's temperament and left much time for leisure and with Betty and the children, and they made their own fun. On fine days they might motor down the loch and picnic with the MacKays at Reidh Cruaidh, making a small fire for their billy. He loved to fish as much as any paying guests of the estate, though it was for Betty's pot and not the trophy cabinet. With the MacKay brothers he passed many a fine night angling for trout, or netting pike at the head of the loch, both a welcome addition to their largely subsistence diet. On their two acres plot they grew root crops, had milking cows and hens and made their own cheese and butter. If on a balance sheet the Thomsons were poor, it doesn't appear to weigh much on the author's outlook. Without a trace of bitterness he states matter-of-factly his salary of eight pounds a week. He mentions that in their first year they bought a cow for £36, which probably tells the reader enough about their finances.

During the stalking season Thomson often lent a hand, usually as ponyman, and throughout his tenure at Strathmore he developed a growing interest in red deer and the practice of stalking. Though only an employee of the estate, the author shares largely the cultural milieu of his wealthy and titled owners, which is the impression conveyed to the reader. Stags are 'aristocratic' and 'noble'; they stand 'proud'. Their spilt blood is a 'red sacrifice'. The actual stalk and killing is portrayed as a kind of duel between equal parties, almost a mind game, the stag having a fair chance of outwitting the gun and escaping. I don't think Thomson is hiding a violent act behind a euphemism here, rather he believes he is revealing something hardwired in the psyche of those who stalk, that the desire to destroy a wild creature is innate in humans and nothing to do with the need for greater biodiversity or the protection of native woodland, which is how it is often dressed up these days. At its heart is a kind of paradox. 'She was feeling that deep strange mixture of lust and regret', he says, when guessing how his employer, Lady Stirling, must have felt as she stood above a beast dispatched by her bullet.

'The act of killing a fine stag as he stands upright, surveying his domain, forms a bridge to man's distant past and is not just an idle fetish,' he writes towards the end of his book. I think he is on shaky ground here, as many cultures have no tradition of hunting beyond what is needed for survival. For the Arctic Sami the reindeer is more than just a meal – the skin and fur made into clothes, antlers and bone crafted into tools. Deer-stalking in the Highlands is quite different. When a stag falls to a high velocity rifle the intestines are removed and left on the hill for scavengers, and the carcass then hauled back to the lodge to be 'lardered' for the market. The only part the modern hunter has any interest in is the head and antlers, which might be bleached and find their way eventually to a space above a door lintel or wall of a hunting lodge, a macabre reminder of a glorious day on the hill.

If I do not always agree with Thomson I cannot begrudge his openness in some matters, which is an enduring trait of the book. He probably enjoys ruffling the feathers of his more delicate readers and at times maybe steps over the mark, as if he wants to make a point about country ways to a woolly urbanite. It's about emphasis, I suppose. One of his duties as guardian of a large sheep flock was to eradicate local foxes, and he sometimes teamed up with a professional fox hunter and a couple of primed terriers. Thomson approaches the task with zeal, and conveys a palpable excitement when they find a den in Toll a' Choin, a high corrie on the south side of Maoile

Lunndaidh. There follows, over a number of pages, an account of how the foxes were stalked and either shot or torn apart by the terriers. 'Our guns roared in union,' he cries. 'Over and over she [the vixen] bounced from the combined impact.' On another occasion he describes chasing a terrified fox. 'Down, down we dashed, blood-maddened man and dogs . . .' When he realises that the vixen had been mauled to death by the terriers, he says, 'The innermost disappointment of not killing I cannot deny nor explain.'

The reader is left in no doubt about the author's sensitivity towards more benign wildlife, especially the migratory birds that made their home on the Strathmore flats every spring. He delights in the annual appearance of a pair of Great Northern Divers and is strangely moved, like every hillman, by the call of the curlew. But a line is drawn at creatures who might threaten his flock or hens. Thomson in those days was allowed to set gin traps, ostensibly for foxes, but I wonder if he tells us the full story. Once in the depths of winter we read how he admires an eagle as it devours its prey. Thomson reckoned it had over-eaten as the great bird struggled when it was time to fly away. Then something that rather disturbed me, which is perhaps a hint at undisclosed practices. 'Had I been equipped with a net,' he writes, 'its freedom might have been in jeopardy.' Why would he want to take an eagle?

Wind and rain that plagued us all night had gone by morning, and when I crawled outside it was to a dewy stillness, the air cleansed and the hills to the north clearly drawn against a pale sky and long streaks of high cloud. I padded barefoot on wet grass and took in deep lung-fuls of mountain air. Two green bundles of fabric a few yards away were as yet unmoving and I appreciated some minutes to myself. I went down to the edge of the tiny loch, sat on a sloping boulder and looked at the view of distant hills, voicing their names in my head. Then something bit me on the back of my hand. Black and the size of a pinhead. A midge. In no time a small group danced about my face, more arriving every second. I went smartly back to my bivvy and began gathering up the pegs. Somehow in the storm of yesterday I'd forgotten that midges might emerge as soon as the wind dropped, even at this height. I'd suffered them three thousand feet up on the Skye ridge, so why not here.

'Hey, you two, there's midges everywhere. Let's grab our things and go. Breakfast can wait.'

Nick wrestled his way out as if from a straitjacket, then Aaron, who flapped in a blind panic as he threw stuff in his rucksack. How could something so small create so much havoc, he asked. At least he had only a little to pack. Nick was more particular. He had his little morning routines and hated to rush the delicate art of filling his large rucksack. But now he fumed and cursed and traced small circles of frustration as the cloud about his head thickened, by which time I had already left and was working up the corrie headwall, Aaron's breathing close behind. We reached Aonach Buidhe summit covered in perspiration. If there were any midges here, a breeze kept them from swarming. Using my sack as a small windbreak I boiled water for tea and we lazed about waiting for Nick. The long views had grown hazy. Warmth was creeping up from the valleys.

Aonach Buidhe and its spacious summit was once a viewing station for a display the like of which I'll probably never see again. At the end of a particularly mild December, with the hills carrying barely a scrap of snow

I came here on a morning of frost with walking pal Dave Hughes. It had rained since we'd left Strathcarron a week before, a single unremitting deluge as I remember, but now cracks appeared in the cloud blanket and light streamed through, great wandering beams that for a magical hour played on the flanks and crests and drew loops of silver in the glens. The rocks seemed to blister at our feet and we danced and shouted with the joy of it.

'What's the safest way off? I see only steep ground.' Nick was studying the map.

I'd never gone east from here before, but found a line that slipped through some crags to a long slope of scree. Tiptoeing over this, Nick felt the strain on his shoulders and thought we should have gone for something easier. We dropped into the warmth of a high valley and to the almost still waters of Loch Mhoicean. An early lunch under a blazing sun, a brief swim, then we crept behind a shady bank for a long siesta. The heat and sun was too much for us, and even for midges.

Our way onward climbed directly behind the loch and we worked up quite a sweat, to an old path into Coire na Breabaig and down to the muddy west end of Loch Mullardoch, by geography one of the remotest spots in mainland Britain. The nine-mile long loch fills the upper reaches of Glen Cannich, and we could see its watershed at a small rise to the west of us. Then we craned our necks and looked up at the ridge. Mullach na Dheiragain rose to over three thousand feet and lay half-shadowed and slumbering and spoke only of a huge effort if we were to reach its crown, especially in this heat. Just then no one was much inclined to move, so in the small shade cast by the crumbling walls of an old shiel we passed the middle hours of the afternoon. Apart from the burn draining into the loch and occasional puff of wind there was no sound; it was as peaceful and lonely a corner as you could imagine. The closest public road is probably the one at Killilan in Glen Elchaig, a dozen miles away.

Had we arrived at the centre? Someone coming here and thinking it wilderness would be under an illusion. The huge drawdown at the edge of the loch and the bare and treeless slopes that rise in front and behind tell a different story, reminders of political expediency and private greed and that continue to this day. Up until the 1950s a visitor to these parts would have found two lochs, not one.

For thousands of years and since the last glaciation Loch Lungard had filled the natural hollow at the base of the great hills of Beinn Fhionnlaidh and An Socach. At its eastern terminus a river, sluggish for the most part, left the loch and meandered for a couple of miles before flowing into Mullardoch, then one of the most beautiful and significant bodies of water in Scotland. Much of the south side was clothed in ancient Caledonian pinewood and on both shores there were lodges and keepers' cottages. A bustle was about the place, and not just when the lords and ladies came for shooting and fishing. In his profoundly sad book, *The Last Highland Clearance,* Iain MacKay writes 'Over the years this glen, without a penny of subsidy, produced thousands of tons of venison, mutton, wool, timber and soldiers for every war.' The upper glen was flooded in 1952 when the dam was finished, inundating the cottages and old rights of way and half the woods and the lovely river that joined the lochs. Bloated by rising waters, Mullardoch crept up the valley and swallowed the smaller Lungard and grew eventually to twice its original size. Today it is a desolate tongue of freshwater that is more reservoir than loch. From the high summits I have seen its drama and beauty when brimful and streaked with breakers. Only when tracing the shoreline does it reveal its sterility, the eroded banks and bare rock and mud where vegetation finds no foothold. Its old purpose gone, it responds now to a different nature. A capricious hand at the wheel, it rises and falls or stays level for weeks. It is like an exiled sea with no moon to stir it.

Iain MacKay was one of the MacKay brothers who lived at Pait in the 1950s, a neighbour and friend of Thomson and a key character in *Isolation Shepherd*. MacKay's book, though, is quite different. A slim, large-format hardback, it contains only a little text and is more a collection of map extracts and captioned photographs that document not only what the Highlands looked like before the construction of large dams and hydro schemes, but how the changes came at a human cost. An angry book in some ways, it is the product of a long-held grievance and sense of injustice. For decades the MacKay family were keepers at Pait, and only left in 1959 when the Monar dam was finished. The text begins with an unsigned letter the author received from an ex-serviceman and amateur ornithologist who, before joining the army in the early 1940s, stravaiged from Fort William to Ullapool. His route crossed and traced some famous glens – Garry, Moriston, Affric, Cannich, Strathfarrar, Strath Bran, Fannich and Strath Dirrie. Although he packed a sleeping bag and ample food, these were hardly used thanks to the hospitality he received from the many keepers and estate workers encountered on the way. He mentions being offered 'a welcome cup of tea at Lungard right at the end of the glen and again at Pait'. He slept in the open on the Strathmore flats and spent the night listening to the constant cries of the waders. 'After a beautiful sunrise the chorus was increased by the blackbirds and thrushes in the woods at Strathmore and Pait answering each other across the loch.' Some four decades later he repeated the walk, and wished he hadn't. Dams had been built, lochs created and raised, the old homes and their inhabitants gone. On his first walk he'd passed some twenty occupied houses; 'most had small but fertile crofts', he writes, and met some forty men, women and children. This time he only saw two people in the distance, who he thought were Munro-baggers. He writes, 'My first walk was the eight most wonderful days of my life and the last walk the saddest and most depressing'.

MacKay gives a broad-brush picture of what happened to the Highlands and he doesn't mince his words: 'Soon after the war ended surveyors appeared in many Highland glens and at the same time the propaganda started.' Highlanders, he says, were promised new jobs, new homes and even free electricity. Landowners were presented with the extraordinary claim 'that [after the dams] scenery and fishing would actually be improved'. MacKay now looks back on the Government campaign with justifiable cynicism. In the two decades after the war, he says, 'over fifty dams and power stations were built, nearly 200 miles of tunnels, 400 miles of roads and who knows how many millions of tons of concrete and steel were consumed.' Was the trade-off worth it? On one hand we have habitat loss and visual impairment, on the other clean renewable energy that is part of a strategy to reduce harmful carbon dioxide emissions. The author makes the claim that 'if all other sources ceased, Highland water would keep the UK going for 29 seconds'.

Interestingly we are given an insight into the public inquiry into the building of the Loch Monar dam, something of a farce, according to MacKay. The inquiry was held in Edinburgh during the winter of 1957/58. When MacKay, who strongly opposed the development, stood to take the stand the Hydro Board objected, saying, 'This person has no legal right to be here – he is simply an employee and owns nothing.' The objection was overruled.

Robert Johnstone QC, presiding over the inquiry, wanted to see the region for himself before coming to a decision, and on a cold grey day in January, with MacKay acting as boatman, a party of some dozen officials arrived at Monar. They never reached Strathmore or set eyes on the unspoilt marshes at the far end. After less than a third of the way up the loch, MacKay was ordered to turn the launch and head back. Mr Johnstone, he was told, had seen enough. The reader is left with the clear impression that the public inquiry into the Monar Dam merely rubber-stamped the proposal by the North of Scotland Hydro Board.

All three landowners whose estates would be affected lodged objections, but these were withdrawn after the inquiry. They were well compensated, the Lovat Estates alone receiving around £100,000. The dam was built and Loch Monar, a body of water created by nature, now extended three miles further west, swamping the alluvial flats of Strathmore, the sand bar and a number of estate dwellings, including Iain Thomson's croft. 'An area regarded by many as the most magnificent example of classic Scottish Highland scenery,' Thomson writes, 'was transformed into an object of vast desolation and ugliness.'

It saddens me deeply that I can never know Strathmore croft nor walk the sandbar at low water or see old Hector's place. I will never experience the four miles of marshy flats at the head of the loch and or the cacophony of birdsong so beautifully described by Thomson. 'Certainly hundreds and perhaps thousands of waders used the Strathmore flats as their breeding grounds. The sound of their calling, courting, feeding and sometimes alarm notes ended the heavy silence of winter and gave us six full weeks of unrivalled song.' I grieve for them. They are gone and we have our few megawatts of hydro power for the National Grid. Our purse is richer, but that cannot be the only measure.

The Last Highland Clearance is much more than the grievance of an ex-estate worker. A good deal of the book is taken up with maps and photographs of the landscape before and after the various developments. We see the beautiful Mullardoch falls in spate and the winding river at Glascarnoch in Glen Dirrie, the marshland and natural mudbanks of Loch Cluanie, all now gone. The map extracts showing 'before' and 'after' chronicle perhaps better than any words the extent of the floodings. But it is the portrayal of the local folk that is most poignant; the keepers' cottages often fronted by three generations of families and each carefully captioned. They are grainy, sepia-toned images that have salvaged something from the loss and keep alive a collective memory, though now slipping into some digital archive. Another sad episode in the ecological and social history of the Highlands, or merely the inevitability of human progress? Take your pick.

The land here of course hasn't been what you might call 'true wilderness' for centuries. Even before the dam a vehicle track reached Benula Lodge, and who is to say it would not have been extended to Lungard had the hydro development not gone ahead. In the last thirty years bulldozed roads have proliferated and now reach just about everywhere. Once just a stalkers' path came crookedly here from Iron Lodge in Glen Elchaig, then in the mid-1980s the overseas owner of this 63,000 acre estate decided to broaden it into a landrover track, presumably to speed up stalking. The lodge has long been derelict, and in more than a dozen visits at different seasons I have never seen the track used, now just another scar on a landscape greatly scarred. There always seem to be plenty of deer. I once saw a herd of about two hundred on the side of a hill not far to the north. Their appetite has greatly altered the land, giving it a plundered look, the ground so heavily grazed that no tree sapling can reach above the grass layer. Tired and threadbare it appears to the visitor today, as treeless as a Dakota prairie. Empty, desolate, wild even, but not a wilderness.

With shadows lengthening and the air a little cooler we picked our way over the soft ground and began ascending, taking Mullach in measured stages with a rest after each. It yielded slowly. For the last furlong we followed a clear-water cascade until it disappeared beneath exquisitely-coloured moss, jade green and purple and cadmium. As this might be the highest water on the hill we drank till bursting and filled our canisters, maybe for the last time before Glen Affric. I slapped freezing water over my arms and let it dribble over my head and down my face. I had no cover for my head, but at least the sun had lost its intensity and was now screened behind evening clouds. The prospect of fine views and a chance to enjoy a midge-free bivouac had propelled us to the crest, and now a little down from the true summit, on a wind-cropped lawn, we set up our sleeping places and sorted our gear, then sat or lay back on our mats and lazed. Who comes to this place? Our approach was unusual and the summit only just a Munro, yet the horizon was crammed with peaks, almost too many to take in. Behind us to the south were the highest tops this side of the Great Glen – Mam Sodhail, Carn Eighe, Sgurr nan Ceathreamhnan, the last of which we hoped to tackle tomorrow. But it was the northwest quarter that our eyes sought, the great army of hills from Torridon to Skye. I reeled off the main ones for Nick and Aaron like someone pointing out old friends in a crowd, their names a strange language and probably unnecessary baggage. There was something wordless about our situation, of being so high, on a crest maybe a dozen yards in width and with flanks on both sides dropping two thousand feet to darkening glens, and the thought of remaining here for the evening and night and next morning. That was wonderful.

At some point that evening the sun peeped through and brushed the foreground hills and tumbled out from clouds to fire diagonal shafts as if a giant hand had been placed over a great spotlight. Photos would have diluted the memory, as old climbers say. We took them anyway.

We slept through dawn and rose to another fine morning, the sun already high over the mountains and blazing from a clear blue sky. Dense mist hid the valley, but the day promised another scorcher. By the time we'd packed and were strolling south along the crest, tentacles of mist crept over the cols and for a while joined the woolly reservoirs in the glens, then the whole mass began to thin and dissolve. It was still and windless and already warm, as we pulled up on the last dip before the climb to Sgurr nan Ceathreamhnan. Three heavily-laden walkers, all men, passed by slowly and with barely a greeting, footing in the opposite direction. A fourth man with a towel over his head was some way behind. Shuffling by, he looked up and his mouth formed a kind of smile but he said nothing. With a big climb ahead our lack of water was now potentially a serious problem. I suggested something quietly to Nick, who managed to convince Aaron to scamper off with our empty canisters and search for a spring or seep in the corrie below.

He was gone a good while, but returned with full bottles and now we felt ready. Even at such an altitude the heat was extraordinary. I covered my head in a spare tee-shirt and sipped water almost continuously; the ridge rising ever steeper, lifting us slowly to the beautiful twin-topped summit from where five ridges radiate. A cool breeze at last. Shadowless hills all around were grilling under the noon sun. Sitting three abreast right on the crown to windward, we lazily watched the recycling mist, in no great rush to exchange this coolness for the promised heat of the valley. Thirst in the end drove us down. A long descent to a shorn-off spur and a final two thousand feet of unrelenting steepness. I eyed one glistening pool on the Affric River where the water eddied between falls, and for the last hour it was every man for himself. Parched and unsteady I waded into the beautifully clear water, clothes and all, and drank and rolled onto my back and closed my eyes and floated with arms cruciform among the disturbed sediment, waiting for the others.

A muddied and eroded trail from here leads downcountry seven miles to Glen Shiel and the main road, but not for us. A better way was a path to Camban bothy, leaving this to ford a river by some rowans, up a tributary to a high and nameless valley dense with heat. We took a vague path through tall grass that bled away before the last sharp climb to the strath head, and from here, after quaking beds and scoured stones, it was the simplest of miles to the main road.

Almost from the first page the reader of *Isolation Shepherd* has a strong sense that this was the end of something, and not just of the author's stay at Strathmore. Thomson frames his short spell at Strathmore in a broader history of the glen. He mentions that in the late nineteenth century the land was divided into a playground for two wealthy industrialists, an American and a German. In the manner of creatures leaving their scent, these two vain men each at loggerheads with the other marked out their terrain with huge deer fences. They had deer-watchers installed and ghillies employed to corral the beasts into cul-de-sacs where they might be slaughtered *en masse* even by the most inept and myopic of guests. Today you can still find tangles of rusting wire and rows of iron stakes drilled here and there into the bedrock miles from any road. Serving no purpose now they have been left to erode naturally. A monument even if it could speak would have nothing to say. The bones of similar fences are everywhere in the Highlands today, often marching over the crests of hills, as one does in the Monadhliath, for instance. I fear the attitude that established them is still alive today, that the hills and land are playthings only and their paper owners can do with them as they wish.

So you might weary a little reading of the random whims of the rich, as I did. Much more fascinating and moving were the accounts of local people and their stories, characters like Hamish Dhu and his father, Alister, who ran an illicit whisky still on the slopes of Lurg Mhor and lived on an island in the loch. Thomson talks of Alister's 'spying stone', which had a commanding view of the Pait river flats and from where he could log the approach of friend or foe, the latter being excisemen on a mission to close such stills and fine their operators. His was never discovered. Thomson ventures that the 'spying stone' marked an old burial ground for infants before the days of registration.

To the west of his place at Strathmore are the 'gaunt ruins of a remote croft house, once the home of a long forgotten family who acted as deer-watchers'. Beside the house was a single large boulder, a kind of natural memorial, as on this a three-year-old boy climbed and fell and broke his neck.

Of Thomson's predecessors at Strathmore, the extraordinarily resourceful Tommy Fleming stands out. He arrived here as a boy in 1912, and apart from a stint soldiering during the First World War was employed as a keeper until 1956, the year the author and his family moved in. A trained engineer, Fleming used the burn behind the cottage to run a small generator to power the lighting and turn a butter churn, much to his wife's delight.

Visitors to the croft were few and far between, but I love the story of when, in the early hours of a January morning, the Thomson family were woken by eight students. The young fellows were exhausted. They'd been blown off Sgurr a' Chaorachain in a blizzard and had to cut steps down an ice slope, arriving at the lochside only after an 'epic descent'. With Betty's restorative porridge and stew inside them, Thomson led them north through Strath Mhuillich to the bealach, from where it was all downhill but still many miles to the public road at Achnashellach.

So-called 'tramps' sometimes appeared, asking for a drink and a bite to eat, homeless wanderers sleeping rough or dossing in ruinous bothies. One gentleman of the road set out for Strathmore from Monar early one spring but never arrived. No one reported him missing, so there was no search party and when his remains were dug from a snowdrift by a shepherd nobody came forward to claim his body. A stranger to the world who now 'wears the turning globe', as Housman wrote.

Most writers can be guilty of personification when conveying the land and elements, and sometimes it is hard to avoid, but for Thomson it is a characteristic hallmark. His landscapes ooze with 'presences', either malevolent or benign but never indifferent: so we read 'white tongued waves swirled with evil menace along cracked, life-hungry rocks', or of 'vagrant shadows cast by aimless clouds'. Blizzards are always 'savage'. While his style might not accord to modern taste, the reader should see his work as part and continuation of a tradition of Highland prose and poetry that interprets place in terms of story. The landscape is not an empty vessel but full of significance.

If a spiritual conviction underlies Thomson's writing it is never defined, nor, I would guess, particularly orthodox, but it is there. During a night sail on Christmas Eve from Monar to Strathmore the author describes setting the tiller of the *Spray* and turning his back and reading some of their festive mail. His mind drifts and he is suddenly in a 'large room with old furniture, pictures and books' and explaining to his employer, John Stirling, about the loss of the *Spray*. Thomson is jerked back to the present to see the *Spray* charging straight for the cliffs of a promontory. He slams the engine in reverse and slows with only yards to spare. Years later, and long after he had left Strathmore, Thomson was invited to visit Stirling at his Fairburn residence. This was his first visit and he was shown into a room, the exact same one he had seen in his dream. Was this a case of what Highlanders call 'second sight'?

Beyond its repertoire of stories is a more general feeling I got from the book, that the author couldn't quite find the words to capture the beauty of what he saw nor articulate what it meant for him. He struggles to achieve the right balance of words when presented with, say, the quietude after a blizzard or the colours of a winter sunset. But can anyone? Can their reality be distilled by any arrangement of words? Some things will always elude us. They are only there in that one moment, then gone but for an ache or echo, the last fading note of some orchestra playing in your head.

For once winter came in layers. It was an accumulation. Everything froze two weeks before Christmas, then a great blizzard swept in to pile snow into corries and hollows and even the hill burns could no longer say where they were. All through January and February the pattern continued. Fresh snowfalls and winds from the tundra and ice on all the lochs, and now with the full weight of winter the mountains appeared reshaped, strangers in their own land. I'd never seen them like this before, not here. A vision of another place come to haunt the old strath.

I wondered how it could feel so cold inside. A quarter year of frost in the thick stone walls now came out and pervaded every corner and hung aloft to clamp around us. I wore all I had, but still shivered. We needed to get moving.

Outside, a low winter sun cast long shadows over the basin. Honeycomb of peat sink and channelway and rock-strewn moorland were all gone, and the burn at the side hidden under a great drift. The Ling was frozen between its banks. Loch Cruoshie lay stilled and opaque as a dried-out salt lake.

Around the bothy were three foot waves of snow blown there by last week's storm. Gavin led out slowly across the drifts and at once sank to his knees. Smooth white slopes rose to the east and to a summit obscured by cloud, while ahead Lurg Mhor was brilliant and gleaming and its snows the colour of egg-yolk. A little wind now. Puffs and eddies, and each trailed whorls of crystals that glittered about us in their millions.

So concealing was the snow-cover it was hard to find a way. It betrayed so little. It took fifteen minutes to reach the loch and we paced easily over the wind-shorn ice. There was no creaking or movement but a dull sound with every footfall. Then we tackled the drifts again. I made to follow Gavin's footfalls whether they went in shallow or two or three feet, so our trail became a trench and when ascending even the smallest rise or hummock we wheezed with effort. At the burn draining Loch Calavie we stopped and rested and broke the ice to drink and top up our water bottles. Then we began climbing straight, and somehow this felt easier, at least for me who was trailing. I appreciated my companion's stamina. But then Gavin cycles thirty miles every day to his workshop and had been 'running his local hills to get fit for winter'.

The slope rose and we climbed and soon the watershed land of Monar and the Ling Valley spread itself like a great shaken tablecloth. A white desert-place. Where was the reindeer herd? Where the wolf-pack? A squall came to shower us with ice pellets and spindrift fingered into warm nooks and I stopped and turned my back and made myself very small. Gavin was already kneeling in the lee of a boulder, but I could see blown snow pour over him as if carried on a conveyor. For minutes and like some tableau we held these postures, rigid and unmoving.

The squall passed and the sun made us squint with its sudden brilliance. We climbed with crampons now, the snow hardening but our spiked boots biting the surface wonderfully, and with every upward step I pushed in the shaft of my small ice axe, having to lean over rather to achieve this. Gavin was way above me by now, and going so fast he seemed almost to be running. He wasn't, but I understood his impatience. The joy of approaching a remote mountain-top in the depths of winter. You can't explain it. The beauty of the ice architecture and rime cauliflowers draped along the crest hardly reward for the two days of breaking trail and effort. But it isn't an equation to be balanced and all the world's words are futile and the moment only is what counts. Just hold it for a little longer.

In deep snow that had piled up on the north side we scooped a hollow to be out of the wind and gazed unobstructed at the pronged summit of Bidean a' Choire Sheasgaich that grew just ahead like an ice peak of a colder clime, then east to the frozen Loch Monar, to the long narrow tongue where the Strathmore flats had been. It was grey and desolate.

I followed Gavin in great bouncing strides down the flank, snow tumbling and hissing, and for a moment I felt the whole slope might collapse, but it held and we came to level ground warmed and flushed, and sought a boulder behind which we could escape the east wind and chew on some lunch. In keeping with his earlier efforts Gavin stormed up the approach to Bidean, leaving me in his wake. The ground was steep almost immediately and I went at a more cautious pace. At some point he waited, and together we veered left towards the south-east ridge, the ground tapering and sunlight flooding a crest disfigured by snow and rime. A near-vertical drop emptied away west, so to feel safe we kept a little right, until this side went as well and there was only dead ground.

A small cairn perched at the narrowest point, and all about was a winter landscape, half foreign, all the hills with new faces – Torridon, Fannich, Fisherfield, Fionn Bheinn, Slioch, Beinn Damph. Across the basin was Aonach Buidhe with its frozen northern corrie and cold footslopes where I once sat by the shieling.

In the manner of tightrope walkers we continued along the ridge, the rock shelving away; and we had to scrape snow from ledges and scramble and kick for footholds until the angle eased and we footed over a half-buried lochan, then steeply north into the corrie where two thousand feet below us were the frozen coils of the Blackwater. We'd come down on the wrong side of the mountain and I hadn't considered how long it would take to get back.

A late sun coloured the snow but gave little warmth. I still wore a balaclava and mittens and cooled quickly every time we stopped. At least the wind by now had largely quietened. We chose a line and stuck to it, keeping just beneath a series of crags and broken ground that bulged with cascades of bluish ice, and finally after what seemed hours, with the sun gone and light fading, we dropped to a rough track by Calavie. Large drifts of soft snow here, so we ploughed to the frozen loch itself and skipped along, though staying tight to the shoreline. Snow lay in a few places, blown sometimes into long crests, but mostly the ice was clear to the shallow loch bed, or else translucent and textured with veins or had an earthen tinge, stones beneath only half-seen and given away by their gauzy imprint. Shore pebbles carried their own ice cradles or a side of rime and a tiny ridge of snow.

The figure ahead was slowing, I was slowing and we still had the basin to cross. For once Gavin asked me to break trail. My head forced my feet onwards but every drift swallowed us and nothing was easy and no line shorter than the one we took. As darkness settled and only the faintest of pale crimson still smudged the high rim of the mountains, we found at last the hard sound surface of Loch Cruoshie.

Only a quarter mile now, Gavin a silhouette, a dark object moving over the still, snowy land, the ring of his bootfalls and something plaintive in his breathing, leading me through the last drifts to the bothy.

The Cairngorms Imagined

You may have been on the same paths many times, but did you ever see Syd Scroggie with his stick and limp and spare hand always on a mate's guiding shoulder? In the quiet of Rothiemurchus or on the path by Luibeg, did you stop and blether? Syd had a natural way with words and could give a shape to what you'd missed or sensed only dimly – the cry of a plover, the scent of some plant, the warmth of sun lately on your face.

I first came across Syd when reading *Poems of the Scottish Hills*, an anthology compiled by the outdoor writer Hamish Brown. I was staying in a hostel in Achnashellach towards the end of a long walk in the Highlands, and although I was unfamiliar with many of the poets I was moved by their words, that chimed with my own experiences. After the walk I managed to track down an out-of-print copy, and over the years it has become a well-thumbed favourite. Even today its spine still brightens my bookshelf. Perhaps in a literary sense very few poets in this collection attain the level of a Hopkins, Burns or Housman but they speak to me, a hillman. Words can somehow soften whatever life throws at you, and here are words full of sentiment and yearning and sometimes loss as they attempt to distill the hill experience. Standing out among them was a handful of poems by Syd Scroggie.

In those days I'd developed a habit of scribbling accounts of my hill days, not just a record of where I went and what I climbed but how I felt, and as it seemed each hill and place was different I tried by some alchemy

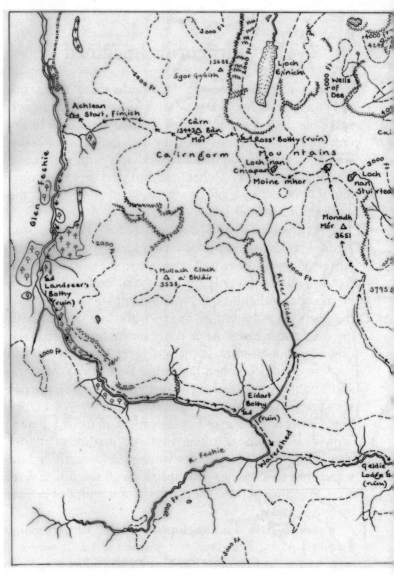

Cairngorms route.

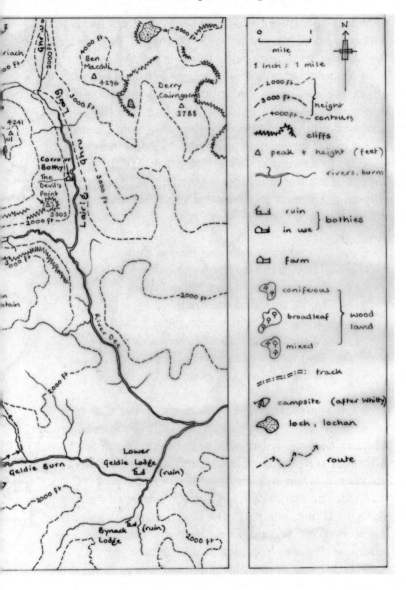

of words to capture their atmosphere. To achieve that without resort to cliché and hackneyed description I found was extraordinarily difficult. Syd's verses have both a quality of immediacy and reflection. They are full of texture and detail and emotion and possess a clarity that brings alive the outdoors. Beyond their descriptive qualities is a rhythm found in the stanzas and the way the sound of the words rises and falls like wind in a corrie or the echo of a mountain burn. The poem *At Last* is the old lament of a mountain lover washed up in the grey streets and caught somewhere between need and desire, always flitting between the two.

> . . . when you cannot hear it calling
> Though the waters tumble down,
> Yet you cannot hear them falling
> In the traffic of the town,
> When you cannot hear them falling
> At the lonely Pools of Dee,
> And the golden plovers calling
> In the hubbub of Lochee . . .

A few years later came Syd's memoir, *The Cairngorms Scene and Unseen*, published in 1989 by the Scottish Mountaineering Trust with a Foreword by Tom Weir. Although at that point I knew nothing about Syd beyond his poetry, when reading the blurb on the jacket I was stunned. The man who had so richly conveyed the hills in verse was blind, and had been since losing his sight in the last days of the Second World War when he stepped on a landmine. He also lost a leg in the incident.

Maybe I was young and impatient, but at first I didn't get on with the book, finding it somehow just a little too discursive and rambling and with a few too many reminiscences of the war. I couldn't see how the various threads came together into a cohesive whole. I loved his poetry, but the book contained only a smattering of verse. And as a teacher I was staggered by his criticism of the underlying principles of the Duke of Edinburgh Award Scheme. But the book grew on me. I began to appreciate better its ironies and humour and how, paradoxically, its faults could actually be its strengths. *The Cairngorms Scene and Unseen* is irreverent and anarchic, but at its core is an attempt by a blind man to understand what impels him time and again to pack a rucksack and walk the hills, and in particular the Cairngorms. Syd's words left a deep impression. Here was a kindred spirit, I thought, someone who felt the same things and shared a similar outlook on the hills as I did.

In order to understand a writer of the outdoors you need to get to the places they went, stalk their shadow and for a while follow their bootsteps. You must make some attempt to inhabit their world. In Syd's case that posed a very real problem. Short of stumbling about blindfolded, how could I ever know what it is like to wander the hills without sight? Syd always downplayed his disability and insisted it did not lessen what the mountains gave him. I admit to being sceptical when I first read this. On the face of it the hills appear to provide a primarily visual experience. Luminous snows, crimson dawns, the iridescence of pebbles in a mountain burn, the memories we take home are of what we have seen. Strip them away and what is there left? For most of his life Syd was reliant on the word-pictures of his friends when imagining a view. But I wonder if our perception of the hills is too loaded towards the visual and the experience communicated rather one-dimensional. After all, sight is just one facet of an encounter with the hills. The coarseness of a granite boulder, the caress of a breeze on your face, the perfume of mountain thyme – these are also part of the picture, especially for someone without sight. Towards the end of his book he writes, 'I am prepared to allot only point five of one percent to the visual side of the hills in their power to awe and impress; the blind man is without that little amount, but the rest, and this is far more important, is as much his as to any climber, deerstalker, laird, or hill shepherd.' But for Syd there was something more. What he found, he says, was an 'inner experience, something psychological, something poetic, which perhaps cannot be fully understood when the physical aspect of things gets in the way.'

If I couldn't honestly emulate the manner of Syd's wanderings then perhaps I might retrace one of his journeys and stop over at some of his old haunts. The stories in *The Cairngorms Scene and Unseen* span some half a century, from pre-war forays to nearly being killed on Carn a'Mhaim when climbing with his second wife, Margaret. During much of this time Syd and his pals would gather at half-derelict lodges or bothies that had been abandoned decades before, places like Altanour, Lower Geldie, Bynack and Corrour. In one way or other these old dwellings feature strongly and they become a theme in themselves. He describes Corrour in the 1930s as in a 'beautifully dilapidated condition'. Altanour was 'silent, dripping and crowded in with queer, tempest-twisted trees'. By chance he found them at the cusp of ruin and with a lingering residue of their former selves. In the detail that remained he could read their stories. In one place was an old box bed and newspapers of a long-forgotten title lining the walls. With crumbling plaster, rusting grate and roof beams that would threaten anyone standing beneath, they had reached a kind of apotheosis of dereliction. They were alone and abandoned and pummelled by the elements, but for Syd these places had soul.

I think the artist in Syd recognised the paradox of how a derelict building could, with a fire in the grate, feel like the cosiest place in the world. Describing a night at Bynack he writes 'and now this fire, which blazed so cheerily up the lum and warmed us through and through, converted this house, which the Dundee Sanitary would have condemned out of hand, into a palace beside which Versailles in all its glory shrank to the status of a hovel'. It was the idea that true comfort was found not in a five-star hotel but in a fire-warmed howff high in the hills.

Of all these places only Corrour is still habitable, the rest recognisable now only by a few standing walls and piles of rubble and signs warning the curious to keep out. On the map they formed a kind of natural route through the Cairngorms, and it seemed obvious that here was my walk. Beginning at the roadhead in Glen Feshie I would follow the valley south, then east, over the Feshie-Geldie watershed, swing north up Glen Dee and over the pass of the Lairig Ghru. Not only was this a classic circumvent of the Cairngorm Massif, but here was the ground Syd covered both sighted and blind, and which more than anywhere else inspired his best writing.

It so happened that the time I had scheduled for this was the first dry day in a run of wet that had fixed the pattern of summer. Coolish overcast weather had brought us to the end of June and the heatwave of spring seemed a long time ago. The seasons were topsy-turvy this year, all to do with climate change, some said. I parked up and went along the footpath around Achlean croft, the last inhabited dwelling on the east side of the Feshie River. Over a burn and across the expansive flood plain then I climbed what I reckoned to be a glacial moraine, now clothed in heather and grasses. In a short minute I was walking a narrow ridge and looking down fifty feet or so to the broad meandering river. The western slopes of the Feshie Hills were planted in exotic conifers decades ago, but here and there along the strath and in patches are still to be found groves of the ancient Caledonian pines, fragmentary survivors of the great forests that once covered much of the Highlands. The heaviest snows for a quarter of a century had damaged these venerable trees, wrenching great limbs from their trunks or leaving them dangling, the ochre wood splintered and torn as if a giant had wanted kindling. Looking ahead, or south, the valley climbed to a moorland fastness and a profile of high hills some 3,000 feet or more, the Munro tops that ringed the Geldie and Tarf watersheds, remote country.

The open ground, and there was plenty of it, was colonised by heather, yellow-flowering gorse and verdant grasses that reached across the flats. The floods and spates on the Feshie, particularly during spring snowmelts, are notorious. 'You can never cross the same river twice,' Syd philosophised. This is especially true of the Feshie, which continually rewrites its course across deposits of gravel and sands, keeping one step ahead of the map-makers.

A recurring theme in Syd's poetry and other writings is the promise of change. In his simple two-verse poem *Change and Immutability* he describes how a young pre-war Syd first began exploring the hills:

When I went up to Clova glen
And I was in my teens
And got there on a bicycle
And lived on bread and beans.
And covered twenty miles or so
And got up Dreish and Mayar . . .

It was the month of May and the oystercatchers were
'madly piping'. He returned four decades later.

When I went up to Clova glen
And I was fifty-five,
And lived on wine and caviare
And had a car to drive.
And managed half a dozen miles
And halfway up the hill . . .

It was May, he writes, and the oystercatchers were
'madly piping still'.

A track through the heather brought me to the bothy
of Ruigh Aiteachean, 'sheiling of the Junipers'. The shrub
in question grows abundantly on the slopes behind. Only
a few yards from the bothy is a chimney stack, about
eighteen feet high and standing entirely on its own. It's
probably the most arresting human feature in the entire
glen. Documentary evidence suggests this was Edwin
Landseer's hut where on the wall above the fireplace he
painted frescos of red deer sometime in the middle of the
nineteenth century. Despite the renown of Landseer the
hut fell into disrepair, and in the 1870s to protect the
precious art a local landowner had an exterior wall con-
structed around it, but even that was not enough. I think
in the end it was just too remote, or successive lairds lost

interest. Without a patron the hut became a rudimentary stop-over for wayfarers and tramps, who stared a little bemused, one suspects, at the fresco in the firelight and its remembrance of a famous Victorian painter. Eventually the ceiling gave way and the Cairngorm winters did it for the fresco. A few of the oldest folk in Strathspey still have it in their memory, and for years after the Second World War traces of pigment could be seen among the piles of plaster and rubble.

The Feshie now spread across its basin, as wide as anywhere on its length, and the sound of it came and went in the breeze as it rushed by gravel islands of its own making and around tree-debris taken down by storms. After about a mile the path rejoined the right bank and threaded along for a bit, sandwiched by river on one side, steep slope on the other. Sections of path had been washed away, undercut by the swing of a meander, and I was forced to teeter over fallen rubble and pick my way. I was entering a steep-sided and flat-bottomed valley, the flanks half-clothed in native woodland, mostly birch, and going now in a more south-east direction. An old track with grass in its centre came from the west side, ran into a ford and for a while carried on parallel with the path, finally joining it. Gazing up and beyond the straggling woodland to grey-brown moors whose summit crowns I could not see gave a shiver of anticipation. The wild land of the upper basin lay ahead, but it would take the remainder of the day to reach.

I was now approaching Syd's country. Although *The Cairngorms Scene and Unseen* hardly mentions the Feshie region it was an area the writer knew well. Syd's base was always Dundee and this I suppose reflected his orbit of exploration, mostly coming to the hills via Braemar and

Deeside or sometimes taking the long corridor up the Tilt. During the war he was a lieutenant with the Lovat Scouts stationed at Alvie and Pityoulish in Strathspey, and from these bases the northern Cairngorms and Feshie were more accessible. Often just with an evening pass he made forays into the hills, and there is something intensely visual about his early recollections. Once after a week of rain he found himself late on the plateau north of Ben Macdui. The cloud suddenly lifted and before him was a wider sunlit world, 'the peaks around glowing with the pristine pigments of an illuminated manuscript,' he remembers. As he dropped a little there was a second burst of light and the land became 'all chocolate brown, shot with gold, and all its algaes and vegetation, invisible heretofore, turned a most brilliant jungle green', and later when the setting sun appeared, 'the hills now seemed mantled in a great hodden-grey plaid stained through and through with the blood of some gigantic wearer'. He'd turned the scene over in his imagination and produced something lasting in the mind of the reader. Whether he'd formed these words from memory or they were what he'd written down that evening, they show an intense observation of the animate world. Then came his blindness, and his experience of the world and hills changed utterly.

After the war Syd became reliant on friends to take him to the hills and guide him once there, so it's no surprise that these characters form an important part of the book's fabric. Their personalities resonate on the page, and through them Syd explores his favourite themes, most of which boil down to trying to answer the conundrum of what is it that draws folk to the wild places. So we eavesdrop on Syd duelling with Les Bowman at Corrour, or with Colin Brand at Old Bynack Lodge just before the war. Another frequent sparring partner was the non-nonsense Bob Maclean, who first answered Syd's advertisement in a Dundee newspaper in 1958 – 'Blind man, due to senescence, indolence, hibernation, or house arrest of friends, requires patient, hardy companion for Clova weekend . . . accommodation cramped, conditions appalling, hours endless, wages nil . . .' Perhaps blindness had softened an innate individualism now that he had to rely on others if he was to spend time in the hills.

Reading *The Cairngorms Scene and Unseen* you appreciate how carefully weighed are his character sketches as he attempts to capture some trait of personality, and they often reveal something of the psychology of his companions. Les Bowman, he says, 'was mordant out of habit, even when he was not feeling that way'. He tells us of the internal struggles of Bob Maclean, a man torn between making the best of what he had or packing in his job and taking to the road. He railed at the world's injustice and the mediocrity of his life in Dundee. 'It was not that Bob had weighed the Lairig and found it wanting,' Syd writes, 'but that its remit was not global enough.' Preoccupied and burdened rather, Bob could become forgetful and he often left his blind companion alone on some rock among the heather until Syd bawled at him. Of his cousin Donald he says, 'the word imperturbable, if it had existed before, would certainly have to be coined in a desperate attempt to describe my cousin.' Gavin Sprott had 'wit and intellect, not to mention his resolution and hardiness.' The legendary Bob Scott, estate keeper at Luibeg Cottage in the decades after the war, flits in and out of the text. Syd manages to avoid caricatures and pens real people with good qualities and flaws, speculating sometimes about what they might be thinking. On occasion he takes us back, not exactly in reminiscence, more in reverie, to a time when the voice of a friend, Jock Mackenzie, who farmed Upper Tullochgrue, details exactly what happened to Syd on that fateful day just three weeks before the end of the war.

Keeping close to the north bank the path climbed steadily through rigid scree, then dropped to the shade of pines, rising again to contour the steepness of Creag Bheag. This was once a droving and trade route; the path was laid on what looked to be very old foundations and cut hard into the valley side. Some years ago a landslide triggered by a spate took away a large section of the old path, and a rough and narrow way has been scratched into the forty-degree slope. The land changed slowly. Distant moors to the south and east came a little closer and the valley was more open. The Feshie itself was boisterous, churning over rock shelves into dark pools and running noisily around boulders. Alder and the pale green foliage of occasional willows lined the banks for a while, then I passed a last twisted birch and before me was the open moor, the empty country of upper Feshie. The sky was now entirely overcast and lowering so that it smudged the crests of Carn an Fhidhleir and An Sgarsoch. The path was faint in places and I had a sense that this way linking the Feshie and Geldie river systems is now relatively little trod, though from time to time I noticed the tyre signatures of two mountain bikes. Perhaps the landslides had discouraged folk, or was it the unremitting loneliness of this high valley?

Where the River Eidart, draining the great hinterland of the Western Cairngorms, joined the Feshie there is the roofless shell of an old bothy. Only a few stout timbers are upright and you might find a more secure haven among nearby boulders. Even in summer it can be staggeringly cold here, which I discovered when passing a night at this spot. The forecast, I recall, promised fine, warm weather and so I'd packed a bivvy sac and only the lightest of sleeping bags. My pal Chris had been bolder and taken only his bivvy. A late start meant it was late when we reached Eidart. We'd sweated up the valley, but now the sun had set and the temperature was dropping. For a make-do mattress I grubbed up a little heather and wormed inside and zipped up. Chris tarried and fidgeted before bedding down, his only protection a wrapping of thin fabric and the clothes he wore. I slept soundly but at some point was woken by noise and movement. In the grey half-light the figure of Chris stood over me and was rooting about in my rucksack. He was shaking and his breath was audible like a strange chanting.

'What the hell are you doing?' He'd got my billy and was now emptying his water bottle into it.

'I need your gas for a brew, and fast.'

'It's three o clock in the morning. Can't it wait?'

'Look, you might be tucked up all snug but I'm freezing my nads off. Haven't slept a wink.'

Scalding tea and plenty of sugary snacks did the trick. 'What a place,' he said later, cradling his mug and munching a third bar of chocolate.

Eidart bothy was well-known to Syd and he admitted to never feeling comfortable there, though for a different reason to Chris. 'A ramshackle comfortless structure crouching in a boggy hollow . . . wire-guy'd roof of rusty tin, unhinged door and uncaulked wooded walls,' was how he described the place, but he struggled to shed the sense that something here was not right. There was an uneasy atmosphere, a feeling of being watched. The matter of 'spookiness' was a theme Syd explores in some depth and with his characteristic mix of seriousness and humour. He has one or two experiences of his own. During the war when staying alone at the remote Shelter Stone by Loch Avon, he saw the silhouette of a strange figure 'pace slowly out of the blackness at one side of the water into the blackness at the other'. His weirdest encounter was again in the war years and when on the path through Rothiemurchus. On a fine evening he became aware of an elderly gentleman standing just off the path. He was tall, stately and ethereal, dressed in old-fashioned garments, and his complexion had a strange 'porcelain quality'. A few and now forgotten words passed between them and it was only afterwards that Syd felt something was not right. 'In his presence,' he writes, 'I seemed to step out of one age into another, as if there on the wooded approach to the Lairig . . . time had got dislocated so that all ages were contemporaneous, and I could as easily have found myself talking with Celtic holy man, sweat-stained Jacobite fugitive or grim cateran as with the preternatural impeccability of this antique apparition'.

On land growing steadily more level the Feshie, much smaller now, ran unhurriedly between banks of peat or into dark pools where I saw a trout jump or shallow over a bed of whitish gravel. With little warning the channel almost doubled back on itself, a bend known locally as the 'turn o' the Feshie'. The river here had cut hard into a rise of moraine, the same deposits that had blocked its path eastwards to the Dee valley and diverted its flow to Strathspey. Today only a narrow boggy bank of moorland separates the two basins. In just a few minutes a kind of hush came over the valley, the Feshie fading into the background as I skipped around a scattering of muddy pools. The sky now was even lower and it seemed to emphasise the widening space, like the unfolded wings of a great bird. The path was gone and there was no sign that a human had ever come this way. Cotton grass bobbed in the breeze. A pipit watched me from its perch on a bank of peat.

Almost imperceptibly the ground fell away. It trended east and from the peat below came the hollow murmur of a burn, this joining another and soon it emerged to flow over bedrock and ruckles of stone. I moved to relatively drier ground a little above the flats and found again the line of the path. The green haugh and pines of the lower Feshie seemed a long time ago and a different world to this barren and treeless land. For a good while the ground hardly seemed to fall at all. The Geldie didn't appear to know where to run, tracing a series of aimless meanders like a blind snake. Feeling tired after much walking, I thought the old place couldn't be far away.

I knew it sat in its moat of pasture high on the south bank, but could see no sign of it, which was strange. I had the map out again and scanned ahead and pushed on. A time-worn track came up from the valley. It forded the river and climbed the slope opposite. Then I saw it, the grey tumbled walls of Geldie Lodge, barely half a mile away. I crossed over and on a level patch of grass by one of the walls pegged my tiny tube-tent. I collected water from the river and laid out my sleeping bag and slid inside. With my flimsy rucksack balanced on its side and with two or three stones I made a pocket of shelter for my stove and boiled water and cooked up a simple meal. Twilight still had some way to run, so after food and a rest I got up and went on a tour of the place, picking my way from room to room, through entryways that were not always obvious. I'd seen a photograph of the lodge in its prime, but now there was no ceiling and no upstairs and the floors were all but buried in fallen masonry. I wouldn't normally have chosen to pass the night by the shell of a laird's holiday home, but this short walk was to be a kind of homage to Syd, and in the late 1950s and 60s Geldie was one of the places where he and his pals were to be found.

Although it sat high on a remote watershed, Geldie in its heyday would have been occupied permanently by housekeepers and servants, keeping the rooms warm and kitchen well-stocked for when the guests arrived to hunt and shoot. In the late nineteenth and early twentieth century the wider Cairngorms were peppered with similar lodges, as well as a network of bothies occupied by deer-watchers and keepers. After the First World War and in the face of increasing costs and taxes, sporting estates began to economise and places like Geldie were used only sporadically or abandoned altogether. The hills emptied, and into this vacuum came the first climbers and hill-tramps, often from the sprawling tenements of Aberdeen and Dundee. Buses were infrequent and expensive, so the early adventurers had little recourse but to cycle to the hills. The Angus glens and especially Clova, which led to the great peak of Lochnagar, were easily accessible on two wheels. As everything had to transported under one's own steam, and with tents being of heavy canvas, most chose to use what rudimentary accommodation they could find in the hills. The once grand hunting lodges, recently patronised by servants and well-appointed guests, became gathering places for proletarian climbers. The clink of bone china and polite talk in the drawing room was replaced by the smell of frying bacon and coarse tales.

By the time Syd appeared in the mid-1930s a generation had already been exploring the hills. Old Geldie Lodge is not mentioned in *The Cairngorms Scene and Unseen*, but the naturalist Adam Watson describes a winter visit on ski in 1949 and wrote that two rooms were still habitable. He remembers rows of servant bells in the kitchen, each corresponding to the many bedrooms. By 1970 only a tiny upstairs room was weatherproof, and that accessed at some risk via a dormer window, then along a corridor of loose planks laid across roof beams. In a few years even this room had collapsed, and now all is open to the sky. The tallest surviving feature is still the red-brick chimney stack, and even tonight in the gloaming this rather contrasts with walls of locally sourced stone. Among the rubble I noted the rusted remains of a cast iron range and a few roof timbers that had escaped the fires of stravaigers. In every room a colony of willowherb wavered in the breeze, at this altitude still some weeks from flowering.

I was up with the sun and sat on the grass in front of the lodge having breakfast. It was still and clear, the ground by me alive with flowering speedwell, buttercup, tormentil and daisy. The soft morning light brought out the colour of mosses and lichens on the walls of the old lodge. I looked over to Beinn Bhrotain, which rose to a blue-grey crown of bare rock four straight miles away. Into the mountain's flanks had been carved water courses, their lines betrayed by the slanting light. I had my map out but didn't really need it, not if I kept to the route. It was easy – downstream to the boarded up 'Red House', which Syd usually referred to as Lower Geldie. A short detour of a mile or so south from here finds the tumbled walls of Bynack Lodge, forlorn in an enclave of singing larch. I would then set my nose north to join the Dee and stride up its valley to a spot just east of the Devil's Point where, at the gates of the Lairig Ghru, is the tiny, single-roomed dwelling of Corrour bothy.

The last leg was over the Lairig Ghru, at first passing the Tailor's Stone and the great bite of Garbh Choire, then rising gradually to bisect Braeriach and Ben Macdui, the path now lost among granite boulders that in the spring tumble down a thousand feet on both sides. The top of the pass is marked by the freezing Pools of Dee, where Syd's friend, Bob Maclean, once bathed to escape the sweltering heat of a summer's day. After a few stony miles of descent the first stunted pines of Rothiemurchus appear as the well-graded path skirts the edge of the great Allt Druidh that drains the entire pass.

It was a journey drenched in Syd's memory, especially the Lairig Ghru and the small bothy which marks its entrance. The former deer-watchers' cottage of Corrour was the heart of Syd's world both before and after the war, and I think in his mind it grew to be a kind of beacon throughout the vagaries he suffered. He'd first entered its gloomy interior with a climbing pal, John Ferguson, in the late 1930s. They'd cycled up from Dundee. Corrour by then was in a fairly decrepit state, not helped by the attentions of some gangrels who'd removed the wall panelling and had ripped up part of the floor for firewood. In the candlelight he noted the grime and usual detritus left by wayfarers, 'packets of tea screwed up at the top, dusty bottles of paraffin and meths, tins of salt gone solid with damp, a can or two of Fray Bentos or Ambrosia rice, a half-used condensed milk tin with matches twisted round with paper to wedge up the holes.' The place was run-down and maybe didn't have too many years left, but he loved it. The war came and despite being based in army camps just north of the Cairngorms and often climbing the hills he doesn't mention visiting Corrour. Two weeks before the end of the war he probably felt he would never set foot in it again.

It happened like this. In the spring of 1945 Syd was part of the Allied campaign which had overwhelmed German forces in the Italian Apennines. The once invincible Gothic Line was in tatters and Lieutenant Scroggie and his team of Lovat Scouts were involved with 'mopping up' operations. On the slopes of Monte Grande he recalls the 'sun-glare on churned up clay, a dead mule here or there, a Sherman tank with drooping gun barrel . . .' With a few men he went on a reconnaissance for a new squadron headquarters. But the ground was riddled with mines. 'My very last sight in the world was the planet Venus,' he writes, 'bright and beautiful, pulsating in the gloaming sky.'

After emergency treatment at a hospital in Naples he was invalided home and moved to St Dunstan's, an institution that helped prepare war-blinded British servicemen and women to live independently. Like many soldiers who felt they'd missed out due to the war, Syd was determined to complete his education and was thrilled when accepted by New College, Oxford, to study History. In this intellectual and stimulating atmosphere Syd blossomed. Weekends saw him at Middlebank near Dundee, where, under the tutelage of Les and Betty Bowman, he learned the practicalities of living without sight. He chopped wood, harvested tatties, and practised with a wooden leg on rough ground. It was ten years before he felt mentally ready for a trip to the hills. Willed and helped all the way by his friend Les Bowman, the pair reached Corrour on a thundery day in April 1955.

In fact some five years earlier the old bothy had been saved from almost certain ruin by volunteers who installed a new roof and gutted the inside, turning it into a simple weatherproof structure, not unlike the purpose-built Cairngorm refuges of Sinclair and Hutchison. But Syd was crestfallen. While I don't believe Syd ever wanted Corrour to perish gracefully, he laments that in turning it into functional watertight shelter its history had been rather beaten out of it. 'The body of Corrour,' he writes, 'had risen from the grave . . . but it had become dissociated from the soul we remembered.'

The route was deeply familiar, and over the years I'd walked and ski-ed and camped and bivvied on it and even dragged a bike over the boulderfields of the pass. But as I stood by the crumbling walls of Geldie and gazed north to the slopes of Beinn Bhrotain and Monadh Mor, the thought of a long walk up the valley waned. Where would Syd have gone? The mountains beckoned strongly and in a way any hillman would have understood. *Give Me the Hills* was the title of Syd's little book of verse and I thought of it now. So much of his writing expresses a simple yearning to be in the hills, and when denied that, it reads like letters of unrequited love. Blinded and lying in a hospital bed in Naples he'd said to a nurse, 'I can live without my sight, but never without my mountains.'

This day would never come again, so I packed and forded the Geldie and cut across gentle, heathery slopes to the Allt Dhuidh Mor and began tracing its meandering bank upslope.

When choosing a line up a hill I like something to hold my attention during the hours of ascent. The burn changed constantly, one minute running smooth and straight in its culvert, the next coiling by a spur or some boss of granite. When the ground began to steepen it divided into four separate channels, spilled over some falls and ran noisily over a great belly of bedrock. A good place to stop. The high sun shone from a mostly clear sky and it felt so warm the heat shimmered in the Geldie Basin. The lodge had gone into its background again and the valley spread itself so I could see its true extent. The upper basin was a place of ghosts, and not just for Syd.

It happened at a time in my life when opportunities could be easily taken. A weekend in March. Snow lying in a deep mantle on the hills and I thought I might attempt to ski from Blair Atholl to Aviemore. It was all spur of the moment, and complications with my transport meant it was early afternoon by the time I reached the snowline above the Tilt. On lightweight telemarks I worked hard to make up lost time, traversing the lonely hills of the Tarf watershed and bedding down for the night at a high col just west of An Sgarsoch.

I slept snugly and as a peachy sunrise coloured the eastern sky I skied off, dropping to cross the Geldie on a snow-bridge, then on a steady incline for some miles of snowfields where I glided almost without effort, as if drawn by a team of huskies. The Geldie behind, and ahead the blue-shadowed Cairngorms. To save time I cut the corner of Bhrotain to Glen Dee, reaching Corrour for a late breakfast, and a couple of hours later I sat by at the Pools of Dee. Not a boulder or heather-tip poked its nose through the blanket, and from here I swept down unstopping for three straight miles until the snow ran thin among the pines. A long ski carry to finish with, but by then it didn't matter.

Today the going was a deal less hurried. The land resolved into a more defined high valley, accentuated by a steep bouldery slopes to my right. Heat was gathering and there was hardly any wind. A large lingering snowdrift lay high on Cnapan Mor where a rivulet had tunnelled through its middle exposing a substantial depth. The land steepened and the burn was stretched so its flow narrowed and had fewer turns. It was also faster and displayed a continual energy, flashing in the sunshine as it ran over a drop of stones. Where Bhrotain and the south-reaching arm of Monadh Mor came together the burn disappeared into the ground, evidenced now only by frills of emerald moss and a dull tinkering sound until it was lost altogether. Reaching the col the land suddenly fell away, making my perch feel quite airy. I peered into the bowls of Glen Geusachan and to the Lairig Ghru two thousand feet below, then across to Devil's Point and Cairn Toul and the high tableland of Braeriach. The cliffs of Garbh Choire showed brick-red in roving sunshine and the remaining snow dazzled like tubes of tungsten, its grain all but lost. I'd never had a clear view from this vantage-point and the arrangement of familiar hills was different and fresh and gave a peculiar beauty whose provenance is the high Cairngorms. In particular I thought of the last lines of Syd's poem, *Summit Cairn*:

> Must panting pause and, pausing, hope to see
> Far more of magic than mere hope can dare;
> Not little loch, not wind-wrenched rowan tree,
> But all Time imaged in each instant there
> And beauty past all thought beneath the skies.

Syd doesn't name the hill which inspired these words. Maybe there is no name or else the piece expresses a general feeling remembered from many climbs. Real places, though, do run through his work, and perhaps none more so than the famous hill pass of the Cairngorms. I think for Syd the Lairig Ghru evolved to become more than just a way through the mountains, a place which for most of his life he could only see in his mind's eye or conjure in his imagination. Time and again it crosses the text in a different form. He comes to it as a teenager and throughout the war years, and later one-legged and blind and being led by friends. In his psyche it evolves to become a kind of metaphor for truth and he refers to it variously as 'mankind's Lairig', a place to aspire to and a symbol for life itself. A journey through it in some sense mirrors the journey of life.

In the end I feel he struggles to say precisely what he means, if indeed it can be reduced to words but he offers a flavour and grounds it in place – 'Braeriach, Macdui and the rest of the wilderness will leave the poet and romantic in the silence with philosopher and metaphysician, to browse on the ambrosia which is invisible to the vulgar eye . . . And the Lairig will be there in all its glory, swept by blizzard or bathed in coral reflection of infinite dawns and sunsets, when mankind and his fatuities have passed away.'

The hills for Syd are never an arena of pure escapism. Whether it was the global uncertainty of the 1930s, the war itself, or the cold nuclear age that followed, the wider world came crowding in, sometimes to provide a contrast but mostly because Syd knew he couldn't just shed the baggage of society when away in the hills. In *The Cairngorms Scene and Unseen* the gulf between humanity's propensity for evil and the beauty of the natural world is never more finely depicted than when Syd passes an evening at the abandoned Bynack Lodge with his friend, Colin Brand. It was New Year's Eve, 1938. Hitler had invaded Austria, Spain was tearing itself apart, and the dead from the brutal Sino-Chinese war were being shovelled into mass graves. High on the Cairngorm watershed Syd writes that it had been 'a day of sunshine, frost and dazzling snow.' The power of his description has the reader with them as they enter the derelict lodge, 'boots clumping hollowly on the wooden stairs', and reaching one of the upper rooms; having lit a candle Syd notes 'bare, dirty floorboards, a dormer window . . . a rusty fireplace with swivel hobs and wooden fender, a low, sloping ceiling. The only furnishing was an iron bedstead with no mattress.' They raise a fire in the grate and settle for the night. By dint of a simple fire the old place was magically transformed. 'Bynack', he writes, had become an 'epitome of home, not just for Colin and me, but to Mankind itself.'

In a flight of fantasy they speculate how they would counter Hitler's army when it reached the soil of Scotland and marched up the Feshie. Syd reckoned he might organise a crack unit of mountain fighters, 'comprising deer stalkers, rock climbers, members of the Scottish Ski Club and stray youth hostellers'. Colin said simply he would 'grab a rifle and take to the hills'. The fire flares and they lapse into silence, lost in their thoughts. I don't think Syd for a minute suggests the world's problems could be solved by a fire at Bynack on a cold winter's night, but sometimes you can believe it. 'Caught in this enormous, retributive convulsion of history,' he writes, 'what could two chaps like us do about it . . . nothing but sit and chat and watch the fire and view the ramshackle stage of the world, not so much with horror at its tragedy, as with ironic amusement at the comedy of it all.' He wrote this after many years, in hindsight of course; but maybe the world has not changed that much in seventy years, only today we recognise that the main threats are found maybe not in governments but in the hardwiring of our own psyche.

I often think you could do worse than to travel back through time and space and find the pinprick of light in the darkness of the Tilt, and there gaze through a frost-furred window at two men bantering in the glow of a fire. An image of sanity in a world teetering on the brink. And as they bantered there, munitions factories worked over-time, armies massed on frontiers, and powerful men were preparing to slaughter their own kind to satisfy twisted notions of race and nation.

I climbed to the stony waste of Monadh Mor, the ground for a while almost level so it was hard to know which of the two cairns marked the summit. For some variety I dropped a little and found the soggy edge of a large snowfield, the surface scalloped and marked by flecks of heather and dead insects and small pebbles. I thought it might last into August. The ground then became more broken and I went slowly over slopes of a hard-set scree, looking now onto Loch nan Stuirteag with its tiny solitary island and the pass linking the Moine Mhor with Glen Geusachan. With some care I descended the slope and tried not to disturb a small herd of reindeer graz-ing the pale-looking pasture. About mid-way I passed a group of four who were sweating up with largish packs and overnight gear. From the way they moved I felt one of them was leading, a private guide or maybe an instruc-tor from Glenmore Lodge. I trundled down to the Moine

Mhor, or 'Great Moss', a bouldery upland puddled with small lochs and hovering at around 3,000 feet, though itself overshadowed by the Cairngorm tops.

Cairn Toul lifted its blue screes a thousand feet just to the north, and the only drama about the place was the view into the trough of Geusachan, its shrinking river dwarfed by acres of slab and rockface. I'd camped by the loch before, but noticed a tent on the far shore so went a little west. On a bend in one of the burns coming off Cairn Toul I found a dryish terrace and here I placed my shelter. The mossy ground was wonderfully soft to lie on. My vestibule framed the slow running burn as far as a gravel bar before it disappeared, and beyond that was a lonely view of the grassland. To the west the bald Feshie tops rose and fell like a chalk downland, and a hole in the cloud cover sent late afternoon sunshine onto the screes behind, squeezing from them stains of purplish lichen and mosses and driving long shadows across the Moine.

Every sound seemed to complement the setting, the slow coursing of water, the cry of pipits, small fingers of breeze in the hollows and about the hillocks. Even the flame-noise of gas working on a small pan of water. It was so far from any road or house I felt at the centre of things. I had fixed my camp by the headwaters of the River Eidart whose confluence with the Feshie I'd passed yesterday, so it was all connected somehow.

The temperature had fallen, but it was still pleasant enough to lie half-napping on my down bag. Every now and then I propped myself up on an elbow and poked my top half out to glance around. I'd heard something. A man was standing not ten yards away looking at his map. I called over and we chatted awhile. He was not far off retirement age, I thought, and offered him a brew but he said he had to keep moving. He only carried a day-sack. Was he staying at Corrour? No, he said, camping in Glen Derry woods. Glen Derry was maybe eight miles or a three hours' walk away. Reckon you better hurry back then, I said, it's getting late. If in fact he was making for the plateau. He had a kindly demeanour and spoke with knowledge about red grouse and ptarmigan and the migratory habits of snow bunting. Natural history had enraptured him since childhood, and only a crook knee now limited his forays. Dodgy knee or not, he was away up the screes of Cairn Toul. I saluted his spirit.

By now it was apparent I was far from being the only soul on the plateau that night, though it was not exactly crowded. I wondered where the group of four had holed up – a bivouac on the summit, or did they play safe and retreat to the valley?

Syd swims against convention with a number of his attitudes and I suppose it is possible that from a selective reading you might draw the conclusion that his views are curmudgeonly and somewhat elitist. As already mentioned, he appears to have had little time for the Duke of Edinburgh Award Scheme, calling it a 'synthetic magnet . . . Bronze, silver and gold are idiot symbols of the craziness of contemporary society'. It is clear he has no quarrel with hard-working teachers and facilitators who run the scheme, but rather is against the idea of reward. Reward for what? Surely the experience of hill and glen are enough. Maybe Syd thought it odd that for something to be beneficial it had also had to be quantifiable.

He is no more polite about Glenmore Lodge, 'a fascist training establishment', he says, 'from which intakes emerge to conquer the hills and in doing so, according to the theory, conquer themselves.' This is an extraordinary attack if taken at face value and he will lose some readers here, which would be a shame. But we cannot unmake our journey to the hills, and I think Syd's attitude is partly a generational thing. He'd got to the wild places under his own steam, often alone, had slept behind boulders and climbed with make-do gear and learned by trial and error or from toughened veterans. It was a rough and ready apprenticeship. The idea that you could learn all this in the classroom or by being towed about the hills by a paid guide was anathema to him. But times have changed. In these risk-averse days it is probably no surprise many folk feel the need for a solid grounding in skills before venturing into the hills, especially in winter, and considering past tragedies it is only sensible that aspiring mountain leaders display a necessary competence.

Maybe Syd's experiences of the war had engendered in him a mistrust of institutions and authority in general – look where they have got us. But I think his unease went deeper. To treat the hills as an arena for sport or self-improvement was somehow missing the point. 'Absent is the poetry, the philosophy, the metaphysics, the dreamy dwam if you like, which is the proper wooing of the hills.' You cannot teach this, though with the right frame of mind you might discover it.

At such a high altitude I was untroubled by midges, and in the morning was able to break camp at leisure. I carried so little that the folding and packing took only minutes. A steady breeze ran over the Moine and played against the current on the burn, making crease-lines and breaking up its reflections. New summer grass wavered and clumps of heather shook gently as I set off. There was no path but I have a good memory of the land here, and headed roughly for Carn Ban Mor, which rose a few hundred feet to the west. In fact I wanted to climb Sgor Gaoith, highest of the Feshies, but it is out on a northerly limb and I needed first to reach the main crest. Pale blotches of sunshine roved across the hill-flanks ahead and picked out the curve of burn, a lovely place to ski in winter and where once a group of us built an igloo. The ground was soft and springy and a delight to walk, despite having to pick my way. I rounded the waters of Loch nan Cnapan, stepped across its outflow, and went through a scattering of smaller lochans to a burn that disappeared over the corrie headwall. I went upstream to where it issued from a mossy spring in a hollow. I filled canister and belly and scouted about for a few minutes. Built into a small west-facing slope at a point where the land began to drop more steeply was the remains of a deer-watchers' howff, a place known as Ross's Bothy. The walls were still sufficient to provide shelter from the wind. The place was tiny, much smaller than other stone-built huts I'd come across, but the hearth would have made it cosy, and for a minute I imagined time alone here a hundred years ago, day after day on the plateau where to meet another human would have been a significant event, lulled to sleep by corrie winds and croak of ptarmigan. The eye was naturally drawn to the length of Glen Einich fifteen hundred feet below, to the loch and river flats and pinewoods of Rothiemurchus, about half a day's walk away. This place was a ruin before Syd was born. The writer Affleck Gray, who knew the Cairngorms better than anyone and lived in the area in the 1920s, recalls finding a box of matches encased in candle grease. Had these been left by Ross?

I didn't stay long and went edging above the broken ground and up gentle slopes of clipped grasses towards

Sgor Gaoith and into a scissoring wind. The summit is a jumble of granite boulders that hang giddily over the gullies and crags of Glen Einich. Across this chasm were the great bald heights of Braeriach and Einich Cairn, dirty patches of snow still rimming their high corries. A small group left as I arrived. On a fine day the Feshies can be a busy place, and so it was good to be alone with the views. I looked west to the Monadhliath and Creag Meagaidh and to the familiar profile of Aonach Beag and Ben Alder some three dozen miles away. Peaks were only hazy in outline further than that. The wind pushed me about, so I wedged myself behind rocks and watched as gusts took bits of grit over the crest, then eddied back in a dull roar. A wonderful place to be.

I thought back to that dreich day in March some years ago when I'd driven down the A9 from Inverness to Dundee. Not entirely sure of my handwritten directions I became snarled in city-centre traffic as I attempted to match my scribbles with the road signs. A sign for 'Lochee' and something flashed in my memory, a line of verse – 'In the hubbub of Lochee', Syd had written,

> When you cannot smell the heather
> In the dingy Dundee weather
> And we cannot go together
> To the Lairig, you and me.

A little later I found his cottage on the edge of the Sidlaw Hills. Margaret and Syd welcomed me and for an hour or so we bantered as naturally as if we'd met in some ruinous hill bothy. Syd puffed away on a cigarette, sipped whisky and took me back to the thirties and tales of Lochnagar and Clova weekends and cycling to the

Cairngorms and back. A kindly man, generous with his thoughts to this stranger. Our time was all too short, and for a while afterwards we corresponded. He reiterated what he'd written, that blindness had not diluted one jot his enjoyment of the hills. His tin leg, he said, was always more of a handicap.

In his words and in real life Syd comes over as modest and without a trace of bitterness at the twist of fate that left him blinded and crippled in the last days of the war. He plays down his disabilities to the point that for most of the time the reader is unaware of them. They were just not important. In the years after losing his sight he achieved some 600 walks and climbs, but we are not presented with a tale of steep rock or even of overcoming disability. Rather he delves into the heart of the matter, to what is inexpressible about the hills and the Cairngorms in particular.

I wonder if there is still a place for Syd and his philosophical outlook in the clean high-tech adventures of today, where labels and gadgets and numbers seem an integral part of the hill experience. We digitise the dawn and count grams and no longer know how to weigh the Lairig. But I like to think the basics have not altered. We still go for challenge, to get tired and full of aches and to feel cold and wet and sometimes anguished. We still place ourselves willingly in the path of danger. The present phase will pass as surely as some day the hills will be as they were. Then Syd will be there for a new generation.

Further Reading

Farre, Rowena, *Seal Morning*, Hutchinson, London 1957; new edition, Birlinn 2008.

Gunn, Neil, *Highland River*, Porpoise Press, 1937; Canongate 1997.

MacCaig, Norman, *Collected Poems*, Chatto and Windus, 1985; third edition, Polygon, 2009.

MacKay, Iain, *The Last Highland Clearance*, Bidean Books, 2004.

Maclean, Alasdair, *Night Falls on Ardnamurchan*, Victor Gollancz, London 1984; new edition, Birlinn, 2001.

McIntosh, Alastair, *Soil and Soul*, Aurum Press, London 2002; new edition, 2004.

Thomson, Iain R, *Isolation Shepherd*, Bidean Books, 1983; new edition, Birlinn, 2007.

Scroggie, Syd, *The Cairngorms Scene and Unseen*, Scottish Mountaineering Trust, 1989.

Index